The Modern Harpsichord

THE MODERN HARPSICHORD

Twentieth-Century Instruments

and Their Makers

by Wolfgang Joachim Zuckermann

ML
651
Z83

OCTOBER HOUSE INC

For Lynn

Published by October House Inc
55 West Thirteenth Street, New York 10011

Copyright © 1969 Wolfgang Joachim Zuckermann
All rights reserved
Library of Congress Catalog Card Number 70–99498
SBN 8079–0165–2

Contents

Preface

A HARPSICHORD is both the easiest and the most difficult of instruments to build. Pluck a rubberband stretched over a cigar box and you get a musical tone. Build a large box out of plywood, stretch wires over it, add a piano keyboard and ready-made plastic jacks and you have a harpsichord with that nice tinkling tinny sound one hears so much on the radio, records and TV. What you have is perhaps the equivalent of a mail-order violin that looks, and sounds—almost—like a Stradivarius. But in that "almost" is contained a whole world of difference.

These differences are not very obvious to the uninitiated—which may account for the wide range of harpsichords, from kit built instruments to the finest copies of antique masterpieces, all presenting themselves to the general public as examples of that precious, forgotten instrument from another time. The harpsichord is suddenly turning up everywhere. You find it in people's homes, in churches, in dormitories, on concert stages, in theater pits, on television, in army barracks, in prisons, and insane asylums. (Yes, I've worked on repairs in a few state institutions.)

In this book I have attempted to sort out the different types, makes, sizes, and qualities of modern harpsichords with which the public is confronted. I have tried to show what makes a harpsichord tick (well, pluck); what are the rewards and pitfalls awaiting the harpsichord maker; what are the strengths and weaknesses of the instrument itself and of particular makes; and what happened to the heritage left by the masters of historical times.

Since the sound of a harpsichord is "different," any harpsichord tone can be judged unusual and interesting, and the tone of almost any instrument will find proponents and defenders, especially since few critics get the chance to examine different instruments side by side. (It is extremely difficult to rely on memory when comparing tone.) An attack on a particular harpsichord is therefore often followed by an attack on the critic himself, and a critic exploring the entire range of modern harpsichord production may have to exile himself to a desert island. (Perhaps this is the reason why in fifty years of the modern revival no one has attempted to write such a critique.)

What, the reader may ask, qualifies me for such a task? For as many years as I care to remember I have been servicing, repairing, restoring, and rebuilding harpsichords of almost all makes both ancient and modern. In addition I have built some 200 instruments of my own, and in the last ten years have supplied innumerable harpsichord kits for construction by amateurs. As the song goes, "Nobody knows the trouble I've seen"—all the trouble the harpsichord is heir to. If I have a bias, it is toward the simple, the practical, the serviceable, and the playable.

Many of the makers discussed in this book I have visited, some of them many times, and I like to think of many of them as personal friends; (a friendship which I hope will survive publication of this book). Those I could not visit I have written, and in general the response to requests for information and photographs has been generous and gratifying. My sincere appreciation is hereby extended to all of the makers everywhere (as well as to many museum officials and other helpful persons) without whose cooperation this book could not have been written.

Because of the popularity of the Zuckermann kit, I have in a way been responsible for the careers of many thousands of amateur builders. Some of the professional builders mentioned in this book began with a kit of mine and went on to more elaborate instruments on their own. I do not think of the kit harpsichord as ideal, except for purposes of amateur construction. Depending on the skill of the builder, it can result in a simple, serviceable, and eminently playable instrument of a pleasant sound, and a tone quality, when properly regulated and voiced, which is probably superior to that of most mass-produced harpsichords.

I do not consider myself a harpsichord maker within the terms of this book (not having made double manuals, nor indeed now making any finished instruments at all), or in any sense a competitor, a term which has little meaning in the harpsichord world.

In reading my critical survey of the modern harpsichord, I would ask the reader to consider me as he would a theater or music critic, who need not be a great playwright or performer himself to be an adequate judge of quality in this area. A critic is entitled to his opinion, backed up by a certain amount of exposure to his medium—radical, unpopular or crotchety though his opinion may be. My own view of the harpsichord has perhaps been negatively colored by constant exposure to repair work—I've seen the instruments and their owners in the most pitiful states of helplessness.

And this is one reason for the book. If it can shed a little light on the confusing issues of what is good and what is bad, what will last and what won't, what works and what doesn't, I won't consider my stay on that desert island completely wasted.

WOLFGANG JOACHIM ZUCKERMANN

New York, June, 1969

Chapter I

The Harpsichord and its Revival

IN SPITE OF the phenomenal modern interest in historical keyboard instruments, a great deal of confusion exists about what these instruments are, how they work, and what they are called.

In the sixteenth, seventeenth and eighteenth centuries, when these instruments were in general use, many different names were applied to them, often interchangeably. We find references to the cembalo, cimbalone, clavesingel, clavesymbel, clavichord, clavichordum, clavicymbalum, clavicytherium, epineta, espinette, Fluegel, gravicembalo, harpsichord, harpsicon, Klavier, ottavino, spinet, spinetta, and virginal.

In modern times, there is general agreement on what name describes which type of instrument, but the confusion lingers in the mind of the general public, often with amusing results. It is not unusual for someone to ask for a cembalo and not be satisfied with a harpsichord, refusing the explanation that these two terms describe the same instrument. The word harpsichord seems to present especial difficulties to the layman. It is one of those words whose pronunciation instantly discloses its users' educational status. The grade and high school segment almost invariably calls it a harpsichord while the college and grad school contingent manage to say harpsichord. In my own files are references to harpiscords, harpsachords, hoppicords, hairpsichords, harp-o-cords, happychards, harpisicopes, horpicarts, tharpsichoids, and harpers cords. (The word comes through French from the old German word harp plus the Greek word for gut or string—harpstring.)

The term harpsichord (*cembalo* in German and *clavecin* in French) is now generally applied to a pluck-action keyboard instrument roughly in the shape of a narrow grand piano, with strings running from front to back. The term spinet describes a similar instrument, but triangular or wing-shaped, with strings running at an angle to the front. (The German word for wing—*Fluegel* —used to be applied to the harpsichord proper, but now means grand piano). The virginal has strings running from side to side and is generally rectangular in shape. The clavichord is rectangular in shape but has an entirely different action which will be described shortly. The word clavier means keyboard and has often applied to any keyboard instrument; in modern German, *Klavier* stands for a piano, specifically an upright.

In order to discuss the modern harpsichord intelligently it will be necessary to arrive at a few definitions, and sketch a brief history of the instrument's development. A harpsichord can be defined as possessing (1) a group of strings, each string having a single pitch; (2) a resonating chamber; (3) a device to activate the strings (by plucking) and produce the sound; and (4) a keyboard to control that device.

By various combinations of these four parts of the definition we can relate the harpsichord to all other stringed instruments. The first element defines the various lyres and simple harps. (The plucking device, not part of the instrument, is the human hand). The modern concert harp and lutes and guitars add the second element, a resonating chamber. The family of viols and

9

Soundboard view of a virginal in the Italian style by William Post Ross, showing the nut at the left of jackrail and curving bridge to right. Keylevers must reach clear across instrument to pluck treble strings at rear.

violins shares the elements of a lute but has in addition a device to activate the strings, a resined bow drawn by hand.

The four elements of our definition are common to all keyboard stringed instruments, the particular instruments being defined by the method of making the string to sound. Clavichords and pianos strike the strings, harpsichords pluck the strings, and the now-forgotten Geigenwerk stroked the strings by means of resined wheels.

Our first three elements were incorporated in various instruments well before the fifteenth century. The application of the organ keyboard to control a stringed instrument occurred near the middle of the fifteenth century and was probably first used in a clavichord. The peculiar pattern of white and black keys preserves the historical fact that keyboards were first developed to render the modal scales on which all European musical theory was based before the renaissance. All the modal scales can be played on the white keys, each starting on a different note. Since modal scales contained only two halfsteps within the octave, the other five halfsteps, when demanded by developing theory, had to be supplied by adding extra contrasting keys.

By the year 1500, then, we have two instruments in common use which control the sound of a harp of strings by means of a keyboard—the harpsichord and the clavichord. Because of the nature of the clavichord action, in which the tangent that strikes the string to set it vibrating also must act as one of the bridges which defines the pitch, the clavichord will always be extremely limited in the amount of tone it can produce. As the clavichord developed, the length and mass of the strings was increased, until by the early part of the eighteenth century a large clavichord became an extremely expressive instrument for solo work, with an infinite range of dynamics reaching the sound level of a modern piano played very softly. In a quiet room the ear quickly learns to accept the dynamic range of the clavichord without any regret for the size of its tone. But neither the human voice nor any other instrument can be added to the sound of a clavichord without overpowering it.

Thus for all concert and ensemble music, the harpsichord came to be the only possible keyboard instrument, replacing the small portative organ or regal that had been used for such purposes in the previous century. But while the harpsichord had a tone of sufficient loudness to blend very well with the voice and other instruments, the variation in loudness that could be managed was very limited. As the harpsichord developed, the severe limitation in dynamics was overcome in part by adding additional string sets to be played by the same keys, until as many as four different sets of strings could be sounded at once. Since multiple keyboards had long been available on organs so that its various tonal resources could be employed in dialogue as demanded by the contrapuntal music of the time, it was a short step to give the harpsichord a second keyboard, and by the early eighteenth century this had become prevalent on the larger instruments.

For almost three hundred years the harpsichord reigned supreme as the solo and ensemble instrument of European music. The orchestra grew up around it, and it was not until the nineteenth century that the conductor moved from the harpsichord keyboard to the podium. During all this time the harpsichord continued to gain in tonal resources and expressiveness, until in the end the problem of gradual variation in dynamics was at last answered after a fashion by the application of the Venetian shutter swell late in the eighteenth century. But by the year 1800 the piano had completed almost a century of development and was ready to take over as the basic instrument of European music.

The death of the harpsichord was comparatively sudden and almost absolute. Production had almost ceased by 1800, and by 1816 the French were

Clavichord action, showing tangents on rear end of keylevers which both strike the string to make it sound and act as one of the bridges to define string length. When key is released, the felt laced between the strings (seen here behind the tangents) damps the whole string. This clavichord is double-strung in the treble to increase the volume of tone.

burning their harpsichords for firewood. Not until the end of the nineteenth century was there to be a revival of interest in what had become an ancient and archaic instrument. At the end of the eighteenth century, harpsichord makers had turned to making pianos. At the end of the nineteenth century, piano makers, some few of them and in small quantities, began to make harpsichords again. Just as the early pianos had been essentially harpsichords with hammer actions instead of plucking jacks, so were these harpsichords made by piano manufacturers essentially pianos with harpsichord actions.

In spite of the conscious attempts of the revivalists to rediscover and recreate the qualities of the earlier harpsichord, it was only natural that they should at first be almost overwhelmed by false analogies with the later piano. And after the first historical reconstructions by Dolmetsch, it was the piano firms of France and Germany who began to produce harpsichords for the general market.

Analogy with existing instruments had played a part in the original development of the harpsichord and clavichord in the late renaissance. The keyboard by which the organ was controlled had developed from broad levers struck by the fist in the early middle ages to the keyboard as we know it today by the fifteenth century, and indeed was incorporated in small portable organs used in ensemble with lutes, recorders and viols. When this keyboard was applied to a harp of strings, it was natural that the strings should be placed above a resonating box analogous to that used with lutes and viols.

An English spinet by Thomas Hitchcock, ca. 1700. Note shape of case which follows shape of strings, and that the spinet plucks close to the keyboard. (The Metropolitan Museum of Art. Gift of Joseph W. Drexel, 1889)

Early harpsichord makers were working out of a long tradition which had achieved, in the construction of resonating chambers, a sensitive and sensible balance between the strength necessary to hold the tension of strings and the fragility necessary for lively resonance. Since lutenists and viol players expected to tune their instruments before playing, it is probable that tuning instability was not considered a grave defect. (It is said of Bach that he was so skillful in maintaining and tuning his harpsichords that he could be ready to play in ten minutes.)

Cristofori, who is credited with developing the first piano properly so called in 1726, was a harpsichord maker, and the earliest pianos were essentially harpsichords with the substitution of a hammer actions. They were built entirely of wood in their cases and frames. But a string at the tension used in harpsichords will give much more sound when plucked than when struck by a hammer. To increase the volume of piano tone it is necessary to increase the mass of the string vibrating, and an increase in the mass of string means that the string must be brought to higher tension to maintain the same pitch.

Thus began the evolution of the piano toward heavier strings and higher tensions, double stringing, and finally triple stringing of the treble, while the bass strings were wound with copper. As the tension mounts so must the case become heavier to withstand the strain, until finally the case can no longer be allowed to participate in the resonance, and iron and finally steel frames had to be used to control the many thousand pounds of tension contained in the strings.* Resonance is exclusively relegated to the soundboard which itself had to be not only thick but heavily reinforced with crossribbing. To gain more tone, the bottom of the case was removed. Multiple unison stringing made any instability in tuning impractical, and still heavier construction imperative.

The modern piano is a feat of engineering developed over a period of 150 years to maintain enormous stress in relative stability. It was only natural that piano makers turning to harpsichords should apply what they had "learned" to the novel instrument. Since the harpsichord had been silent for so long, they were not disturbed by critical comparisons with the sound of the classical instruments.

Unfortunately, while the earlier analogy to the resonating chambers of lutes and viols had been useful and valid for harpsichord makers, the later analogy to the problems of piano construction proved false and useless. Massive cases and steel harp frames are unnecessary to carry the lesser tensions, and such members cannot participate in resonance. The soundboard does not need to be deadened with excessive thickness and heavy cross-ribbing, and the heavy keys, weights and bushings required by an increasingly complex action mechanism for the piano defeat the light crisp touch needed for harpsichord playing. Harpsichords must of necessity be more fragile and less stable than pianos if the thin strings and delicate pluck of the action is going to excite the bridge, soundboard and case. Encasing all this in steel would still not prevent the movement (and resulting instability) of the essential parts unless

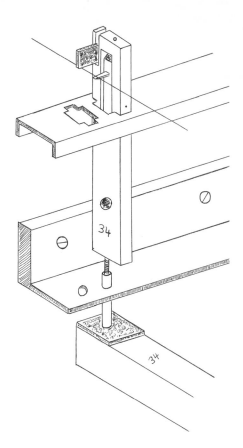

Schematic diagram of harpsichord action, showing key end padded with felt, jack guide, jack with adjustable end screw, tongue and plectrum, and felt damper. Jack rises through jackslide which can be moved left or right to change amount of pluck.

---

* It is calculated that a modern grand piano must control more than 38,000 lbs. of tension. In contrast, a harpsichord with 2 × 8′ + 1 × 4′ disposition develops tension of no more than *6000* lbs., less than a sixth of that of the piano.

all of these were made of metal, a conclusion drawn by John Challis as we shall see.

The harpsichord, then, may be said to have originated when people thought of equipping plucked instruments, which had existed for centuries, with mechanical plucking devices. These devices, called jacks, are basically rectangular pieces of wood riding past the string on the end of the key lever. In order to pluck the string, it is necessary to insert the plectrum (plucker) into a swivelling tongue set into the jack, so that the plectrum, having done its plucking job, can get out of the way of the string on its return journey to rest position. The tongue is allowed to swivel only backwards, its forward motion being stopped by the body of the jack itself, thereby forcing the plectrum to pluck the string on its way up. On the way down, the plectrum briefly touches the string, but since the tongue is free to swivel backwards, the plectrum is pushed out of the way when, in its movable tongue, it collides with the stationary string. The tongue is then returned to rest position by means of a spring. The key, and the jack riding on its end, descends to rest position by gravity, i.e., by the player releasing the key.

Anyone interested in the harpsichord should understand thoroughly how this mechanism works. Without a complete grasp of the characteristics of this action it is not possible to either maintain or play a harpsichord properly.

In the old harpsichords the jacks were generally from three to eight inches long, half an inch wide and about 3/16 in. thick. They were often made of pear wood, which is particularly well suited, being fairly soft and easy to work, yet possessing a close grain and smooth surface. A slot was cut into the upper part of the jack and into this the tongue was set, pivoted by a pin inserted laterally through jack and tongue. The pinhole in the tongue was large enough to allow it to swivel freely. At the bottom the tongue had a diagonal slant which butted against a matching slant in the jack, thus preventing forward movement of the tongue. Next to the tongue a smaller slot contained a piece of cloth which acted as a damper, resting on the string to stop its vibration. From the tongue at right angles projected the plectrum, usually bird quill but sometimes leather.

The jacks were held upright by passing through slots in two strips of wood. The lower one, the jack guide, was near the keyboard and fixed in position. The upper one, the slide or register, was approximately level with the soundboard. It was capable of being shifted from side to side to allow the plectra to engage or miss the strings. Sometimes both strips were combined to form a boxslide which was deep enough to hold the jacks upright without a second guide.

Since the early days of the harpsichord people have constantly tried to improve this simple action, but basically without any great success. Some modifications make the modern jack much easier to adjust: notably, an adjustment screw controls the rest position of the tongue which in turn controls the amount of plectrum projection; and a bottom screw called the end pin now controls the height of the jack and thus the vertical distance from plectrum to string. (In the old jacks the plectrum itself was pushed backwards and forwards to control projection, which often made it too loose; and the height was adjusted by shaving the bottom of the jack or adding cardboard shims, a cumbersome procedure when you have to adjust several hundred jacks. Frank Hubbard suggests that small screws were expensive and hard to make, and therefore not used by the old makers.)

The reason for the dissatisfaction with the jack action was that then, as now, the majority of harpsichords were usually not in first class playing condition. The action was often uneven, some jacks would fail to speak altogether, others would pluck with too much force, still others would not repeat quickly enough or speak only every other time. In an article on the harpsichord appearing in an eighteenth-century French encyclopedia, the writer states that "so many complications denote the imperfection of the harpsichord. It calls for too much skill on the part of the workmen and patience on the part of the players. The mechanism is too constraining and repairs are too often necessary,

Piano by Bartolomeo Cristofori, Florence, 1720. Note the "jackrail" still used to limit the dampers. This is in all respects a harpsichord save that the tone is achieved by striking the strings with leather-covered hammers instead of plucking with jacks. (The Metropolitan Museum of Art, The Crosby Brown Collection of Musical Instruments, 1889)

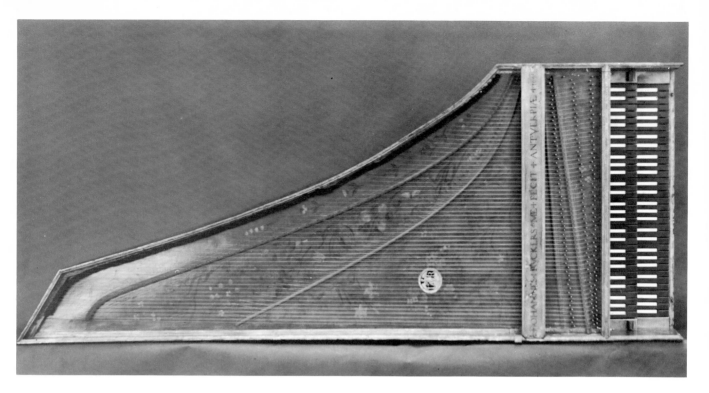

Harpsichord by Johannes Ruckers, ca. 1620, showing the eight-foot and four-foot bridges. The disposition of this harpsichord is 2 × 8´, 1 × 4´. It was rebuilt by Blanchet in 1750 to increase the range and to make both keyboards playable at the same pitch, and restored by Dolmetsch in 1908. (Yale Collection on loan from Belle Skinner Collection)

for instruments that require them frequently are not very rare." (Quoted by Frank Hubbard, *Three Centuries of Harpsichord Making*, p. 258.)

The solution to these problems is to be found in the choice of material for the jack, plectrum, spring, register and keyboard, as well as in the skill with which these parts are made, fitted together and adjusted, rather than in a radical change of the principle of the action. A radical "improvement" in the action would turn the harpsichord into some other instrument, as indeed happened with Cristofori's *gravicembalo col piano e forte*, which became the modern piano.

It should be mentioned in passing that the brief contact of the descending plectrum with the vibrating string causes what many consider an unpleasant buzz or snarl. Elaborate mechanism have been suggested for avoiding this, but they have been so complex as to make the jack unwieldy. In addition, this little snarl has been accepted as part of the basic harpsichord sound. It may even be said to add a bit of dryness and chatter to the total sound.

All harpsichords, spinets, and virginals have a jack action as described above. The difference between them is to be found in size, shape and complexity.

The harpsichord proper has at least one set of strings running from front to back (one note or key for each string), but more often it has multiple sets of strings. The strings start at the wrestplank or pinblock, where they are tied to the tuning pins. Then they pass over the nut or front bridge, continuing to the bridge, which is glued to the soundboard, and terminating at the hitchpin. The sounding section of the string extends from nut to bridge.

The first set of strings is pitched so that middle C on the harpsichord corresponds to middle C on the ordinary piano. This is called 8´ pitch, the term 8´ being derived from the organ, the most ancient of keyboard instruments. (The pipe for C, two octaves below middle C, is 8´ long.) A second set of strings, still at the same pitch and added to the first set, would turn this into a 2 × 8´ harpsichord. The two unison strings are not used as in a piano or clavichord where they are struck together; in a harpsichord each set of strings has its corresponding set of jacks, which can be played independently or together. Unlike the piano, where three strings produce one tone, three strings on the harpsichord produce three separate tones which may also be sounded in unison. In a $2 \times 8'$ instrument, two notes of the same pitch sound differently, because the tone quality varies with the precise point at which a string is plucked. As the plucking point is moved from the nut to the center of the string, the tone changes from nasal to mellow and fluty.

A third set of strings added to this will usually be an octave higher, producing an instrument possessing $2 \times 8'$ and $1 \times 4'$. When still a fourth set of strings, pitched an octave lower, is added, an instrument with $2 \times 8'$, $1 \times 4'$, $1 \times 16'$ results. In all these cases hand stops, knee levers or pedals usually enable the player to combine the various sets in any way he desires. Still adding to the variety of tonal colors is a buff or harp stop which is found on most harpsichords. This consists of a series of felt or leather pads which can be brought into contact with the strings, resulting in a pizzicato effect. This stop is often though erroneously called lute stop (from the German *Lautenzug*). In this book we will call the partial damping of strings a buff stop, while a special course of jacks plucking close to the nut will be called a "lute" stop.

A second keyboard is usually added to larger harpsichords, even though it may be possible to operate all the different sets of jacks from one keyboard. It must be remembered that all the jacks riding on a given key go up and down each time this key is depressed; whether they play or not depends on whether their particular jack slide has been moved to allow their plectra to engage the strings. If it has not, they go for a "free" ride while other jacks on the same key speak.

The second keyboard was first made by the Flemish builders and was used for transposing. It differed by a fourth from the first (or upper) keyboard, so that singers or instrumentalists could be accompanied at two different pitches without having to transpose. (In 1739 the Dutch organist van Blankenburg chided the earlier keyboard players for being "so inexperienced in transposing that in order to transpose a fourth lower they made expressly a special second keyboard . . .".)

Later it was decided that a second keyboard would add versatility, especially to a solo performance, if it enabled the player to use the second keyboard for additional or different stops. Thus the principal 8' was brought down to the lower keyboard along with the 4', and the upper keyboard was used for a solo 8'. If the two keyboards were capable of being coupled, all three sets could be played together. The upper keyboard could also be used for an "echo" effect—a passage is first played on the lower 8' & 4', then repeated on the upper 8'. The two keyboards could be played simultaneously by both hands, one on each keyboard, for special effect, or to give that complete freedom to the separate contrapuntal notes of which the organ had long been capable. (Pianists often find difficulty in playing baroque music written for double-manual harpsichords, witness Kirkpatrick's rescoring of the Goldberg Variations.)

The large harpsichords had three sets of strings, $2 \times 8'$, $1 \times 4'$, and often four sets of jacks, the extra set comprising a "lute" stop. These jacks would

A fretted (gebunden) clavichord, German, first half of the eighteenth century. By striking a string in different places with the tangent, different pitches are obtained. Thus one string can serve for several keys of the keyboard, reducing the total amount of tension that must be sustained by the case. Since the music to be played on such an instrument was largely "horizontal" and the harmony relatively simple, the player would have no need to sound major and minor seconds and some minor thirds together. (The Metropolitan Museum of Art, The Crosby Brown Collection of Musical Instruments, 1889)

pluck one of the 8′ sets very close to the nut to achieve a nasal sound. The 16′ is largely a modern development; it is occasionally found on the old German harpsichords, but even on these it is sometimes a later addition.

Spinets have one set of strings and jacks. The strings run at an angle to the keyboard, giving spinets their triangular shape. Since the spinet layout forces the jacks to pluck close to the nut, the spinet tone often tends to be somewhat nasal. To save space, the strings are usually arranged in pairs, so that two jacks are contained in the space between pairs, one of them plucking the upper string to the right, the other the lower string to the left. Both strings of a "pair" are thus separated by a semi-tone. (This is not to be confused with string pairs of a 2 × 8′ harpsichord, where strings of a wide pair have the same pitch.)

There is also an octave spinet in 4′ pitch, often called octavino, ottavino or octavina; these are very small, since 4′ strings are theoretically only half as long as 8′ strings. Because of their small size, ottavinos are often contained in carrying cases which enable the players to move them around like luggage. Although musically the 4′ pitch by itself is not very useful, players like to carry these little spinets with them for practice purposes. Many modern makers do not make ottavinos or have discontinued them, because they are as difficult to make as the larger spinets (there being still one jack and one string to each key, and the tight spacing making adjustments even more difficult); and obviously their prices had to be lower than those of the larger spinets.

The virginal is also rarely made nowadays, although the old builders made it in large numbers. Virginals are rectangular in shape, with strings running from side to side. Unlike spinets or harpsichords, virginals have both nut and bridge on the soundboard. This characteristic, plus the fact that virginal jacks pluck close to the center of the string, give virginals a pleasant and fluty tone. Strings are arranged in pairs as in the spinet, but the virginal outline, unlike

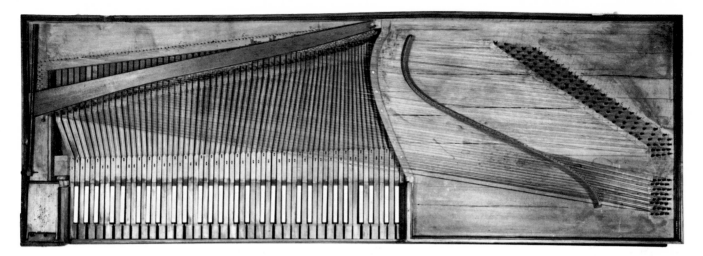

that of the harpsichord and spinet, is not very efficient in following the natural form of the string band. The space saved by paired stringing is lost again at the corners of the rectangle. This may be one of the reasons why virginals are not made much nowadays; although extremely handsome, they take up almost the same space as a harpsichord.

We come now to the clavichord, which is quite separate from the preceding instruments. The clavichord has the simplest of all keyboard actions. Mounted on the end of the key is an upright metal blade, the tangent, which strikes the string when the key is pressed. The tangent serves both as striker and as nut. Its function is to set the string in motion and provide one of the two points between which the string vibrates, the other being the bridge. The rest of the string, between tangent and hitchpin, is damped, since it would produce an extraneous sound if allowed to vibrate freely. After striking the string, the tangent stays in contact with it until the key is released. Since some sort of escapement is necessary to achieve unhampered vibration in a string by striking, clavichordists pay for a somewhat inefficient sound production by obtaining a tone ranging from triple pianissimo to piano. However, by holding the tangent against the string, every nuance of the player's touch can be transmitted to the sound. The clavichord is the most sensitive keyboard instrument, the tangent being only a direct extension of a finger. Since the tone responds to every nuance of touch, the clavichord was a favorite instrument of J. S. Bach, and its capacity for varying dynamics (within its small range) made it important to the early romantic composers before the efficient development of the piano. They were especially fond of the *Bebung* (quake), a vibrato which can be achieved on the clavichord by pressing the key up and down while the tangent remains in contact with the string. Clavichords are rectangular in shape and can have either one or two sets of strings (tuned in unison and struck together). Clavichords have often been electronically amplified, but unfortunately there is much distortion. When the tangent strikes the string it also lifts it, thus stretching it and increasing its pitch. (Stretching has the same effect as tightening a tuning pin.) This little pitch increase, when amplified, sounds like the "wow" of an electric guitar, an effect completely out of place in clavichord sound.

So much for a brief introduction. The points touched on will be discussed in much greater detail when we consider the different modern builders and

An unfretted (bundfrei) clavichord by J. M. Voit, 1812, Germany. This has a separate key for every note, and two strings for each pitch. The increased tension that must be borne by the case of such an instrument usually caused the right front corner to twist up. (The Smithsonian Institution)

see how they have attempted to cope with the challenge of making these instruments sound well and work efficiently.

In considering the contemporary harpsichord, it might be instructive to touch briefly on the phenomenon of the modern revival, which, after all, is responsible for the resurgence in harpsichord making described in this survey.

It is interesting to note that only sixteen years after the English maker Kirckman made his last instrument about 1800, a large number of harpsichords in the Paris Conservatoire were broken up and used for firewood during the cold winter of 1816. An instrument that had reigned for 300 years was dead, buried and forgotten in the space of little more than a dozen years. We've often been told about the advent of romantic music and its striving for great volume and range of dynamic expression, for which the harpsichord was pitifully inadequate, but the suddenness with which this instrument fell out of favor is somewhat reminiscent of the passion with which many people suddenly turned against lush romantic sounds after World War II. Just as early nineteenth-century man must have had his surfeit of the harpsichord, so the postwar musical population had heard Stokowski transcriptions of Bach once too often.

Apart from the constant swing of the pendulum from one fashion to its opposite, there are, of course, many reasons for a revival of this kind, and some of them have to do with the *Zeitgeist*, the pervasive spirit of an era. Ours is, of course, the age of science, and as such we feel a kinship with the eighteenth century, the age of reason, and an alienation from the nineteenth century, the age of unrestricted sentiment. In addition, we envy the eighteenth century its sure sense of order, an antidote for the doubts and insecurities of our own time.

There are, of course, also practical reasons for the revival. For one thing, long playing records, developed after the war, spread the gospel of old music and proper instrumentation. The sounds, strange at first, of renaissance and baroque instruments became common in most musical households. At the same time, and for many of the same reasons, a resurgence of chamber music playing occurred in America which was somewhat reminiscent of early nineteenth-century Vienna. As soon as people heard the new-old sounds they wanted to produce them on their own, not only for the novelty but because the music sounded so much better on these instruments. It was soon found that the sound of plucked harpsichord strings was able to blend with a string ensemble infinitely better than the reverberating sounds of the hammered piano strings.

But perhaps the most important reason for the revival of baroque music and its appropriate instruments has to do with the return of linear, horizontal, polyphonic music in the past fifty years.

From Haydn to Wagner (to use convenient if not exact terminals) composers explored the possibilities of homophony—the embellishment of a single melody by means of vertical harmony, and modulations from key to key until with Wagner these manipulations of chords and tonality could go no further. This "romantic" music, with its vertical chords and thick textures, degenerates into mere noise when played on a harpsichord. The initial pluck of the string which is out of pitch until the string settles into its pure tone, and the rattle of the plectrum against the string before the damper can act, the rapid

decay of harpsichord tone, the fixed dynamics, the rigid brightness—all these "deficiencies" of the harpsichord in terms of the music that was being written and played in the nineteenth century were eliminated by the piano.

Wanda Landowska at the Pleyel Harpsichord.

But by 1900, vertical, homophonic, tonal music had come to a dead end. Composers abandoned verticality and tonality and returned to the horizontal, linear, polymelodic and polyrhythmic thinking which had characterized all ancient, oriental, and primitive music, as well as all European music to the time of Bach. (Bach, in popularizing the well-tempered scale, had made the great adventure into vertical, homophonic tonality possible.)

The movement "back to Bach" or back to baroque, is thus not merely archaizing, but rather a rediscovery by musicians, after a long diversion, of the greatest potentiality in musical thinking—a rediscovery which has now permeated popular music.

And for the delineation of polyphonic voices and polyrhythms, the harpsichord has no equal among musical instruments. All its "deficiencies" become virtues, all its "vices" become necessities.

Thus it was a nostalgic hankering for the past, a dissatisfaction with our own time, the novelty of the harpsichord sound, its adaptability to the modern idiom, the ready example on long playing records, and considerations of sheer musicality and taste, which impelled people toward the harpsichord.

21

Even then the harpsichord might not have staged its comeback if it had not been for pioneers like Landowska as performer and Dolmetsch as builder to set the stage. Once that stage was set, though, it seems that the harpsichord made its appeal not only to lovers of the old; modern serious composers as well as popular music groups seized on the "new" sound. Just as there seemed to be a relation between our age and that of the baroque, so the sound of the harpsichord seemed well suited to modern music.

Hardly a day passes in New York, for example, in which a recording studio is not using a harpsichord. One musical instrument rental service alone possesses a fleet of 18 harpsichords which it was my lot for many years to tune and service daily. These instruments are used in Muzak for banks and supermarkets, incidental music for Shakespeare dramas, advertising jingles for television, background music for documentary films, Christmas music, children's music, cha-chas, rock and roll, jazz, folk songs, ballads, Broadway plays, off-Broadway plays, and now and then Vivaldi and Corelli. In one of my earliest exposures to modern uses of the harpsichord, composer-conductor and TV personality Mitch Miller nearly threw me out of a recording studio for having had the temerity to provide only a "single bank" instead of a double harpsichord. The occasion was the setting of a short poem extolling the virtues of a chemical fertilizer, to be broadcast to farm areas.

Day after day musically unsophisticated people walk into harpsichord shops asking for an instrument they know nothing more of than that they must possess one. How long this fad (if that is what it is) will last no one can say, but it still seems to be gathering force. Whether it will all collapse one day as suddenly as it did 150 years ago is anybody's guess, but modern life, which shows every sign of becoming increasingly frantic, will continue to produce an equally strong reaction, driving people back to the safe haven of an earlier time, its music and its instruments.

Chapter II

A Few Notes
of History

IN A DISCUSSION of the modern harpsichord it is essential to trace at least briefly the history of harpsichord making. Serious students are referred to three excellent books which have recently been published, and are free from the misinformation of earlier studies. The three works, by Donald Boalch, Raymond Russell, and Frank Hubbard, approach the history of harpsichord making from different points of view and cover the field as thoroughly as it is likely to be covered. *Harpsichord and Clavichord Makers 1440 to 1840* by Donald H. Boalch (London, 1956) is a biographical listing of all the makers, and a detailed description of all their surviving instruments, with 32 photographs. *The Harpsichord and Clavichord, an Introductory Study* by Raymond Russell (London, 1959) is an excellent and scholarly history of the instruments which also reprints a number of the historical documents; 103 excellent photographs. *Three Centuries of Harpsichord Making* by Frank Hubbard (Cambridge, Massachusetts, 1965) covers the period from the maker's point of view; a profound and scholarly text, with hundreds of excellent drawings of construction details of all the different schools; for accuracy, clarity, and patient research this book is not likely to be surpassed.

The history of harpsichord making has been divided into five schools, more or less chronologically—Italian, Flemish, French, English and German—and we will follow this division with a brief discussion of each.

ITALY: Harpsichords of the Italian school are the ones taken least seriously by the modern builders, probably because Italian instruments were invariably simple, lacking the means for tone and color changes that made the later Northern instrument so suitable for the performance of large virtuoso pieces; the musical compositions seem to have kept pace in complexity with the instruments for which they were written or vice versa.

An Italian spinetta, ca. 1540, showing the instrument proper enclosed in an outer protective case. Note the arcaded fronts of the white keys, an ornament found on many old instruments. The lid at the left rear of the case covers a compartment for tuning wrench, quills, etc. (The Metropolitan Museum of Art, Purchase 1953, Joseph Pulitzer Bequest)

Thus we find that no great demands were made by either composers or players on the Italian harpsichord makers. Burney, the famous English eighteenth-century traveller, and other observers, could hardly disguise their disdain for the unsophisticated and mechanically noisy instruments they found in their travels through Italy. Yet the Italian school represents the purest form of harpsichord making.

The earliest dated example of an Italian harpsichord stems from 1521, but they were certainly made earlier than this, and continued to be built well into the eighteenth century. In all this time the design was hardly changed. The Italians seemed to have had little curiosity for exploring and enlarging on the possibilities of the harpsichord; once the form of the Italian harpsichord had developed, the makers were satisfied to leave well enough alone.

It is perhaps interesting to note here that the modern piano has not changed much from 1860 to the present day, in a period when almost everything else has undergone complete transformation. This may be because the piano, like the Italian harpsichord, is basically satisfactory on its own terms. The Italian harpsichord makers were, like modern piano makers, on the whole quite conservative.

The Italian harpsichord might be likened to a guitar or lute; its case is a box, built and ribbed as lightly as is feasible; the box follows the pure outline

Italian harpsichord by Jerome de Zentis, 1658. The elaborate decoration of musical instruments called forth the skills of the best artists that could be obtained. Compare the legs of this instrument with those of the Buecker & White instruments in the alphabetical section of Chapter IV. (The Metropolitan Museum of Art, The Crosby Brown Collection of Musical Instruments, 1889)

of the string band. The outline of a harpsichord is usually derived from the sounding lengths of the strings and their lateral spacing. Thus, if the key centers, for example, are $1/2$ in. apart, the width of a four octave harpsichord will be about $27^1/_2$ in., if one allows $1^1/_2$ in. on each side for case and frame (49 keys × $1/_2$ in. = $24^1/_2$ in. + 3 = $27^1/_2$ in.). The key centers are laterally spaced the same as the strings, since each key is underneath its corresponding string.

It is well known that the string length of a given note should theoretically be twice as long as its octave above. Thus, if the highest C in our four octave instrument is 5 in. long, the next C down will be 10 in., middle C will be 20 in., an octave below that 40 in., and the lowest C 80 in. This is called a "just" scale and is usually not followed in practice because the extreme length of the bass strings would make the instruments too long for practical handling; the bass strings are usually shortened and provided with heavier wire to compensate for their loss in length.

Nonetheless, the Italians adhered closer to the just scale than any other school. It was easier for them to do this than for the others, since they used a very short scale and the keyboards did not extend very far in the bass.

The scale of a harpsichord is usually expressed by citing the length of c^2, the C above middle C. From the length of a single note the entire scale can be laid out, since one need only double the length as octaves descend into the bass, and halve them as they rise into the treble. Having established the length of five C's, one can draw the curve of the bridge, and the remaining strings will fall into place. Harpsichords range in scale from $c^2 = 9$ in. in some Italian instruments to $c^2 = 17$ in. in some modern instruments with metal frames. Needless to say, the shorter the scale, the smaller the tension of the string will be.

Going back to our example of the four-octave harpsichord which was $27^1/_2$ in. wide at the keyboard, we now find that the vibrating length of the lowest string should be 80 in., given a 10-in. scale. Allowing 6 in. from the nut to the key front, and another 4 in. from the lowest bridge pin to the outside of the case, we get a total of 90 in. of instrument. Since we are dealing with a small, single manual instrument, we might want to reduce the overall length by deciding to make the speaking length of the lowest string 60 in., and thus end up with a harpsichord 70 in. long and $27^1/_2$ in. wide. (An Italian harpsichord which came through my shop actually measured 28 × 70 in.) The short scale forces the bridge to bend in sharply at the treble, and the bentside of the case follows the outline of the bridge, keeping a respectful distance of three to four inches.

In actual fact, the Italian harpsichords often had only 45 keys, ranging from E to c^3, but their key centers were more than $1/_2$ in. apart. The lowest E was tuned to C, and the D and E were apparently provided by the low F♯ and G♯ for which there was little need. This arrangement of the lowest octave was called a "short octave" and was to be found on many Italian harpsichords. The narrow keyboard made the instrument very slim in front and, combined with its length, gave it its characteristically elegant appearance.

Italian harpsichords almost always had two sets of strings, both tuned to normal or 8-foot pitch. These were plucked by two rows of jacks facing in opposite directions. The two jacks for a given note ride on one key, but pluck

Detail of one of the three carved roses found on the soundboard of an Italian harpsichord of the seventeenth century. (The Metropolitan Museum of Art, The Crosby Brown Collection of Musical Instruments, 1889)

unison strings. The strings were arranged in what appears to be pairs, roughly ¹/₈ in. apart, with ³/₈ in. between pairs. The wider space allows the jacks to rise between strings and, facing in opposite directions, pluck to the right and to the left. Thus, the narrow pairs are a semitone apart, being plucked by jacks of different keys.

The two 8-foot registers were not provided with movable stops, and it appears that the player never varied the tone by allowing only one or the other set to engage, thereby taking advantage of the difference in tone color produced by the two different plucking points. For tuning purposes, however, it was necessary to isolate the sound of only one register at a time, and the player evidently accomplished this by moving the jack slide itself, since no levers projected to the front for this purpose.

The registers were usually boxslides, which were deep enough to combine the upper and lower jack guides into one. The deep slide meant that the jack made contact with its guide for almost half of its length. This necessitated a fair amount of play and would have created the mechanical noise of which Burney complained.

The case of the Italian harpsichords was extremely thin, about ³/₁₆ in., and case as well as soundboard were usually made out of cedar or cypress, both

Harpsichord and stand in gilded gesso relief, Italian, seventeenth century. Its function as a musical instrument has been overwhelmed by the decorator's art. (The Metropolitan Museum of Art, The Crosby Brown Collection of Musical Instruments, 1889)

softwoods in the evergreen family. There was as little bracing as possible, and it usually consisted of triangular knees glued to the bottom and sides. In one Italian harpsichord I restored, these knees extended only $2^1/_2$ in. along the bottom, yet the case was basically in good condition after 300 years. Another Italian instrument which came through my shop would not hold pitch and I was forced to conclude that the bracing was weak and the case was giving. Since the only way to verify this suspicion was to get a glimpse of the interior, I soaked out the soundboard, a tedious procedure, and was rewarded with an unusual sight—there were no braces or knees of any kind, nor were there any traces of knees ever having been in the instrument. I did not solve the mystery of how such an instrument came to be (it was genuine in most respects), but

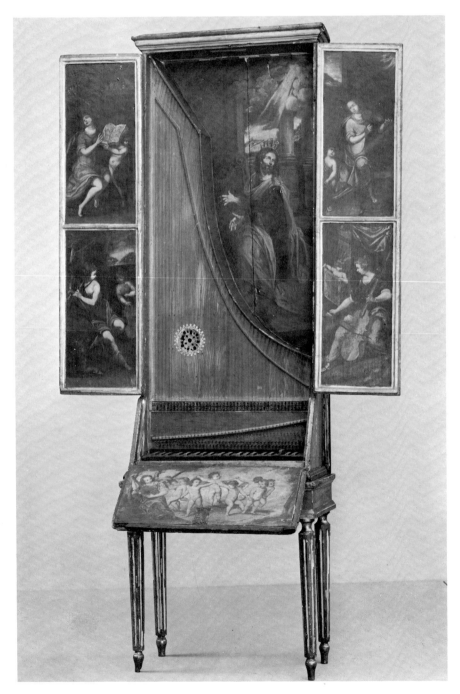

Upright harpsichord (clavicytherium *or cla-*vicembalo verticale), *Italian, seventeenth century. Jacks are returned by springs instead of by weight. (The Metropolitan Museum of Art, The Crosby Brown Collection of Musical Instruments, 1889)*

the addition of a few knees did prove extremely effective in restoring the usefulness of the instrument.

The ribbing on Italian soundboards is also minimal; there are four or five thin diagonal bars, perhaps $1/4$ in. thick, in one system of ribbing; a second system utilizes the cut-off bar associated with Northern instruments, coming to within a few inches of the bridge, with one or more smaller ribs between cut-off and spine. The entire instrument was light enough to be carried under one arm, without, of course, the storage box, which later developed into a separate outer case, from which the inner instrument could be removed.

The keyboard usually had boxwood naturals and black sharps, and the keys were pivoted on thin balance pins. They were guided in back by a rack with vertical slits in which wooden slips extending from the key ends rode. Any decoration was usually reserved for the outer storage case which completely concealed the plain inner case.

Italian harpsichords were most often voiced with bird quill, and I have found the modern substitution of delrin unsatisfactory. The short scale, resulting in fairly slack strings, does not seem to accept the "tearing" resulting from a pluck with the stiff plastic. Even quill has some of this tearing effect, and it seems that leather results in the gentlest pluck of all.

The Italians also made many spinets which seemed to have enjoyed a popularity equal to harpsichords. They were often polygonal with five or six sides, and the jacks came through slots cut directly in the soundboard. Octave spinets were also popular and used in the home to accompany singers.

In summarizing the Italian harpsichords, it may be said that these instruments were deceptively simple and for that reason tend to be dismissed by the modern builders. In truth the Italian harpsichord could be likened to a Buckminster Fuller construction in which a large dome can be erected with extremely thin, even fragile components, if these components are combined in the right order. The Italian system of thin cases, braced by knees and capped by mouldings providing rigidity, made an instrument as strong as a case many times as thick, but much more live. The custom of making separate inner and outer cases not only allowed poorer people to possess and play the inner case and defer purchase of the outer case until they could afford it, but permitted the makers to concentrate their art on the inner or working case and leave the outer case to cabinet makers who needed no knowledge of musical instrument making. It is a system which might well be copied in modern times.

ANTWERP: The Flemish harpsichord makers concentrated their activities in the city of Antwerp, which was a flourishing commercial center in the sixteenth century. Harpsichords were made in Antwerp soon after they were made in Italy, but quickly developed their own style. Although many makers worked there, by far the most celebrated name among Flemish builders is that of the Ruckers family who were active for about 100 years. It is a curious fact that many Ruckers instruments survived and very few of all the other Flemish makers, and Frank Hubbard speculates that since Ruckers harpsichords were famous and sought after, they were not likely to be discarded even when in bad condition, and that further, many Flemish harpsichords were later passed off as Ruckers to fetch higher prices.

In 1557 ten Antwerp harpsichord makers applied for guild membership as harpsichord makers, a category which up to then did not exist. Their request was granted, and they became members of the Guild of St. Luke, which also contained painters, framers, printers and bookbinders. Since the guild regulated standards of work and stipulated a strict system of apprenticeships, it tended to unify and standardize a national style and is an important reason why the old harpsichords, unlike those of today, were easily identifiable by nationality. It must not be supposed, however, that the effect of the guilds upon harpsichord making was only beneficial. Frank Hubbard examines the guild statute of 1599 in France and finds that it encouraged nepotism since it favored the sons of the masters; it eliminated true competition between masters and tended to protect the incompetent at the expense of the talented; by limiting each master to one apprentice it discouraged the masters' enterprise and prevented talented apprentices from seeking out the best masters. (Hubbard, pp. 85, 86.)

In 1579 Hans Ruckers was admitted to the guild. His ten children laid the foundation for the Ruckers dynasty. Two among his children became notable harpsichord makers: Hans the younger, often called Jan, born 1578; and Andries (Andreas) born 1579. Andries had a son of the same name in 1607, Andries II, who worked with him. There was also a Christopher Ruckers, whose connection with the family has not been established. A nephew of Hans

A double virginal by Hans Ruckers, Antwerp, dated 1581. The larger instrument, played on the keyboard at the right sounds at normal pitch. The keyboard at the left belongs to a completely separate instrument that could be removed from its shelf under the large soundboard; this instrument sounds an octave higher. Block-printed papers were often used by the Flemish makers to decorate their instruments. (The Metropolitan Museum of Art, gift of B. H. Homan, 1929)

29

II named Jan Couchet entered the guild in 1642, and his son, Jan II, was admitted in 1655, after his father died. Two more Couchets, Abraham and Joseph, became guild members, the last of the Ruckers family to do so.

The Ruckers instruments were valued for their beautiful tone. I have heard very few Ruckers harpsichords—not many of them are in circulation in this country. When one hears of an antique harpsichord owned by someone, it is a safe bet that it will be an Italian (if, indeed, it doesn't turn out to be some kind of piano—an English square, a giraffe, or a huge American square). Italians turn up quite frequently and in the most unexpected places—the window of a Third Avenue antique shop, as a planter or bar in someone's apartment, or in an auction sale. (I recently had dinner in an Italian restaurant on New York's West Side and discovered a beautiful Italian harpsichord, lavishly decorated and in unrestored condition, in the cloakroom.) Next in frequency are the English harpsichords and spinets. Few French and German instruments have survived, so their scarcity is not surprising, but Russell mentions over one hundred Ruckers personally known to him (Boalch lists 137), so the absence of Ruckers from general circulation must mean that they are hoarded in the way special currency and stamps are hoarded. I did get the chance to examine and play a Ruckers in the Berlin Musik Instrumenten Museum, where instruments are kept in first class working order, and found it to be superb.

The question of tone in the old harpsichords is fraught with uncertainties, since most old instruments are either in poor condition or have been badly restored. (In New York's Metropolitan Museum many instruments are kept a fifth low, which makes it impossible to judge them.) The problem of evaluating what the old instruments sounded like in their day is further complicated by the effect of aging on the wood; my guess would be that in most cases the aging process tends to improve the tone. Here again we must defer to Frank Hubbard who has examined more old instruments than anyone else. He de-

Another double virginal by Hans Ruckers, ca. 1590. The keyboards are modern replacements. (Yale Collection of Musical Instruments)

30

Two-manual harpsichord by Hans Ruckers, dated on soundboard 1613. This instrument was restored by Hubbard & Dowd in 1951. (Rhode Island School of Design, Providence)

scribes the tone of the Ruckers as one in which "the initial energy imparted to the string by the pluck is not drained off quite so quickly" (as in the Italians); he ascribes this quality to heavier construction and longer scales. He finds that "the best Ruckers tone has enough individuality to be interesting but does not impose its characteristic upon the performer." He goes on to say that most modern harpsichords are likely to have a sound "much like that produced by a Ruckers when a heavy mass such as a hammer or flatiron is permitted to rest on the bridge near the string being sounded."

The soundboards which produced this extraordinary tone were made from quartered spruce and were extremely thin. The underside had a cut-off bar,

Detail of Hans Ruckers' 1613 harpsichord showing modern jack (with screw end-pin) and tuning pins. Note that wire is seized to pins, the end of the wire being held behind the windings. At right, another detail of the same harpsichord. Note divided D sharp key in base.

and smaller ribs were placed at right angles to the spine. The cases were made of softwood, and braces went across the instrument from bentside to spine, unlike the Italian knees. Ruckers scales averaged $c^2 = 13\frac{1}{2}$ to 14 in.

Since the soundboard is often considered among the central mysteries of the harpsichord maker's art (in Ruckers instruments especially it seems to have been of vital importance), the wood used for soundboards bears some examination. Italian soundboards, as we have seen, were mostly made of cypress. In some cases this was quartered, like the spruce Ruckers used, but often it was cut from a slab. In quartering, the log is cut into four wedge-shaped quarters and each quarter furnishes narrow boards instead of the wide ones obtained from the width of the trunk. Quartering keeps warpage down to a minimum and results in prettier grain figures.

Cypress is not as stiff as spruce and cypress boards were therefore left somewhat thicker. A typical Italian cypress soundboard examined by Hubbard was found to be about $\frac{3}{16}$ in. ($\frac{10}{64}$–$\frac{13}{64}$ in.) under the bridge and about $\frac{1}{8}$ in. ($\frac{6}{64}$ to $\frac{9}{64}$ in.) around the edges. The Ruckers soundboards averaged

Harpsichord by Ionnes Dulcken, Antwerp, 1745. (The Smithsonian Institution)

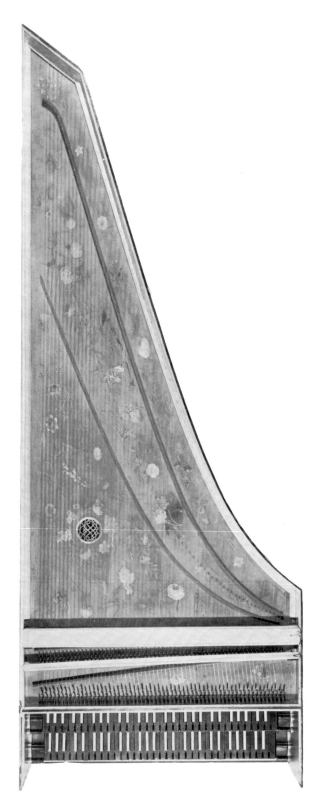

Soundboard view of Dulcken 1745 instru-
ment. Note "reverse" keyboard, and separate
jackrail for lute stop plucking close to the nut.

$^3/_{32}$ in. in thickness, tapering to as little as $^1/_{16}$ in. at the edges. The soundboards were rarely even in thickness throughout, but then the old makers lacked modern planing machinery for making uniform thicknesses. In any case, it is doubtful that they desired uniform thickness; most of them planed sound-boards thinner toward the edges, and this was done more by "feel" than by accurate caliper measurement. We will see that the better modern instruments also tend to have thin soundboards and planed-down edges.

Although the Ruckers made their soundboards with extreme care, what we would call "craftsmanship" on their instruments leaves a lot to be desired by modern standards. Both the Italian and Flemish instruments were almost sloppily put together, inside pieces showing knots, glue drippings, and imperfect joints. From this it may be learned that it is risky to judge an instrument by the "craftsmanship" as is often done today. The Italians and Flemings exercised great care where it counted, in the tone production and the working of the action, and the fact that some of the instruments have lasted to this day would tend to prove the point. Today's harpsichords often show immaculate craftsmanship but a poor tone and hopelessly complicated action, so that the effect of the fine cabinet work is wasted.

The Ruckers built various types of single manuals (mostly $1 \times 8'$, $1 \times 4'$), 8′ virginals, 4′ virginals, and double virginals (an 8′ and 4′ in a single case). The most far reaching in their effect on later builders, however, were the two-manual instruments. There is no evidence that Ruckers ever made two-manual harpsichords for other purposes than transposition. Most of them contained $1 \times 8'$, $1 \times 4'$ available on either manual. The lower manual was offset to the left by a fourth so that "middle C" on the lower manual plays the fifth string below that played by middle C on the upper. We have already quoted the organist van Blankenburg voicing his astonishment that two keyboards were necessary just for the purpose of transposing. He goes on to say "this seems incredible, but the proof . . . will confirm this: viz., that the famous Ruckers from the beginning of the previous century until more than thirty years later only made instruments in which, first, there were for the two keyboards only two (sets of) strings, but nevertheless four registers . . . so that one keyboard had to be silent when the other was sounding; secondly, the lower keyboard stood a fourth lower than organ pitch and had at the top five keys too many so that the upper keyboard could have had the same overflow in the bass, but instead of making the beautiful bass of the lower keyboard sound to this end they not only left it without keys but they made in their place a wooden block and next to it a short octave . . ."

However, in later years most of these instruments were converted (not by Ruckers) to double manuals as we know them—each register possessing its own tone color or pitch, and all of them capable of being coupled or played individually.

The outside of the Ruckers cases was sometimes painted but often marbled, with wide bands of green or brown to simulate panelling. Inside were usually found the distinctive block-printed papers, which were glued to the nameboard, cheeks and the casework above the soundboard. The lid might also be decorated with paper or might have a genuine painting inside it. The soundboard was decorated with paintings of fruit and flowers. Bone and ivory were used for covering the key naturals, and the wooden accidentals were stained black.

FRANCE: In the sixteenth and seventeenth centuries, judging by the extreme scarcity of surviving instruments from that period, the French relied mainly on imports from Italy and Antwerp. In the eighteenth century the story of French harpsichord making revolves around the Blanchet family: father

Nicholas, son François Étienne, and grandson, also François Étienne. When the grandson died, his widow married their apprentice, Pascal Joseph Taskin, who became the most famous of the French harpsichord makers. He was succeeded by his nephew, Pascal Joseph Taskin II.

The Blanchets and Taskins spent only part of their time making their own instruments. The greater part of their time was occupied with remaking Ruckers, which were prized highly for their tone, but were not very useful for the French music of the time. As we have seen, they had two keyboards, each working $1 \times 8'$ and $1 \times 4'$, with no manual coupler, and one of the keyboards often contained a short octave like that found in Italian instruments. To do justice to the music of Couperin and other French masters, the bass and treble had to be extended from FF to f^3 and made chromatic (one key for each semitone). This involved widening the instrument on both sides, widening the soundboard, and putting in a new wrestplank. While they were at it, the French builders made a new keyboard and action, which were much more accurately made than those of Ruckers. (Taskin's keyboards are said to

Harpsichord by Ioannes Goermans, Paris, 1754. (The Metropolitan Museum of Art, anonymous gift, 1944)

be the best of all.) Essentially there was not much more left of the old Ruckers than the soundboard, and even that had to be enlarged, but the French makers evidently thought this elaborate process, called *ravalement*, worth doing.

It seems that the French makers were quite capable of making fine instruments in their own right, although few have survived. However, it may be that the converted Ruckers with the Ruckers initials in the soundboard rose fetched a better price; and the passion for converting one instrument into another has been found in many a maker. It seems somehow easier to start with something, although in the end it turns out to be a lot more work than building an instrument from scratch.

When making keyboards for Ruckers instruments, the French makers were faced with the task of turning the former transposing doubles into true

Harpsichord by Benoist Stehlin, Paris, 1760. (The Smithsonian Institution)

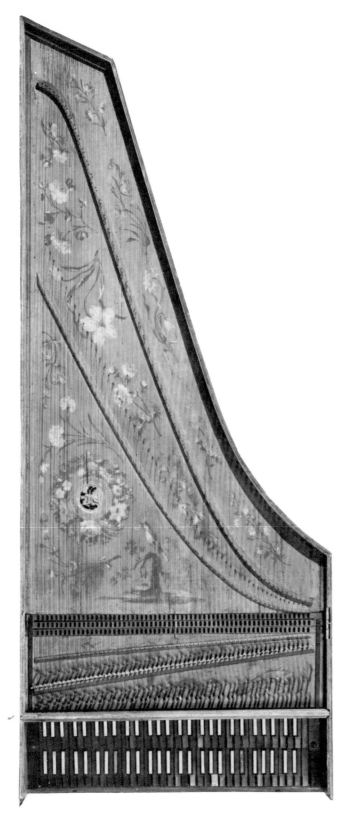

Soundboard of Stehlin 1760 harpsichord. Jack rail has been removed to show jackslides and stops.

two-manual instruments, so that keyboards and jack sets could be combined in any fashion. The method of coupling which had been used up to then consisted of a set of dogleg jacks which were capable of being worked both from the upper and lower manuals. These jacks had a long extension reaching to the lower keyboard, while the remainder of the jack was poised over the ends of the upper keys. Since dogleg jacks are rarely used on modern harpsichords, we need not go into the intricate reasons why they are unsatisfactory from the players point of view (see Hubbard, pp. 80–81).

The keyboard coupling mechanism developed in France was as simple as it was ingenious, and is still used on many modern harpsichords. Mounted on the rear surface of the lower keys were short sticks called dogs which were able to push up the rear of the upper manual keys, thus activating their jacks. To disengage the coupler the upper keyboard was pulled forward, allowing the dogs to miss the upper keys. Called a push or shove coupler, it is the simplest of all manual couplers. With this coupler, the player can use the *forte* of the lower manual (lower 8′ + 4′ and upper 8′), then change to the sudden *piano* of the upper 8′ only, which, though the coupler is engaged, will sound by itself.

Taskin was extremely inventive and in his later work often used knee levers instead of handstops. He also used in one set of jacks a soft leather, called *peau de buffle*, instead of quill. This is not, however, to be taken as the ancestor of the modern sole leather plectra; Taskin's leather was extremely soft and stroked rather than plucked the string for a pianissimo tone.

Taskin, in his own instruments used a shorter string scale than Ruckers, and usually had three registers, $1 \times 8′ + 1 \times 4′$ on the lower keyboard, and $1 \times 8′$ on the upper. Taskin's bracing ran from bentside to spine, like the Ruckers, but unlike them the upper braces were placed perpendicular to the bentside, thus presumably increasing their efficiency. His cases were $3/4$ in. compared to Ruckers $1/2$ in. and the Italian cases of $3/16$ in.

The importance of the French harpsichord for the modern era is that the French prototype has had an enormous appeal for some of the best present

Soundboard of harpsichord by Pascal Taskin, Paris, 1770. (Yale Collection of Musical Instruments)

day builders. Considering the five national styles as prototypes of the modern instrument, we find that the Italian harpsichords are considered too simple and limited, having only one keyboard and a short one at that. The Ruckers, as we have seen, were not expressive doubles and also lacked the keyboard range necessary for the literature. The English harpsichords came toward the end of the harpsichord's heyday, and contained some complex features designed to compete with the rising popularity of the piano, which today are irrelevant. The German instruments were also late and complex, encumbered with such additions as 2′ and 16′ stops, which makes them far from ideal to copy.

French harpsichords stand midway both chronologically and in complexity among the national styles of harpsichord making. Consider its two keyboards extending from FF to f ^{3}, coupled by means of the mechanically sound push coupler; its two rows of 8′ jacks separated by the 4′ row, resulting in the right plucking position to give the two 8′s just the correct amount of difference in tone color, allowing them to contrast when played separately yet mix when played together; and its registration of $1 \times 8' + 1 \times 4'$ on the lower keyboard and $1 \times 8'$ on the upper—and you have an instrument complex enough to be interesting, yet simple enough to work and sound well; in other words, the ideal harpsichord to copy.

Toward the end of the eighteenth century Sebastian Erard made harpsichords with pedals. He later founded the well known French firm of piano makers.

The French harpsichord cases were painted inside and out, and then varnished. Often the inside was a bright vermillion, and the outside black, or

Bottom removed from Taskin instrument, showing underside of soundboard, bracing, and repairs made to soundboard.

A pretty ottavino spinet by Pascal Taskin dated 1778. (Yale Collection of Musical Instruments)

green (*merde d'oie*, according to Russell). In the more elaborate instruments there were gold leafed panels, paintings inside the lid, the usual flowers and fruit on the soundboard, and an ornate stand.

ENGLAND: The early period of English harpsichord making produced mostly virginals derived from the Ruckers design. However, rather advanced harpsichords from the 16th and early 17th centuries survive which contain three sets of strings, and indicate, according to Russell, that the early English virginal music need not necessarily be performed on a single 8′ virginal or spinet to be considered historically correct.

The spinet became quite popular in eighteenth-century England, occupying the place of today's upright piano. The eighteenth-century English spinets were rather large, with a five-octave compass and a very long spine to provide the longest possible speaking length for the low bass notes.

The most important English makers were two immigrants—Jacob Kirckman from Germany, and Burkat Shudi from Switzerland. Their large harpsichords are among the best of any school; Frank Hubbard considers that they "may represent the culmination of the harpsichord makers' art," and this judgment is certainly borne out by the Kirckmans and Shudis I have seen.

40

Both makers had well organized workshops, turning out hundreds of instruments. Kirckman especially seems to have been a shrewd businessman. Both Kirckman and Shudi were apprentices to a maker named Hermann Tabel. Shudi left Tabel first (in 1728) to set up his own shop. Kirckman stayed on and became Tabel's foreman. When Tabel died, Kirckman is said to have come down to breakfast one morning and to have spoken as follows to the widow Tabel: "Madam, today I am going to get married." "And to whom?" asked Mrs. Tabel, her female curiosity aroused. "You, Madam" was the answer, and thus did Kirckman get the widow, the shop, and everything in it. In later years he carried on a side line of lending money at interest.

Curiously, neither Kirckman nor Shudi employed the manual coupler

A handsome and imposing English harpsichord by Josephus Kirckman, 1798. This instrument has all the machinery and refinements of the late harpsichords competing with pianos. The underside of the Venetian swell mechanism is clearly visible. (Boston Museum of Fine Arts, gift of William Lindsey in memory of his daughter, Mrs. Leslie Lindsey Mason)

used in France, but instead used the old system of dogleg jacks, which is less satisfactory. Their large harpsichords had a lute stop (a set of jacks plucking near the nut and producing a nasal tone) and a dogleg set on the upper manual; on the lower keyboard they had 1 × 8′, 1 × 4′ and the same dogleg working from the lower keyboard. The lute stop, being extremely nasal, did not mix well with the other stops and was therefore pretty much confined to solo use.

One innovation of theirs which survives to this day on pianos was the use of front key pins to guide the keys, rather than the "rack" system with a slotted rear guide. The front pins allow individual dip adjustments by means of card punchings. Their use of ivory naturals and ebony sharps has also survived in the modern piano. This is probably no accident, since the modern piano owes more to the early English type developed by Broadwood (who was Shudi's son-in-law and whose piano firm continues in England to this day) than to the Italian or Viennese type of piano.

Kirckman's cases were not quite $3/4$ in. thick, and the soundboard thickness averaged $1/8$ in. The bracing ran crosswise from bentside to spine, but there

An English square piano of the same period as the Kirckman harpsichord, by Clementi & Co. Note how tension has pulled up right corner of case. Muzio Clementi was a composer, and virtuoso pianist who also profited as an astute businessman; when pianos were replacing harpsichords he became a piano manufacturer.

were elaborate sloping braces to strengthen the belly rail. A weakness was the absence of blocks upon which the pinblock rested, and this often caused its upward warp, something which is common even in pinblocks resting securely on frame blocks. Since the strings exert a constant pull on the tuning pins, they tend to "tip" the block.

Russell points out that the big harpsichords of Kirckman and Shudi actually represent the harpsichord in its years of decadence. These instruments post-date the compositions of Bach, Couperin, Handel, Rameau and Scarlatti by at least 25 years, and the fashion was rapidly changing. Probably for that reason, Kirckman and Shudi added various features to their instruments to make them more expressive, anticipating the competition with the piano. One of these was the famous Venetian swell, which was a Venetian blind shutter lid that could be opened while playing to let out more sound. Another was the machine stop, a complicated pedal-operated device to switch registers quickly for piano-forte effects. A Shudi with Venetian swell which I heard in England worked remarkably well. The result of the swell is indeed astounding, but one wonders if the music really requires such effects.

English harpsichords were invariably veneered (except at the spine which faced the wall), and often cross-banded and inlaid; they usually rested on a turned trestle stand.

GERMANY: Few harpsichords of German origin have survived from the 16th and 17th Centuries. There are a few virginals and spinets, and a great number of simple small clavichords. The clavichord has always been more popular in Germany than elsewhere, although small clavichords were also made in Italy in large numbers. The simple German and Italian clavichords were very much alike and seem to have been made for those customers who wanted a keyboard instrument but couldn't afford the more elaborate harpsichord.

These simple clavichords were usually fretted (gebunden), which meant that several tangents would strike the same string, but at a different place to get a different pitch. Thus a low C tangent would strike a given string furthest from the bridge, and the C# enough closer to achieve the semitone difference. This meant, of course, that these two notes could not be played simultaneously, but this was not an objection in the music of that time. Even on fretted instruments, a number of the keys in the center of the keyboard were frequently unfretted (bundfrei). Fretted clavichords were not only compact, but used a greatly reduced string tension, allowing a light construction. For some reason no modern builder makes fretted clavichords; perhaps they are too simple for our taste. In fact, the clavichord is altogether, and unjustly, neglected by the modern makers.

The two important German families making instruments in the 18th Century were the Hass family (father and son), and Gottfried Silbermann and his nephew Johann Heinrich. The Hasses were responsible for the best German harpsichords and clavichords. Their clavichords were large and elaborate, and some of them had 4′ strings in the bass in addition to a compass of $5\frac{1}{2}$ octaves, FF to c^4.

The Hass harpsichords were equally elaborate, some of them having 16′

and 2′ stops in addition to the usual 2 × 8′ and 1 × 4′. When the 16′ was used, it was treated to a separate soundboard at a higher level with its own bridge. The 8′ hitchpin rail was then anchored to the braces and even reinforced with iron angles, since it did not have the solid support of a bentside. Curiously enough, as in England, the French manual coupler was not used, and the old dogleg system was pressed into service. A dogleg which speaks from both manuals makes dialoguing from one keyboard to the other very difficult, but Hass allowed the lower manual to slide out and disengage the dogleg.

German harpsichords usually had a double "S" curve to the bentside. They were often elaborately decorated (one lid painting shows that very instrument being presented to a lady and Hass standing next to it), and had heavy, framed stands. The natural keys were sometimes covered with tortoise shell, and accidentals with ivory and mother-of-pearl.

The question of the so-called "Bach" disposition has been dealt with exhaustively by both Hubbard and Russell. This question is of great importance in a discussion of the modern harpsichord, since many German harpsichords made today are based on or copied from the so-called "Bach" harpsichord, said to have been in that composer's possession.

The disposition of the "Bach" harpsichord was 1 × 8′, 1 × 16′ on the lower manual, and 1 × 8′, 1 × 4′ on the upper, and this is what most modern German builders employ to this day. Recent research has uncovered two facts about this instrument: one, that there is no evidence whatsoever to connect this harpsichord with Bach; and two, that the disposition was not original and has been rearranged at a later date.

Readers who are interested in the painstaking and fascinating process involved in the unmasking of the "Bach" disposition are referred to the authors cited above. It remains to be said that the results of accepting as a model the spurious Bach harpsichord are twofold: one, it has brought the 4′ to the upper manual, thereby radically altering registration possibilities from what they were when the music was written; and two, it has emphasized the 16′ which was practically unknown in the great days of the harpsichord.

SUMMARY: In summarizing the features of the old harpsichords as they bear upon the modern makers, the following rather startling facts emerge:

1. There were at least five different national styles with only superficial resemblances to each other. The majority of modern harpsichord makers do not recognize this fact or defer to it in any way.

2. The case thickness of the old harpsichords practically never exceeded 3/4 in. The majority of harpsichords made today have cases more than double or triple that thickness, or frames of steel or aluminum.

3. All old harpsichords had a closed bottom. The majority of harpsichords made today have no bottom at all.

4. The scale of the old harpsichords rarely exceeded $c^2 = 14$ in. Many modern harpsichords have longer scales, some reaching over 16 in.

5. Almost all old harpsichords used some kind of bird quill for plectra; practically no modern harpsichords do.

6. With the exception of the Ruckers transposing harpsichords, which

Harpsichord by Hieronymus Hass, Germany, 1734. This elaborate instrument by one of Germany's greatest builders has a disposition of 2 × 8′, 1 × 4′, 1 × 16′, and a lute course. Note the checkered skunk-tail sharps with mother-of-pearl and tortoise shell.

are a special case, the 4′ was never found on the upper manual of old instruments; in a large number of instruments made today, that is where the 4′ is.

7. Only a tiny number of harpsichords have survived with an original 16′ stop; yet the overwhelming majority of modern concert harpsichords have this stop.

8. Pedals on the old instruments were extremely rare; on modern concert instruments they are invariably present.

9. The old harpsichords never had more than three or four soundboard ribs, and these did not cross under the bridge. On the majority of modern instruments there are twice and three times that number, many of them crossing under the bridge.

10. The keyboards of the old harpsichords were unbushed, light, shallow and minimally weighted; many modern harpsichords have piano-type keys heavily bushed and weighted.

11. The soundboards of the old harpsichords practically never exceeded $1/8$ in. in thickness. Many modern harpsichords have boards almost double that.

12. The jacks in the old harpsichords were simple rectangular slips of wood, with a tongue returned by a boar's bristle. The majority of modern harpsichords have complex jack mechanisms, made of plastic or metal, with a number of adjusting devices.

From the above it will become apparent that the modern harpsichord is a different instrument from the historical one and often shares with it only the name. In discussing the modern harpsichord, we must endeavor to consider it on its own terms (whatever they may be); it would be quite useless to compare an Italian harpsichord possessing a case of $3/16$ in. thickness to, say, a Neupert with a case over thirteen times as thick. Instead, it will be illuminating to find out what the modern makers consider important; and how they solve the problems of tone, mechanics, and construction.

Chapter III

The Modern Harpsichord

Discussing the modern harpsichord is a little like describing the modern house. Not only do houses vary radically from early to modern times and from one architect to another, but houses by the same architect differ greatly from one another.

In modern times we encounter some 100 harpsichord and clavichord makers in the world. Contrasting this figure to more than 1,100 names listed in Boalch for the historical period, we must recognize that our celebrated revival is still in its infancy. It is true, of course, that Boalch covers a period of over 300 years and the modern revival began only fifty years ago (projecting our current number of harpsichord makers over the next 250 years we arrive at about half of Boalch's figure). Moreover, the production of some modern shops is far greater than that of the historical workshops. Further, a comparison of the modern shops with earlier makers is complicated by the question of defining who is a professional. Due to the guild system and the strict regulation of production, we can be fairly certain that all historical instruments were products of professional makers. Today many talented (and otherwise) amateurs have gotten into the act.

On the whole, though, the picture of harpsichord production today is not unlike that of former times. In the age of computers and space travel, harpsichords and clavichords continue to be made mostly in small shops, often by a single person working alone or with one or two assistants. Oddly enough, small and meticulous instrument-making is even truer of America, the land of mass production, than of some European countries, notably Germany.

Even the time-honored custom of apprentices setting up their own shops after a time with the master is often followed by the modern builder. Thus Hubbard and Goble, for instance, worked for Dolmetsch; Rutkowski and Dowd were at John Challis' for a time; Bannister worked for Hubbard and Dowd; Senftleben worked for Ammer, Zahl for Sassmann, Ross for Hubbard, Schütze for Mertzdorf, etc.

In trying to define or describe the "modern" harpsichord, we must soon realize that, while it was simple to group historical makers by nationality because national building styles were fairly consistent, this is not possible today. With more success we may attempt to describe the harpsichord in the 20th century by dividing the makers into half a dozen categories according to their general philosophy of building. These categories which easily overlap, would be: (1) faithful individual copies of historic instruments; (2) faithful copies in production; (3) free copies; (4) commercial production; (5) new designs; and (6) complete break with tradition.

Faithful individual copies are turned out by the makers generally working completely alone, slowly and painstakingly assembling as close a copy to the original as they can. Skowroneck, Hyman and Hugh Gough might be examples of makers working this way.

Related to this style of working are the shops of Hubbard and Dowd, for instance, who copy faithfully but on a more elaborate scale, turning out a greater quantity and working with a number of assistants.

47

Arnold Dolmetsch, father of the modern revival of the harpsichord and other ancient instruments, and one of the makers discussed in Chapter IV. The caption supplied by the Dolmetsch firm for this picture tells us that when he heard someone bid £5 for this lute he leapt to his feet and shouted, "No, fifty pounds."

The builders who make free copies, such as Goble, Bannister and a host of others, will base their designs loosely on those of particular historical makers. They may try to copy the scale, plucking point and general geometry, but will make many concessions to modernity, such as heavier construction, plywood, plastic jacks and the like. (Indeed, even Hubbard and Dowd often use plywood, metal slides and plastic jacks.)

The commercial production shops like Neupert and Sperrhake are usually run by former piano men who base their designs on a mythical harpsichord or their version of what a historical instrument looked like; they will generally have a set number of "models" with names like "Bach," "Telemann" and "Vivaldi" which are made in large quantities. Although these harpsichords and clavichords bear no relation to historical ones, their makers usually claim a vague connection.

The makers of the fifth category break forthrightly with the past to experiment with the most advantageous use of modern materials and technical knowledge. John Challis is a good example of this approach; by using materials like annodized aluminum for soundboards he has advanced the science of harpsichord making, so to speak, the way each historical group used to make advances over the preceding group. To advance the knowledge of building does not necessarily lead to an improvement in the instrument itself, but it does add to the knowledge *about* the instrument (if only to teach us what not to do).

Last are the makers who turn their backs on any tradition and are concerned with what is essentially a new instrument for the performance of new music. The electronic harpsichord designed by Caleb Warner and now manufactured by Baldwin is such an instrument. In this connection the Allen electronic harpsichord should be eliminated altogether since it merely simulates the sound electronically without using strings or jacks.

It should be understood that individual makers must not be forced into one or another of these categories. They are presented here to give the reader some idea of the wide range covered by harpsichord production in the 20th century. In the next chapter we shall consider the individual makers in detail and it will be apparent that almost none of them fit exclusively into only one of these divisions, but span at least two or three in their building activities.

In tracing the 19th-century origins of the modern harpsichord revival, credit should be given to Alfred Hipkins (1826–1903), who was active in the English firm of Broadwoods, the piano-forte makers who got their start in Kirckman's day. Hipkins became interested in the harpsichord through a study of C.P.E. Bach's music, and through his writing and proselytizing awakened English interest in historical instruments. In the 1880's Hipkins met Arnold Dolmetsch, who had come to England from his native France.

Arnold Dolmetsch (1858–1940) was to have a profound influence on the revival of not only historical keyboard instruments, but lutes, viols, psalteries, recorders and many others. Dolmetsch was a rare combination of builder, restorer, performer, teacher and writer, and soon became identified with a group of poets, craftsmen and artists that included William Morris, Yeats, Swinburne and G. B. Shaw. Artists and writers attended the Dolmetsch concerts given on old instruments and encouraged him in his projects. When Hipkins suggested that Dolmetsch restore some harpsichords stored at Broadwoods, he pursued this task eagerly, and soon found himself making these instruments.

Meanwhile, two venerable French firms of piano makers, Erard and Pleyel, started building harpsichords. The reason that the name of Pleyel is more prominently associated with harpsichords lies in the fact that Wanda Landowska commissioned this firm to build instruments to her specification.

The first decade of the 20th century saw other piano makers getting into the harpsichord business, including the German firm Ibach & Sons in Barmen, Hirl of Berlin, Pfeiffer of Stuttgart, and Seyffarth in Leipzig. The French piano makers Gaveau and the American firm of Chickering manufactured harpsichords for a time, both under the direction of Arnold Dolmetsch, whose influence reached everywhere. Neupert in Bamberg, Steingraeber in Berlin, and Maendler in Munich began their construction of historical keyboard instruments at about the same time, *ca* 1907.

Before discussing the individual builders, we should turn to some of the broad objectives pursued by the modern makers. What should be the goal of the modern builder? Should he, indeed, make precise copies of the old harpsi-

Frank Hubbard in his workshop.

chords? Should he use modern materials and production methods? Should he experiment and try to improve the tone and action?

It may be argued that we should duplicate the early instruments when we intend to play early music. This is, in fact, the argument of Martin Skowroneck, who maintains that while most good violinists have an instrument made by an old master, many harpsichordists have never even seen or heard an original, and musicians can usually not compete with museums for the few which become available. This has led to a situation in which the harpsichord makers could by degrees develop an entirely new instrument which has nothing in common with the old ones except the name, and no one would be the wiser for it.

Skowroneck goes on to list some of the differences between the old harpsichords and the modern German product which we have summarized at the end of Chapter II. He takes the modern German makers to task for their hankering after silvery (*silbrig hell*) trebles and booming (*dumpfdroehnend*) basses (which, incidentally, they rarely achieve) instead of the reedy trebles and sonorous basses possessed by the old harpsichords. The result of a non-singing tone will be to emphasize the constant "explosion" of continuous plucking, which then takes precedence over the sustaining qualities of a tone. The net effect of such a tone is an emphasis of rhythm at the expense of melody, and this, Skowroneck feels, is proper for the performance of modern music but not for early pieces.

It is true that Skowroneck's own work bears out his theories, since his instruments have the live, singing tone associated with the old ones. It is also true that these copies will, of necessity, be fragile, expensive, rare (since they take a long time to make) and unsuited to mass production. It follows that the insatiable demand for modern harpsichords could not be met by these copies.

The question now arises: How far can one go with substitution of modern materials and production methods without sacrificing the genuine tone? The danger here is that the maker is seduced by the new materials into more and more radical departures. Further, the modernizing could start what we may call the "complexity cycle" which is associated with so much of modern life. In harpsichords this cycle is described by Hubbard: "In an endeavor to make

Martin Skowroneck at the keyboard of one of his instruments.

them strong their makers increase the size and number of frame parts. They soon discover that in order to make such heavy instruments sound at all well, the strings must be heavier and longer than the norm for old instruments, but such a scale and stringing greatly increases the tension. The next step is to install even more weighty members to hold the instrument together."

The same principle could be applied to the jack mechanism. Wooden jacks and registers, for example would change dimensionally to match changes in the case, whereas rigid metal slides and plastic jacks needed to be made adjustable because the string band, which rests on wood, would be at odds with the fixed position of the jacks. Furthermore, the introduction of "half" stops, an intermediate position of the jacks requiring great accuracy, which developed in response to the modern demand for the greatest number of registration changes, would require minute adjustments. As we shall see, some of the complex modern jacks are so intricate that their net effect is to make the instrument less stable than a simple old one.

In theory it should be possible to preserve the historical sound (which, though it varied from one national style to another, was usually far superior to the modern tone in that it sang, sustained, and carried easily) and yet use modern materials and production methods. But in practice this is rarely achieved. (This argument is complicated by the fact that many performers make such distinctions between the different styles that they would consider it incorrect to perform Bach, for example, on a French style harpsichord, or Handel on an Italian instrument. But how many players, one might ask, could afford five different harpsichords, all exact copies of their prototypes?)

One should not blame the machine for the weaknesses of modern production methods. It must be stated flatly that a machine can do a better job than the human hand, in most cases. A machine will cut a piece of wood straighter, smoother and more accurately than the human hand; a machine can drill a more precise hole, can make a more perfect miter, can do a better sanding job, can polish a finish more effectively. The weakness of mass production lies not in the machines themselves, which are, after all, only extensions of the human hand. The flaw in mass production is precisely the human element. It is humans who set up the machines and operate them, and the ease of opera-

William Dowd.

tion, the dulling effect of constant repetition, and the frightening efficiency of the machine will lead to mistakes being made and then multiplied many times.

Skowroneck rightly points out that the moment a shop has numerous workmen, the instrument must be designed in such a way as to allow tolerance for mistakes by workmen which the master may never see. Therefore all glue joints must be doubly reinforced, all framing members thick enough to withstand string pressure even when fitted badly etc. This is given as one reason why production instruments cannot be as good as individually built ones.

Thus an ideal shop set-up would seem to be one or two craftsmen working with a complete set of machines at their disposal and making a certain number of similar instruments. This number should be large enough to warrant the time spent in production jigs and set-ups, but small enough not to dull the makers' faculties.

The modern makers working alone on exact copies often do not use machines if they can help it. They feel that the hand tool is a more immediate extension of the hand (perhaps analogous to the clavichord tangent as extension of the finger) and that the "feel" of the workman which was so important to the old makers who passed each board through their own hands, can more easily be applied to the work with hand tools. It should be pointed out that a good craftsman can become so adept at using woodworking machinery that the "feel" need not be lost. When the machines are properly oiled, run silently and smoothly in unworn bearings, when blades are sharp and guide fences true, when saw table surfaces are polished and belts have the right amount of give, and when the workman lets the machine do the work without forcing it, a relation of intimacy and "feel" can be built up between the workman and his machines.

In some cases both the way a shop is run and the quality of the product are determined by economic factors. Although the historical workshops seemed to earn a good living for their masters and in some cases even helped them amass a small fortune, this is hardly true today. It is probably not accidental that many of today's makers have rich wives or independent incomes. This is especially true of the better makers with smaller outputs. Harpsichord making

John Challis chipping (pulling to rough pitch) one of his harpsichords.

could hardly be considered a well paying profession, yet many are attracted to it by the rare promise of meaningful work.

A harpsichord maker working by himself might be able to make two large harpsichords a year selling for $5000 each, or perhaps seven smaller ones averaging $1400 each. In either case his turnover will be around $10,000—of which almost half will go into overhead and materials, unless he is well organized and works economically. His actual salary will then be considerably below that of a waiter, bricklayer, nurse, plumber or auto mechanic, not to speak of doctors, lawyers and stockbrokers.

Those makers who are in it for the money (there aren't many) may perhaps think in terms of the modern piano. Pianos which are, structurally at least, considerably more complicated than harpsichords, sell on the whole for lower prices. But pianos are made in enormous quantities, with true utilization of modern mass production techniques. Although the harpsichord market is brisk at the present, it is as nothing compared to the demand for pianos. The largest piano manufacturer in the world, Japan's Yamaha (200,000 a year) at one time considered going into harpsichord production but rejected the idea because it was not economically sound. (One rather shudders to think what the results would have been although the Yamaha piano is an excellent instrument.)

Nonetheless, one can at least conceive of a well organized, modern shop, turning out a good harpsichord like the French prototype, low priced and of high quality, in quantities to meet the demand easily. That this has not been done may be due to a number of factors. There is, first, the impossibility of getting capable, eager young apprentices who do not either want to dabble in something "interesting," or set up their own shop after one year. There is, second, the system of distribution, in which harpsichords have invariably been sold direct from the shop to the retail customer; putting them in dealers showrooms, aside from upping the prices considerably, has not worked. People interested in harpsichords tend to seek out a maker they have heard of rather than buy on impulse from a piano store; and dealers are usually not equipped to cope with service problems even in their own showrooms, let alone in the customer's house. And lastly, and perhaps most important, there is the personality of the harpsichord maker himself; he must be an ideal blend of craftsman and businessman; in most cases he is one or the other—or neither.

Let us now look at the most damaging modern departures from the old building styles. These can be summarized under the headings of (1) construction and materials (2) scale and tone (3) disposition (4) soundboard and ribs, and (5) action.

In the construction of the case the modern builders have departed most radically from the old harpsichords. We have seen that historical instruments never had cases more than $3/4$ in. thick, usually less, and always had bottoms. Since the modern revival was started by piano-makers, they immediately determined that an open bottom on a harpsichord would provide more sound, something they had decided was true for pianos. (The early pianos had, of course, closed bottoms.) Since the bottom provides an immense amount of strength, the lack of one had to be compensated for by heavy frame

Typical harpsichord made in the grander than grand piano tradition. Massive case, massive framing inside the case, and less tone than is achieved by less ponderous means. (Sperrhake Model 260)

members and a rim at least three times as thick as that found in old instruments.

Far from considering such subtle points as the effect of an enclosed air space or "baffle" on the tone, the piano makers thought of making the open bottom more efficient by doing away with the wooden frame altogether and substituting steel, and indeed Pleyel started manufacturing steel frame harpsichords.

Once the heavy case construction is used, the choice of material seems to make little difference. Some modern German makers use plywood filled with pressed wood chips, and aside from the fact that this material does not hold screws, it seems neither to improve the tone nor detract from it.

As a matter of fact, even many of those makers who adhere to the old case measurements use plywood today because of the ease of construction it affords. My own experience with plywood has been that if a high grade wood of the correct thickness is used it will have little effect on the tone, as far as such matters are capable of being measured. In this, however, I would be contradicted strongly by such builders as Skowroneck and Hyman. The

As a contrast to the massive Sperrhake, consider this elegant instrument by William Dowd. The "modern" lines of the Sperrhake are already dated, while the simple lines of the Dowd instrument will continue to be timelessly modern.

difficulty of proving this and many other points about harpsichord construction is that it is practically impossible to set up a scientifically controlled experiment, in which of two identical harpsichords, one, for example, receives a plywood and the other a lumber case. Aside from the fact that no two instruments are ever identical or sound alike, few makers can afford the time and money for such an impartial experiment.

Some modern harpsichord makers do not realize that in the older instruments the case was a part of the resonating system. When I constructed an Italian style harpsichord which had a plywood case $1/4$ in. thick the case was so live that each blow of the hammer would resound and echo before the soundboard was even installed. (It might, incidentally, be interesting to contrast the modern method of pre-forming the bentside with the Italian way of bending the side right to the instrument, thereby pulling it tightly over the frame like a drumskin.)

In addition to dropping the bottom, thickening the case walls and adding heavy frame members, the modern German makers also shortened the length of the instrument considerably, replacing the long brass wires in the bass with short, thick, overspun strings. This encouraged the muddy bass often called *dumpf droehnend* (muffled boom), especially in the 16′, which was hung on the already foreshortened 8′ bridge. As if to emphasize the short squat appearance of these instruments, the grain of the outer veneer was run vertically.

The scale and its effect on tone is perhaps the most disputed and confused issue in harpsichord construction. Adding to the confusion is our lack of knowledge of the exact pitch used on the old harpsichords. Pitch and scale are of course intricately related, since a string 10 in. long would sound entirely different if tuned to c^2 rather than a fourth higher to f^2.

We must consider here Frank Hubbard's statement that as the scale is progressively elongated the tone becomes louder and plainer, losing the silvery fuzz of harmonic development, until it becomes dull and coarse (and breaks). As the string is shortened the tone becomes weaker and more complex and overtone-ridden until it is rejected as false.

We are therefore moving between two extremes, approximately represented by $c^2 = 9$ in. and $c^2 = 17$ in., on either side of which the tone becomes unacceptable. (It should be kept in mind here that the custom of expressing the scale by citing c^2, though convenient, is only a rough approximation, since from middle c on down scales are often severely foreshortened.) The modern makers have been moving in the direction of the longer scale for two reasons. They are after increased volume, and they claim that a tightly stretched string will minimize the drop in pitch which follows after a plectrum has just plucked the string, a process involving lifting, stretching, and increasing the pitch of the string for an instant. With increased volume, however, the longer string will also lose complexity, going towards the plain and dull. Of course, the considerably increased tension entails heavier construction. It should also be kept in mind that volume alone is a questionable goal to strive for. A harpsichord with a clear, singing, sustaining tone will fill a concert hall more effectively than an instrument with a louder tone which carries with it the percussiveness of the pluck, and whose tone falls with a dead thud at the listeners' feet.

An example of the massive machinery inside a modern piano-maker's version of the harpsichord, including mechanical fine-tuning devices, separate dampers, and piano-style metal framing. Detail of a Pleyel harpsichord.

The question of disposition has already been discussed in the historical section. From the point of view of construction it is not a good practice to hang the heavy 16′ strings on the 8′ bridge, thus encumbering that bridge and often spoiling the tone of the instrument. In the so-called Bach disposition that is frequently the case; in the few surviving instruments with genuine 16′ stops, these were always given their own separate bridge. But aside from the fact that the Bach disposition (1 × 16′, 1 × 8′ on the lower, and 1 × 8′, 1 × 4′ on the upper) was never found in historical instruments, it is not particularly practical for the player. The lower combination of 8′ and 16′ is not very pleasant by itself, and does not dialogue well with the upper 8′ and 4′, whereas a lower combination of 16′ and 4′, or all three lower stops will contrast nicely with the upper solo 8′.

The modern soundboard construction has again been derived from the piano which, after forcing the harpsichord out altogether, has had an unhealthy effect on that instrument, as if to say; you can come back again, but only by copying me and following my ideas.

In pianos, soundboards are quite thick to withstand the enormous pressure of the heavy strings. Numerous ribs run straight across the soundboard, passing right under the bridge. All of this presumably makes little difference to the tone, since the drumstick-like force of the hammers will set the strings in motion, no matter what kind of board is under them.

With the much lighter harpsichord strings the quality, size and ribbing of the soundboard becomes critical; the harpsichord string will have less force to activate the soundboard and thus will be less able to overcome obstacles. We find, therefore, that a rib run under the bridge will "kill" the tone at that point. For that reason the old makers never crossed under the bridge. In the space of some 50 years many of the modern makers have not yet questioned

57

Underside of Neupert "Couperin" model, showing massive framing, and ribbing of soundboard at right angles to bentside crossing under the bridges. Round buttons on soundboard insulate heads of screws from touching soundboard.

For comparison with the Neupert construction, the interior of a Skowroneck harpsichord patterned after a Dulcken harpsichord.

the wisdom of ribbing straight across the soundboard or using boards $^1/_4$ in. thick. As long as customers continue to write them letters of praise for the sound (one must realize that customers who have no means of comparing the sound of their instruments can do little else than admire the unusual tone of a harpsichord no matter what it sounds like, and this is why almost any tone will find some proponents), they will presumably continue to make harpsichords in this way. Many other modern makers have a haphazard attitude toward the ribstructure; they change from one system to another frequently, and their attitude seems to be never to cross the bridge till they come to it.

The question of plywood or laminated soundboards should be considered because plywood gets around the problem of cracked soundboards. In America, especially, the difference between the dry steam heat in the winter and the high humidity in the summer will result in radical soundboard changes. These boards can easily expand $^1/_4$ in. in each direction, and it stands to reason that a solid board, glued down firmly, will crack when it shrinks. The practice is therefore to install these boards when they are at their driest so that they cannot shrink any further but only expand. This they will often do, resulting in a large bulge, sometimes touching the strings and causing buzzes.

Since plywood boards will not crack but are quite capable of expanding, they are usually glued in when they are at their largest (most humid) so that they can expand no further. In what way they interfere with the sound is a matter of conjecture. No matter how many theories are advanced by physicists and acoustical engineers (and they are quick to jump into the fray), this point is best settled by practical experience.

Since no two instruments sound exactly alike, a comparison of a plywood and solid board in two similar instruments might not tell the whole story. I recently had an unusual occasion to test this point when I was forced to remove a solid spruce board from one of my clavichords which had gone through an especially humid summer in the country and replace it with a soundboard of the same thickness, but triple laminated basswood. Oddly enough, I found the tone of the laminated board to be somewhat louder and clearer, and to have more definition.

However, before one jumps to conclusions from this example it may be well to consider the general quality of an instrument before assessing the effect of particular construction methods. On the whole, the finer the instrument, the more critical each change would be because of the harpsichord's sensitivity. This particular clavichord was of a medium quality, so a change did not seem to make much difference. Had the instrument been a carefully worked out copy, the plywood board might have had a deleterious effect.

It is interesting to note that laminated soundboards were successfully tried in the eighteenth century. Hubbard cites a maker called Carl Lemme who is quoted in *Musikalische Erfindungen* 1781 (p. 277):

In the year 1771 we received an order from a friend who was staying just then in Amsterdam, to send two claviers with the express condition that their soundboards must be injured neither by his proposed tour to Batavia nor by the heat nor by anything else. We were convinced that the risk was too great for us to depend on using merely good dry wood and sending the claviers off, for in this case we must be absolutely certain.

We set aside on this account a room in which we hung a Farenheit thermometer, and specially heated it to the temperature found below the Equator; and all experiments were fruitless even when we used the driest baked wood. Even if it did not split in the heat, it did when it was returned to the cold, or at least it warped. Finally we had the idea of making a double soundboard which I called "gepreszten" in my catalogue. Admittedly the fear arose that the tone might lose its perfection. Only unwearying diligence, numerous and often fruitless experiments, and many changes to the specially made clamps satisfied us. The commissioned claviers arrived at the specified place without the least damage, and many more have followed thither with the same good fortune.

The language in this, incidentally, making use of such phrases as "unwearying diligence" "numerous and often fruitless experiments" sounds very much like that found in many modern makers' catalogues.

Last of the modern offenders is the action. Again, the modern harpsichord inherited its keyboard from the piano makers. Piano keys are almost 1 in. thick and heavily bushed at points of contact with pins, since these keys receive a great deal of punishment. Aside from the fact that they are often subjected to brutal and continuous pounding, the greater volume of the piano, and the need to withstand greater playing force, necessitates a sturdy key.

This is not so on a harpsichord. Players soon find that no matter how much or how little force is exerted, the tone has practically the same amount of volume. The intelligent players therefore soon develop the light touch associated with harpsichords, for whose key half the size and weight of a piano key is sufficient. A light and unbushed key will have the advantage of bouncing up and down with great facility, helping to achieve lightning speed and instant repetition. Further, a light unbushed key "trembles" (*zittert*) under the finger, according to Skowroneck, actually vibrating with the sound and giving the player an intimate "feel" of the action.

We have already mentioned the "cycle of complexity," as it affects the jack. Again the ideas derive from the modern grand piano action which is capable of infinite and minute adjustment. The ironic fact regarding this is that perhaps only one piano technician out of ten has mastered the difficult art of regulating a grand piano, so that only one in ten pianos is in good adjustment. Although in theory this is capable of correction (one merely needs to regulate the action, the manufacturer might say) in practice it is not (who will do it, with technicians becoming rarer and more expensive all the time?).

Two small examples of self-defeating complexity should be cited here. On the old jacks the damper was wedged into a slot, within which it could be pulled up and down for adjustment. Some modern makers follow this sensible arrangement, but others, notably Neupert, go it one better and glue the damper to a little brass extension which is slotted on one side and can be moved up and down for adjustment. What happens in practice is that the workman gluing the damper to the brass shelf also gets glue on the jack body so that the damper will stick to the jack itself, making it in fact not adjustable. This is so common that I have rarely seen a Neupert rectangular jack without it (in their round "OK" jack they have abandoned this method).

Another example of complexity for its own sake concerns a jack first developed by Maendler, and continued by Wittmayer for a while. They reasoned that the small amount of play necessary to keep the jack moving up and down in the slide might cause adjustment problems. They attempted to solve these problems by attaching to the bottom of the jack a long spring pointing upwards whose function it was to keep the jack to one side in its slide slot. What actually happened was that these springs got caught under the strings when jacks were removed for servicing. Once the spring was bent it was hard to straighten, and the repairer would frequently just clip it off. Since the slide slots had a considerable amount of play in anticipation of this spring, once the spring was gone the jack was extremely unreliable. It should be pointed out that the presence of play between jack and slide slot was objected to in the first place because the precise point at which a leather plectrum plucks is of extreme importance. The spring would have been unnecessary with quill, which can be plucked at the very tip or farther in without altering the tone, thus tolerating a certain amount of play. A leather plectrum is tapered, and the slightest play causes string contact at a different point in the taper, resulting in variation in volume.

These examples could be multiplied and will, indeed, be discussed under the individual makers. They should suffice here to illustrate the point that each "improvement" brings in its wake a problem which must then be overcome with another improvement. Anyone with an idea for improving the jack action (and improvements have been suggested since the sixteenth century) should think through his idea most thoroughly and test it out in practice before advancing it. On the whole, mechanical things work best when they are left in their simplest possible form.

Having looked at the damaging departures from traditional ways of making harpsichords, let us now consider the imperfections which are in the nature of the harpsichord itself, so that we may know at the start what the makers are up against.

The first problem concerns the production of the pluck itself. To date no satisfactory plucking material has been found. Leather has the severe disadvantage of gradually getting duller and softer as the point gets used again

Jack of a seventeenth-century Italian harpsichord signed F. F. Pearwood with hardwood tongue, flat brass spring. Plectrum was quill, now changed to delrin. Note loose damper which has been tightened with cardboard shim. To make room for a small adjusting end pin, ¼ in. has been cut off the bottom.

Soundboard of an Italian seventeenth-century harpsichord undergoing restoration in the Zuckermann shops. This instrument has a 2 × 8' disposition without handstops; in order to throw jackslides to off position for tuning, you must reach under jackrail.

and again until, by imperceptible steps, the owner has a different harpsichord from the one he originally possessed. In addition, leather is extremely sensitive to the slightest changes in humidity. A harpsichord must stay in perfect regulation, i.e., the relationship between jacks and strings must be constant, in order for leather to work well. Needless to say, this is asking more of a harpsichord than it can reasonably be expected to deliver.

Quill has been the subject of complaints from the old days to the present. It is true that quill from such birds as goose and chicken has given this material a bad name, since feathers from these fowl are not satisfactory for the purpose. However, even primary wing and tail feathers from such birds as raven, condor, crow, eagle and turkey, which are suitable, have caused their share of problems. It is hard to find a constant supply, and selecting suitable feathers and shaping the quill itself are all tasks fraught with uncertainties; in terms of modern production they are not to be considered.

Next, the various plastics are considered. Modern man has an unshakeable faith in plastics, but it may come as a surprise to learn that no plastic has yet been equal to the task of plucking a string over and over again. Some plastics, like corfam, get "tired" or lose their resiliency, some like delrin seem to undergo a subtle change from the repeated shock of plucking, until they become hard and brittle. Still others are affected by moisture, like leather. In addition, plastics don't have the advantage of uneven organic materials like quill and leather, which negotiate the pluck somewhat gradually; a uniformly structured material like plastic will bend evenly under pressure until it reaches the point when it will bend no longer. It will then straighten out with such suddenness that this process is likely to be accompanied by a small sound of an explosion, in effect an unpleasant mechanical sound. The feel of such an action will also be unsatisfactory because it will be rubbery leading to a sudden departure of any resistance.

It seems that constant plucking of a thin, stretched steel string puts an enormous strain on almost any material. It can be calculated that in a given piece, like Bach's C major Prelude, lasting about 138 seconds, middle C gets plucked 69 times, or once every two seconds. Thus in one hour middle C will receive 1800 plucks, and in one week of two hour a day practice it will get plucked

Wormeaten pinblock removed from restored Italian harpsichord.

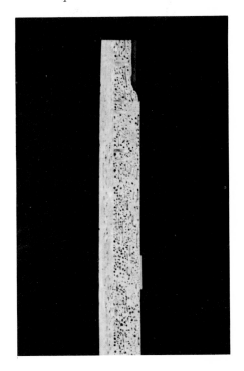

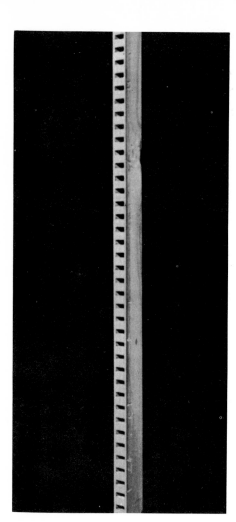

Box jackslide from Italian harpsichord (one of two). Jack slots are carefully carved from solid wood, eliminating need for lower jack guide.

about 25,000 times for a yearly total of one and a quarter million plucks.

The second source of imperfection in the harpsichord is the necessity for a jack to ride up and down freely in a guide without allowing any play. Further, the jack must return by the force of gravity alone, and still allow the plectrum to slide past the string. This is something of a feat, depending on closely but carefully fitted parts, stable materials, stable weather, smooth plectrum undersides, rust-free strings, cases matching jacks and slides in expansion, exactly the right jack spring tension and many similar prerequisites. To expect it of one jack may be reasonable, but to expect it of 250 jacks at all times is perhaps asking for too much.

The third imperfection is the matter of spacing; there is just too much that must be fitted into a small space, both laterally and from front to back.

Since keyboards are designed in such a way as to make the key tails about $1/2$ in. wide, there is a maximum of $1/2$ in. (less the diameter of the string) between two strings. When a second set of strings is added, the space gets reduced to less than $3/8$ in. The second set must be at least $1/8$ in. away from the first to avoid the famous damper problem. This occurs when two jacks of different 8′ sets, facing each other, ride up and down in the $3/8$ in. space between strings, left to accomodate them. The damper of each jack must rest on the string assigned to it. Since the jack must be capable of being completely disengaged, a movement of over $1/16$ in. is necessary to allow the plectrum to miss the string. During this movement, the damper must continue to rest on the string to avoid sympathetic vibrations. It follows that the damper must start out by protruding more than $1/16$ in. beyond the string it is resting on, if it is to have string contact even after the move disengaging the jack. On the other hand, the damper must not be allowed to touch its neighboring string; thus a healthy amount of clearance is called for, especially when it is considered that a vibrating string takes up more space than a silent one. This is how we arrive at the minimum of $1/8$ in. between narrow string pairs.

The scant $3/8$ in. that is left between the wide pairs must now be allotted to a jack and to clearances both in front and in back of the jack. As we have seen, the jack must be allowed a certain amount of movement, thus in effect decreasing the availability of space. The jack itself cannot be made very slim since it must contain a swivelling tongue usually slimmer than the jack itself. This tongue holds the plectrum and a certain amount of "meat" is necessary both for the plectrum and the tongue axle pin. If the tongue is $1/8$ in. thick, the jack will be about $3/16$ in. It is easy to see that this leaves not much more than $1/16$ in. clearance between jack and strings. Since the tongue has a habit of flinging backwards right after an explosive pluck, it often touches the neighboring string. Kirckman recognized this problem by placing a staple in back of the tongue to limit its movement. Some modern makers place a thread in back of the tongue, especially in the bass where the larger amplitude of the vibrating string throws the tongue back even further. The staple or thread will usually hamper easy voicing, since it prevents the voicer from swivelling the tongue out completely for easy access. But then, many modern jacks prevent swivelling-out of the tongue altogether by the way they are designed and voicing procedures adjust to this.

Bannister and others attempt to solve the lateral space problem (which is

compounded by the narrower key span used on old harpsichords) by splaying out the keys in the back to gain more than the $^1/_2$ in. key width in front. This works, but makes keyboard construction cumbersome and adds width at the front at the expense of an elegant appearance.

The front to back space shortage is even more severe. Four registers containing jacks must often fit into a space which is limited by the top or shortest string. In an average scale the length of f^3 on the 8′ is about $5^1/_2$ in. Into this space must be crammed the treble tip of the 8′ bridge with enough free soundboard around it not to kill the tone; the 4′ hitchpin rail and the 4′ bridge tip, again with free soundboard space; the thickness of the belly rail; four registers containing jacks; the top 4′ nut and tuning pin; and the rail for the 8′ buff stop.

Allowing an absolute minimum of just over half of the available space to the soundboard area, we are left with little more than 2 in. for the gap containing the registers and the section of pinblock containing the 4′ nut, etc. Now the registers themselves must have some thickness, a minimum of $^1/_{16}$ in. on each side of the jack, and since there must be play as well the jacks cannot be over $^3/_8$ in. in width. Even at that we have used up the allotted 2 in. without considering some play for the registers themselves to prevent jamming when the pinblock bowes in under string pressure, or the room needed for the pinblock section of the top string. But a jack $^3/_8$ in. wide leaves little room for a damper slot, and some makers get around this by having special damper jacks which carry the dampers for all the damper-free jacks. The damper jacks themselves take additional space, of course, nullifying most of the space gained.

The severe space shortage both sideways and front to back causes many maintenance problems of jacks sticking or touching backs or fronts of strings, and slides jamming. I have known plumbers who have given up plumbing because in that trade one is forever forced to work in the tightest and most inaccessible areas; the same could be said for harpsichord technicians, and it is not surprising that they have frequent nightmares.

So far we have dealt with three flaws of the harpsichord, none of which are easily correctable—the wear and tear of constant plucking, the gravity controlled jack movement, and the extreme space limitation for the jack

Keyboard and rack of Italian harpsichord, showing slits in rack at back of keys. Wooden slips in the key ends slide up and down in the slits. Keys are boxwood, with arcades; sharps are ebony.

63

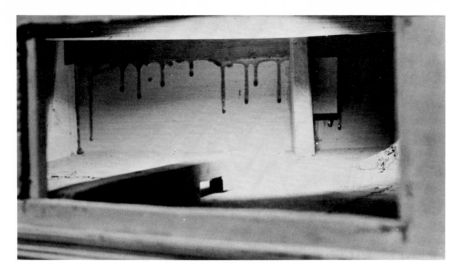

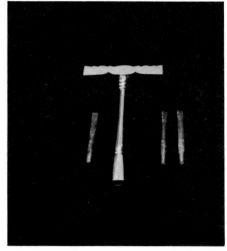

Interior of case of Italian harpsichord showing two of the knees supporting bentside. Note glue drippings below liner—probably from the original construction. Photo taken through cut-out in spine.

Threadless, flat-headed tuning pins from an antique harpsichord. The tuning key is a copy by Hugh Gough of an eighteenth-century tool.

Section view of Italian harpsichord.

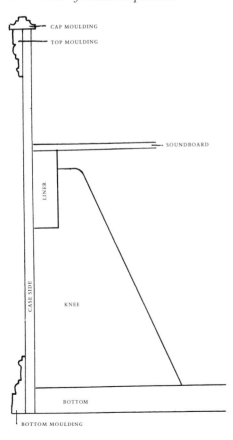

CAP MOULDING
TOP MOULDING

SOUNDBOARD

LINER

CASE SIDE

KNEE

BOTTOM

BOTTOM MOULDING

action. Two further flaws concern the 4′ hitchpin rail and the general instability of the harpsichord.

The 4′ strings are usually anchored on the soundboard itself, since they are only half as long as the 8′ strings and cannot reach the 8′ hitchpin rail because the 8′ bridge is in the way. Although the 4′ hitchpins are supported by a rail underneath the soundboard, this rail must be reasonably light so as not to interfere with the sound. The pull that the 4′ strings exert on the hitchpin rail will lift that section of soundboard, so that it is quite customary to find the 8′ and 4′ bridges lying in a "valley" with the hitchpin rail on a mound between them. Oddly enough, far from interfering with the sound, this peculiar topography sometimes seems to enhance it, and most good harpsichords seem to show this to some degree. In extreme cases, the soundboard may come up to touch the strings.

The three or four ways of getting around this are not very satisfactory. The 4′ strings can go all the way to the 8′ hitchpin rail through holes drilled into the 8′ bridge; the 4′ hitchpin rail can be attached firmly to braces inside the harpsichord; the 4′ strings can be attached to pins coming up through holes in the soundboard; and numerous ribs can be run straight across the soundboard. (The German harpsichords never show the wavy soundboard topography because of their ribbing straight across.) Some of these solutions interfere with the tone, others are mechanically awkward.

The general instability of the harpsichord, which in the mind of the public is intimately associated with this instrument, is practically a function of its tone. In order to get a good sound, a harpsichord must have fine wires, must have a thin soundboard, must have a reasonably thin case. Even if metal reinforcement is used, the thin strings and thin soundboard will see to it that there is expansion, contraction and shifting, with resultant tuning and action instability. John Challis has done more than anyone else to resolve these problems and he has come close, but there is general agreement that the tone he achieves is unlike that of a fine old harpsichord.

The picture presented here of the harpsichord as a flawed instrument is uniformly gloomy, but in actual practice these problems can be held down to manageable proportions. For the purpose of this study, it is important to keep these problems in mind, especially in trying to evaluate the work of the makers we are about to consider.

64

The Modern Makers

THE QUESTION is often asked which is the "best" harpsichord made. It is argued that there is a leader in every field—there is a "best" piano, motorcar, hearing aid and what have you. The question of best is not easily applicable to harpsichords. In such a question the instrument's various properties would have to be considered and evaluated; thus we would investigate the instrument's physical appearance, its tonal qualities, its capacity for staying in tune and regulation, its ease of servicing, its response to climatic changes, its behavior during transport and rough handling, and its size and weight. No harpsichord could be rated best in all of these departments; some of them, like a singing tone and extreme stability seem to be mutually exclusive.

While there is no "best" harpsichord, one could easily find candidates for the worst (indeed, it would be difficult to choose from among many applicants), since it is quite possible to make an instrument that is ugly, unreliable, mechanically complex, heavy and difficult to transport, and possessing no tone at all.

The question of "best" is further complicated by a consideration of best for what? Best for a performer to practice six hours a day on? Best for a housewife to play once a week? Best for accompanying chamber music? Best for Scarlatti, for the *Fitzwilliam Virginal Book*, for rock and roll? Best for playing in a large hall, in an apartment in the middle of the night? Best as a show piece in a pretentious home, or (as I recently had occasion to supply) as a furnishing for a builder's model apartment? And further, best at what price, and what delivery time?

In considering the modern makers, I have at least attempted to be objective, describing the instruments in text and pictures so that the reader may draw his own conclusions. In evaluating how an instrument performs it is, of course, unavoidable to make some value judgments; from closely following the career of the various makers' instruments in the cutomer's home, on the concert stage, or in the repair shop, I have been forced to draw some conclusions with which I should acquaint the reader. To write a study on the modern harpsichord by quoting from advertising brochures would not prove very enlightening to the reader.

In the last chapter we discussed the many shortcomings of the harpsichord. To acquaint the reader with my own bias, let us now briefly look at an instrument as close to the ideal as I could conceive of, perhaps an amalgam of the various makers' products.

This instrument would be physically handsome—harpsichords, after all, were objects of beauty, enticing artists to lavish extravagant care on their decoration. Since a harpsichord has only an average of about 50 to 60 keys to the piano's 88, it is capable of having a much more elegant shape, being slim in front but of approximately the same length. The width of the grand piano in front determines its bulging curve, its bulky action is responsible for its deep case, and its heavy construction neccessitates its fat legs. All of this is not required in a harpsichord; it can be slim, light, possessing an elegant curve, and resting on delicate legs or stand. It has a tradition of being decorated in bright colors and patterns, unlike the somber nineteenth-century piano. Thus our ideal harpsichord would perhaps be 7 feet long (long enough to achieve a good bass in the lowest 8′ strings, but not so long as to create a problem in handling or room placement); it would possess a gentle bentside and perhaps a fishtail at the end; it would have a painted case, perhaps in the French or Flemish tradition, with a decorated soundboard, or a natural wood case with the grain running lengthwise to emphasize its length; it would have keyboards with arcaded or moulded fronts, wooden or ivory naturals, and wooden sharps; it would have elegant hinges and hardware, a music desk of pleasing size and shape, and a stand or legs of the right proportion.

The instrument would have two five octave keyboards, FF to f³, close enough together to allow playing the upper and lower with one hand, and far enough apart to allow easy crossing of hands from one keyboard to another. There would be 2 × 8′ and 1 × 4′, arranged so that the 4′ is between the two 8′ rows of jacks, thus giving the two 8′s enough contrast from varying pluck-

Double manual harpsichord by William Dowd, inspired by a Ruckers transposing double except for the disposition: 2 × 8′, 1 × 4′, compass BB–b².

MVSICA DONVM DEI

QVOD CANTVS FLORERE FACIT

ing points. The 8′s would have a live enough bass to make up for the lack of a 16′, and the lower keyboard would work the 4′ and back 8′, while the upper would bring the closer or "nasal" 8′ into play. There would be a shove coupler on the keyboards, handstops to control the on and off positions of the registers, and buff stops on both 8′s.

The action of my ideal instrument would work smoothly, noiselessly, and effortlessly. The jacks could be of a stable plastic, and the plectra could be of delrin, carefully voiced. The jacks would be carefully fitted to the slide to leave enough play for smooth operation under all climatic conditions, but not so much as to cause imprecision in repetition. The slide could be wood, allowing it to expand together with the case, and covered with leather for noiseless operation. The lower guide could be a stable material like plexiglass, through which the jack end pins glide. The jacks would be adjusted to pluck the three strings in quick succession, so that the resistance of the pluck is not tripled when all three strings are plucked together. The jacks would possess top adjustment screws which would be set to allow plectrum movement either forwards or backwards. The plectra would project about $1/_{32}$ in. beyond the string, resulting in an action light enough, yet preventing the plectra from missing. The jack springs would be resilient enough to return the tongue quickly to rest position, thus assuring quick repetition, yet not possess so much tension as to prevent the plectrum from sliding around the string on its way down. The keys would be light, unbushed, minimally leaded, allowing a frictionless performance.

The tone would sustain easily, and its singing quality would swallow up any explosive or percussive sound emitted by the pluck itself. The bass would be neither thuddy nor boom out, the tenor would be clear without being raucous, and the treble would be fluty and without harshness. The tone would carry easily so that the listener could trace the patterns of different melodies played against each other, without imposing itself on the performer or listener, or forcing the shape of the music. It would be neither lushly romantic nor boringly dry, would neither whimper nor blast. It would accept whatever music was played on it, neither adding to nor detracting from the music, but allowing the player to form his piece to his own desired shape.

I would expect to give my instrument a thorough tuning and adjusting session of two hours once a month, and would be prepared to touch up sections of the instrument once a week, unless it were used in performance, when I would expect to tune the whole thing. To expect more stability than this would probably mean sacrificing a balanced tone.

So far it is perhaps possible to find actual instruments measuring up to my ideal. But I would further expect this instrument to cost only about $2500 and be delivered within three months.

Now these may sound like unreasonable requirements, but we must keep in mind that both pianos and motor cars, which are infinitely more complex, sell for lower prices than harpsichords and can be delivered much more quickly. Are harpsichords, then, really so difficult to make?

Consider again the ideal harpsichord. Once the design has been carefully worked out, it should be possible, at least in theory, to make such an instrument in a large plant. The cases are capable of being mass produced and yet made accurately, as is easily proved by the German harpsichord production. The jacks, slides, guides, and keyboard are no more difficult to make than countless other industrial products. That leaves us only with the soundboard, voicing and regulation, which are not so easily adaptable to mass production.

But the theory and practice of harpsichord making are two different things. The mentality of the craftsman and the businessman do not mix easily. William Dowd, for example, maintains that he does not want to enlarge his shop any further, forcing him into the front office and away from the bench. He is looking forward, as are many of us, to making two instruments a year, without help and without taking customers' orders to force him into the whole expansion cycle all over again. John Challis spends part of his time building exquisite record and sheet music cabinets for his own use, and Frank Hubbard makes violin bows. I am forever building mediaeval furniture in my shop. This is surely not the attitude of a serious businessman.

The concept of an educated man being allowed by this society to work with his hands is relatively new and the credit for this must go at least in part to Dolmetsch and William Morris. Perhaps to punish society for this long delayed and grudgingly given permission, the educated man takes rather a cavalier attitude toward the business aspect of his craft. In continental Europe

Diagram of a shove coupler showing "on" and "off" positions.

Diagram of a dogleg jack.

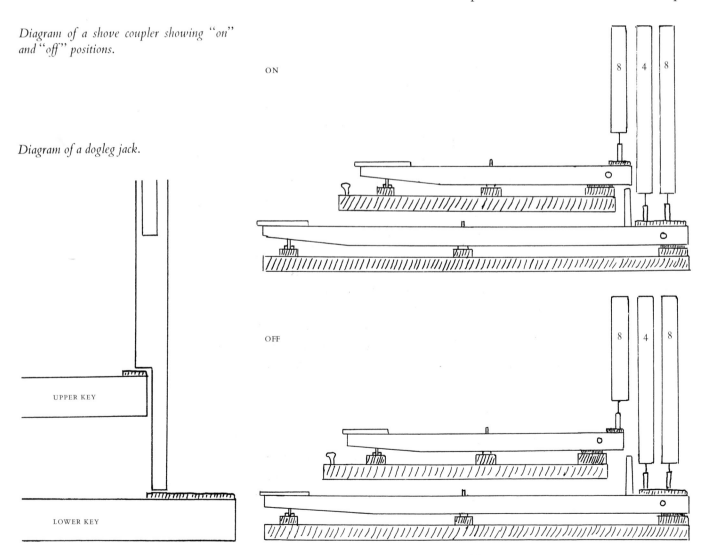

ON

8 4 8

OFF

8 4 8

UPPER KEY

LOWER KEY

where modern harpsichord making started much earlier than in America, its practitioners are more deadly serious and professional, with a consequent lack of imagination.

This brings up the difficult question of who *is* a professional harpsichord maker; with the appearance of harpsichord kits the line between the professional and the amateur gets very thin indeed. John Challis, half in jest, defines the professional maker as one who is willing to buy back his own instruments. This would presume that the professional maker's instruments are recognized, desirable and subject to long waiting times (after all, why buy back your own if you already have surplus stock).

Perhaps a more charitable definition would be concerned with a combination of factors: length of time in business, number of instruments made (and sold—some beginning makers keep piling up instruments until their houses are full, and then move to larger houses), percentage of time devoted to building, portion of income derived from it, and seriousness of purpose. Charles Mould, in his study of modern English makers for the *Galpin Society Journal* (XIX, April, 1966), defined the professional as follows: "A professional maker is one who builds his instruments primarily for sale to the general public, or a builder whose instruments have been used and acclaimed by performers of international rank." I have erred on the side of leniency in including everyone who has made a few instruments of his own design and sold them, and whose intention it is to continue. The extent of his professionalism should become apparent from the description of his activities.

The builders given here are arranged in alphabetical order, a system Boalch uses successfully with the old makers, where Ruckers is preceded by someone named Roze who may or may not ever have built anything (no instruments have survived), and followed by Rudloff, also with no surviving instruments and a scanty record. No attempt has been made (or could easily have been made) to set apart the important makers from the beginners, semi-professionals, or former builders. It must be pointed out again that the opinions given here are those of one man. The reader is invited to seek out as many harpsichords as he can find and form his own conclusions.

No claim is made that this listing is complete. Some makers listed here should perhaps not have been included, and others who should have been, may not have come to light in time. Some makers did not fully co-operate with this survey and information on them may contain inaccuracies; others co-operated too fully and may have stretched their production figures a bit. Still others, like some of their historical predecessors, may purposely have supplied misinformation. Within these limits, however, an effort has been made to be as inclusive and accurate as possible.

JEREMY ADAMS
211 East Main Street, Gloucester, Massachusetts

The Boston area has become the Antwerp of the modern harpsichord. Around the workshops of Frank Hubbard and William Dowd are clustered a number of small shops of their former apprentices turning out harpsichords based on the best of the French and Flemish predecessors.

The pioneering work done by both Hubbard and Dowd can best be appreciated by looking at the work of their apprentices. Here is the same scrupulous attention to historical models, the same meticulous craftsmanship, the same dedication to the craft. (Sentences like this always sound like excerpts from some harpsichord maker's brochure, but here they are justified—and, in any case, neither Hubbard nor Dowd nor their apprentices issue brochures more elaborate than descriptions of their instruments and price lists.)

After working a year in a store front in Cambridge diagonally across from a place called American Variable Star Observers, Jeremy Adams has now established himself in Gloucester, Massachusetts.

For six years Adams worked for William Dowd, and before that he worked for an organ builder. Since Dowd has an average staff of only six, an apprentice gets to do almost everything from keyboard-making to stringing and voicing. A Dowd apprentice will often build an instrument for himself, using Dowd's shop facilities—perhaps his "masterpiece." Adams has only built two instruments, a single manual harpsichord based on a 1640 Ruckers, and a double based on Dulcken, the eighteenth-century Flemish maker who followed Ruckers by a century and whose instruments have served as models for a number of modern makers. (Dulcken's harpsichords had a lot more in common with the eighteenth-century English harpsichords than with the earlier Ruckers, and usually included a "lute" stop, the set of jacks plucking close to the nut and producing a nasal tone.)

Adams, unlike many beginners, makes his own jacks and keyboards. The jacks, in contrast to Dowd's, are wooden, but this is not a case of the apprentice outdoing the master with regard to authenticity. Plastic jacks require an expensive mould, and unless he is willing to buy plastic jacks from another maker, the beginner will have to do the laborious work of making wooden jacks himself. (We used to make them in quantity and counted 32 different operations in the process.)

Adams uses wooden slides and follows Dowd in the use of plexiglass lower guides. His soundboards, like those of the entire Boston school are of spruce, barred in the conventional classical manner and tapered toward the edges.

KLAUS AHREND
2951 Veenhusen-Kolonie 21B, bei Leerlostfriesland, West Germany

The importance of Klaus Ahrend lies in the fact that he is one of a small number of makers working in Germany today in a one-man shop building copies of historical models. Until recently this was unheard of in the land of the mass-produced harpsichord and the infamous Bach registration.

Ahrend was born in 1937 in Göttingen, and has been making harpsichords for the past five years. He has produced a total of 17 instruments, and is currently making an average of three instruments yearly, doubles and singles. He makes his own keyboards and jacks, which is generally a clue to an entire style of working. It will usually mean that he is very particular as to what goes into his instruments (though in Germany one can actually buy very well made keyboards), that he is copying old harpsichords of a specific style, and that he is not lazy. Ahrend's jacks are made of beech, one of the woods used for jacks in Germany, which is quite stable but not as smooth, easy to work or attractive as pear. Pearwood comes from Switzerland and is almost impossible to get

Ahrend jack: wooden body and tongue, delrin plectrum; no adjustment screws.

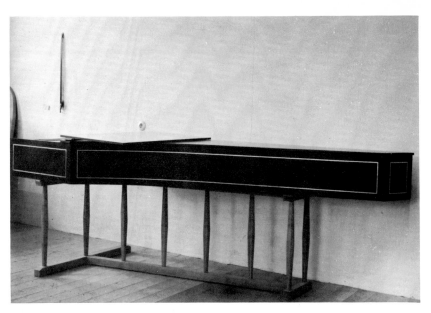

nowadays. (The last pearwood I had was so gnarled and full of knots and blemishes that an entire half log yielded but a pitiful quantity of usable material.) The jacks are 15 mm ($^1/_2$ in.) wide and 3.5 mm ($^5/_{32}$ in.) thick, and plectrum material is delrin or quill.

Ahrend uses *Fichte* for his soundboards, which I take to mean spruce.

Klaus Ahrend is in frequent communication with Martin Skowroneck and Rainer Schuetze, two of the other German historical workshops; the three builders have had an interesting effect on the production shops in Germany as we will have occasion to see.

A handsome double manual harpsichord by Klaus Ahrend in the late Flemish style. Specification: 5 octaves; upper manual 1 × 8′; lower manual 1 × 8′, 1 × 4′; push coupler; 37½ × 102 in.

Klaus Ahrend at the keyboard.

JAN H. ALBARDA
14 Riverdale Drive, Thistletown (Rexdale), Ontario, Canada

Jan Albarda started his building career in 1962 at the age of 52. As is often the case nowadays, he first started with a kit and later developed his own designs.

Born in The Hague, Holland, in 1910, he graduated in architecture and engineering from the Technical University in Delft. After practicing and teaching architecture for thirteen years, he left Holland in 1951 to settle in Canada with his wife and two children. It was there, in the liberating environment of the new world, that he was able to indulge his interest in music to the extent of embarking on a career as a harpsichord maker.

Albarda has made a total of 25 instruments, including doubles, singles, spinets, virginals and ottavinos. His pitch c^2 is that golden mean of scale averages, 13$^3/_4$ in. He works by himself, being interested in "quality, not a large output." Albarda makes his own keyboards, and sometimes jacks, but often uses the plastic jack of Frank Hubbard's design which is now commercially available from a Boston piano supply house. (The day that supply houses everywhere start stocking keyboards and jacks is the day we are going to see a great flowering of harpsichord making everywhere.)

Jan Albarda has published a book called *Wood, Wire and Quill* (Coach House Press, Toronto, 1968) which is intended for the layman as an introduction to the harpsichord. He has restored eighteenth-century spinets and early nineteenth-century square pianos. Restoring early squares, the rectangular ancestors of the modern piano, is, incidentally, a job frequently tackled by the instrument enthusiast, simply because these instruments are plentiful and cheap, and the closest one can usually get to antique harpsichords or clavichords. It is a restoration which should not be undertaken lightly.

Albarda uses both solid spruce and poplar plywood for soundboards. The only commercially available poplar plywood is Italian poplar, which comes in 4′ × 8′ sheets of three glued-up layers totalling $1/8$ in. in thickness. I feel somewhat responsible for spreading the use of this material for soundboards, since we supplied it in the early years of the Zuckermann kit. We have long since abandoned it in favor of basswood made up specially, since it turned out to be unstable, full of blemishes and skipped inner layers, and tonally not as successful as other plywoods.

Next to keyboard and jack making, the soundboard is the biggest stumbling block to the beginning harpsichord maker, and lacking the sophisticated machinery necessary for making solid spruce boards of $1/8$ in. thickness, he

Single manual harpsichord by Albarda: AA–f³; 1 × 8′ delrin, buff; 1 × 8′ lute with quill.

will cast around for a suitable plywood. Thus he will consider Philippine mahogany, birch, or anything else that comes in sheet form of the right thickness. Since soundboards were always made from softwoods like spruce or cypress, it would seem that a hardwood like birch would be the wrong thing to use, and indeed harpsichords with such soundboards usually do not have a a very distinguished sound. One may argue that the stiffer hardwood board allows the tone to sustain longer, but one will pay for this by sacrificing the beautiful singing tone achieved by the softer woods. The question is hopelessly complicated by the use of plywood, which may act differently altogether from lumber.

Albarda is now working on a single manual harpsichord with a divided (organ) manual—1 × 8′, ½ × 4′, ½ × 2′, and a clavicytherium. The clavicytherium is an upright harpsichord in which the jacks were pushed horizontally and returned by springs. The entire harpsichord is set on a stand and projects upwards. The modern piano makers were later to borrow the idea of the upright harpsichord, but to save space they turned the harp around so that the bass pointed to the floor, occupying the formerly empty space behind the stand. The German firm of Neupert has in turn borrowed the idea of the modern upright to make an upright harpsichord.

Walnut virginal by Jan H. Albarda, compass BB–f³, 1 × 8′, buff.

AMMER K. G.
652 Eisenberg, Thüringen, East Germany

With Ammer we come to the first of the German production shops, making what are called *Serien Instrumente* ("series" instruments, i.e., mass-produced instruments). The reader may have gathered that I do not hold the modern German product in very high esteem; and this is, for once, not an erratic personal opinion, but the general consensus of the entire harpsichord world including players, makers, critics, and listeners. It will, of course, be easy for anyone to cite one particular player or critic praising the German factory instruments, but such isolated instances do not point to a consensus. Moreover, there are sometimes excellent reasons why such praise is given; in Germany, highly respected professors unashamedly accept commissions from the manufacturers, and players are often forced to use a particular make instrument because it is the only one available in a given location, or the only one that can be serviced free of charge.

Whenever non-Germans criticize the German factory instrument, charges of prejudice can be levelled at the critic, so we are fortunate in having the support of the fine German harpsichord maker Martin Skowroneck, who takes vigorous issue with his fellow German makers (we will discuss this in detail when we consider Skowroneck himself). Other enlightened Germans have taken a stand against *Serien Instrumente* (see W. Schroeder in our discussion of Wittmayer) and the climate of opinion in Germany itself is slowly changing and going away from the current factory product and toward the classical model.

The German factory harpsichords (and the instruments of Ammer, Neupert, Sperrhake, Wittmayer and others are so alike that they can be lumped together) can be faulted for the way they look, sound, and work. Having said that, it is only fair to point out their plusses: ready availability, good cabi-

73

net craftsmanship, well-made keyboards (often not made by themselves) and, until recently, low prices. The current practice of selling these instruments through dealers where they go through not only one but sometimes two and three hands, has upped their prices to such a degree that in many instances they are no cheaper than the products of the small workshop, sold directly to the consumer.

The makers of the *Serien Instrumente* have managed to do away with the natural advantage of the harpsichord over the piano. As we have seen, the harpsichord's narrower keyboard and lighter body allows this instrument to appear slim and elegant when compared to the piano. Just as stout women wear black while those with beautiful figures disport themselves in colorful dresses, so do pianos most often appear in slimming black to the harpsichord's gaily decorative colors. The German makers, most of whom started as piano builders, took the following steps in changing harpsichords to the piano "look": (1) reduced the length demanded by a natural string scale to an extra short scale in the bass with the substitution of heavy wrapped or overspun strings (copper winding on steel core, as found in pianos) for solid brass; (2) extended the width at the front by allowing a generous space on each side of the keyboard to house the elaborate stop or pedal mechanism on each side of the jack slide; (3) thickened and deepened the cases considerably, adding to the bulkiness of the appearance; (4) allowed the grain of the wood to run vertically, thus emphasizing the squatness of the case (akin to a chubby girl wearing a dress with horizontal stripes); and (5) set the instruments on three heavy legs instead of a stand of slimmer legs. In addition, having accomplished the piano look, they used light colored wood as if deliberately avoiding the slimming effect of darker colors. (Ammer, for example, offers cases in elm, oak, or ash.)

Next, in considering the sound of the German harpsichords, we find that their makers' ways of constructing them would seriously impair the tone of any harpsichord. Again the German penchant for making things immeasurably heavier than they need to be (we might call it "overkill" in modern terms) results in cases five and ten times as thick as the old ones, and structural members big enough to support a house. We have already seen that much of this excess lumber was added in view of the inexplicable absence of the bottom found on all old instruments; but further, these heavy cases did not notably improve the stability of the harpsichord. In addition the thickness of the soundboard, size of bridges, and frequency of ribs was greatly increased; ribs were made to run under the bridges, the bass was severely foreshortened, and thick 16′ strings were hung on the 8′ bridge. Many people are familiar with the peculiar sensation of facing an enormous and impressively heavy German harpsichord, only to realize that the little whispered sound it makes is the total product of that complex piece of engineering!

Considering now the stability of the German products, we find ourselves most disappointed of all. One could appreciate structural changes which may detract from the tone and appearance if at least they resulted in better tuning stability and less maintenance; but this is not the case as we shall have occasion to discuss when we consider the other production shops whose instruments are more plentiful in this country.

Ammer jacks. Left, wooden jack and tongue, steel spring, round hole for plectrum. Right, black plastic, steel spring, square hole for plectrum.

Ammer is second only to Neupert in being the oldest German firm currently making harpsichords. They have been in business for 40 years, and the
shop is now run by Frau Renate Schulz-Ammer who claims to be the only
Cembalo-Baumeisterin in Germany. Ammer has made a total of 2100 instruments and their current production averages 25 doubles, 20 singles, 50 spinets,
and 20 clavichords yearly. They employ 25 workers, and this makes them
considerably smaller than their West German colleagues. The fact that they
produce so many more small instruments than large ones makes them less
objectionable than some of the other production shops; most of the defects
recited above apply to a much larger degree to the big doubles. Some of the
Ammer spinets look almost graceful, and the sound is at least tolerable.

As is common both with beginners and large production shops, Ammer
makes neither keyboards nor jacks on the premises. They are now using both
plastic and wooden jacks. The plastic jack is black, $^{7}/_{16}$ in. wide and $^{5}/_{32}$ in.
thick and has an adjusting screw protruding at an angle near the top; the
wooden jack, of about the same dimensions, has the adjustment screw under
the tongue, forcing the adjuster to remove the jack. It has a round hole in the
tongue, raising the question of how easily a square piece of leather can be
fitted to it.

A most unfortunate habit, luckily restricted almost exclusively to German
shops, is the naming of different models after a famous composer or harpsichord maker. This is at best confusing, and at worst a fraudulent practice.
Thus we find that the Ammer model "Scarlatti" is a one manual harpsichord
with compass AA-f^3. Now Scarlatti is one of the few composers whose music
demands two keyboards and a compass FF-g^3, so what possible justification
was there for associating his name with that particular model? The case for the
"Vivaldi" is the reverse, since that composer's music calls mostly for continuo
parts, single manual use, and four octave compasses, yet we find his name
wedded to a five octave double manual, with a 16′ stop—a novelty of which
Vivaldi could have had no knowledge.

More serious is the case of the "Ruckers" and "Bach" models. The term
"Ruckers Model" ought to mean a reasonably close copy of Ruckers. The
extent to which Ammer copied the Ruckers is in the length of pitch c and the
registration. But an 8′ and 4′ registration is common enough, and the scale,
also common, is only one of many characteristics of those famous instruments
that deserve emulation.

Without even examining an instrument, a glance at the Ammer brochure
can tell the story. The Ammer "Ruckers" has five octaves, black naturals,
white sharps, weighs 220 lbs., has slanted cheeks, vertical graining, and three
modern legs. Ruckers usually had a short keyboard, ivory or bone naturals,
stained sharps, weighed much less than half as much, had square cheeks,
marbled or painted exterior, decorative paper interior, and was set on a stand.
Needless to say, the framing, ribbing, and soundboard construction are
radically different from the real Ruckers. We have already seen that the
"Berliner Bachfluegel," on which all German "Bach" models are based, belonged neither to Bach nor was its 16′ original; it remains to be said that even
this instrument has not been copied very accurately.

Years ago, when I was new in the harpsichord business, I came across an

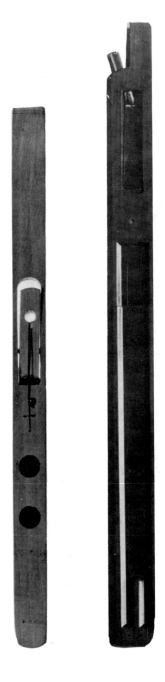

Ammer "Vivaldi" model.

Ammer "Bach" model for sale, for the ridiculous sum of $700. The fact that almost no tone issued from within its massive outline I laid to poor voicing. "I can soon fix that," I thought, with the enthusiasm and confidence of the beginner. It so happened that a poor and talented student of Fernando Valenti's needed a big, cheap harpsichord at the time, so the instrument was bought with the expectation that I would make a concert harpsichord out of it.

I quickly realized that a total revoicing would be an enormously time consuming job—it would mean a patient removal of the old leathers which were firmly glued in, insertion of new leathers, and then cutting some 250 plectra to size. But voicing does not only entail the cutting of leathers; it means making each jack work, probably re-setting spring tension, adjusting dampers, end pins, and set screws, freeing keys, setting the amount of key dip, and the many other steps necessitated by total revoicing. (The new leathers, being stiffer, will be positioned higher and require total jack re-adjustment.)

Figuring an average of ten minutes spent on each jack, this job required over 40 hours. Now in an ordinary workshop where one builds instruments and attends to customers, phones, and the business of the shop, it is not possible to count on more than one hour a day for repair work. This meant that the Ammer was to stay in my shop for nearly eight weeks; in all this time it would arouse the curiosity of all shop visitors who would ask time-consuming questions, and in addition would take valuable shop space which could yield a higher return. Testing a few jacks with new leather and not finding the expected improvement, I decided just to re-cut the existing leather. This meant advancing the registers until more leather projected past the string, and then cutting off the "tired" end of the old leather and allowing a fresh section of the plectrum to pluck. This usually works if enough leather is left.

This particular Ammer had an odd feature—one of its two 8's had "up-bearing" i.e. the string left the bridge on its way to the hitchpin going up rather than down. This was caused by a complicated system of hitchpin rails; there seemed to be no room to hitch that particular 8' set anywhere else. Now contrary to common belief that there must be firm down-bearing on a bridge by the pressure of the string, some of the better builders double-pin the bridge in such a way as to relieve pressure on it. The string presses sideways (in one direction) and down against the first pin, and to the opposite side and up against the second (double) pin. The idea here seems to be to insure *firm* contact of strings with bridge without unduly encumbering the bridge. On the Ammer, however, the strings were not contacting the bridge very well, which resulted in a dull tone without definition.

People sometimes defend the German harpsichords on the ground that they "sound like an organ." This they do, to the exclusion of sounding like a harpsichord. What we finally achieved with the Ammer "Bach" model was a thick, soupy sound somewhat reminiscent of a quiet organ. To be sure, when all four sets were on, and it was in tune and in maximum working efficiency, the instrument had a charm of its own; but whatever that was, it was hardly right for bringing out the best in the harpsichord music played upon it.

An unexpected way in which such an instrument can be damaging is in its capacity as representative of the genus "harpsichord." Thus there is a large Ammer in Moscow, a city with few harpsichords, giving the poor Russians an odd idea of the harpsichord's virtues; and the only maker in Japan is said to have used an Ammer as a model for his own instruments.

Is it fair to judge a maker by one or two instruments? Probably not, but in the case of *Serien Instrumente* it is fairer than with the small makers who sometimes make no two instruments alike. The factory products have changed little over the years, but we will see that their makers seem now to be waking from a long sleep. Ammer now uses closed bottoms (this in itself may only mean a bottom added to the usual heavy structure), and cases which seem to be somewhat thinner than those of the other shops.

PRODUCTION MODELS BY AMMER

1. Clavichord: 5 octaves, single strings; $59 \times 19\frac{3}{4}$ in. 110 lbs.
2. Spinettino (4′ ottavino): 4 octaves c–c4; 48½ lbs.
3. Spinet "Delin": 4½ octaves C–f3; $1 \times 8'$, $61 \times 39\frac{3}{8}$ in., 99 lbs.
4. Spinet "Silbermann": 5 octaves; $1 \times 8'$, buff and half stops, $76\frac{3}{4} \times 37\frac{3}{8}$ in., 143 lbs. Two hand stops.
5. Single manual harpsichord "Scarlatti": 4¾ octaves AA–f3; $1 \times 8'$, $1 \times 4'$, divided buff on 8′; 64×37 in., 121 lbs. Handstops.
6. Single manual harpsichord "Ruckers": 5 octaves; $1 \times 8'$, $1 \times 4'$; $86\frac{5}{8} \times 41\frac{3}{8}$ in., 220 lbs. Three hand stops.
7. Two manual harpsichord "Vivaldi": 5 octaves; upper manual $1 \times 8'$, $1 \times 4'$, buff on 8′; lower manual $1 \times 8'$, $1 \times 16'$, buff on 16′ (here called "theorbo"); $80\frac{3}{4} \times 41\frac{3}{8}$ in., 352 lbs. Five pedals and two hand stops.
8. Two manual harpsichord "Bach": 5 octaves; upper manual $1 \times 8'$, $1 \times 4'$, buff on 8′; lower manual $1 \times 8'$, $1 \times 16'$, buff on 8′ and 16′; $102\frac{3}{8} \times 42\frac{1}{2}$ in., 385 lbs. Keyboard coupler; 7 hand stops, or 5 pedals and 2 hand stops.

OLIVER ROBIN BAGOT

Levens Hall, Kendal, Westmoreland, England

English television viewers may have been somewhat surprised recently when, during a program on motorway routing, they encountered O. R. Bagot playing "Les Barricades Mysterieuses" on one of his harpsichords. This happened because the English authorities wished to push a motorway (their answer to America's freeways) right through Mr. Bagot's estate.

Bagot, who is a prosperous English landowner and director of several large companies, naturally protested. Needless to say, Bagot does not make harpsichords for a living, nor does he even sell them (courtesy of the British tax system).

He has been active since 1956 and produced a total of four large doubles, three of them with pedals and 16′ stops. He works with Robert P. Davies of Holly House, Levans, Kendal, who is now putting together Hubbard kits. His first instrument was based on a Goff, perhaps a case of the blind leading the blind, but he is said to have copied a Dowd since then, with better results.

BALDWIN PIANO COMPANY

1601 Gilbert Avenue, Cincinnati, Ohio

The brochure on the Baldwin "combo" harpsichord is apologetic about what it is. "Sure, we *call* it a harpsichord and you *can* play chamber or baroque music on it, but don't make the mistake of thinking it's some kind of dusty antique. You can make sounds as exciting as today's, probably even more exciting." It goes on to tell the prospective buyer that "there's no delicate resonance chamber to worry about" (so much for those dusty ancients like Ruckers, Taskin and Kirckman), and that it (the sound) "can *all* be changed with a foot operated mute control. And by change we mean really changed."

The "combo" harpsichord is appropriately handled by Fred Gretsch Co., the electric guitar makers who have been bought out lock, stock, and barrel by Baldwin, a firm whose aggressive advertising and business methods are as exciting as today's, probably even more exciting.

The Baldwin electric or "combo" harpsichord was designed by Caleb Warner, who was at one time associated with Eric Herz in Cambridge. The idea presumably was to manufacture a stable all-around harpsichord for the market requiring specially loud volume, like jazz, rock, and concert work in large halls and with large groups. The actual result was a glorified electric guitar operated by a keyboard.

Physically, the design is not very successful; it uses an aluminum channel section in place of wooden case, and three legs without any charm whatever. The lucite top and music rack give this instrument an outer space quality not easily associated with harpsichord design. One could perhaps swallow the design (a bitter pill!) if the instrument had a pleasant sound and worked satisfactorily. This, unfortunately, is not the case.

When Caleb Warner and Herz dissolved their joint operation, Baldwin bought the rights to this design, thus becoming the first major piano firm in the United States to enter the harpsichord market. Needless to say, no one at Baldwin knew much about harpsichords; and if anything is a bad beginning in attempting to cope with harpsichords, it is a background in piano work. (Two Baldwin harpsichords which I was unable to repair were returned to the factory and came back in worse condition than before.)

The Baldwin electric harpsichord.

The electro-magnetic pick-up bar of a Baldwin harpsichord.

The soundboard in the Warner-Baldwin is made of some sort of masonite; it is obviously intended only for decoration. The sound of the strings is received by magnetic pick-ups positioned in a bar running directly above the strings. The sound picked up in this fashion is then fed into an amplifier and speaker, and its volume can naturally be regulated from very soft to very loud. There is also a "swell" pedal similar to the organ swell. The resulting sound is extremely crude. It must be remembered that the sound of a harpsichord is the result of a complex interaction of the plectra, strings, soundboard, and case, combining to produce a timbre rich in overtones. With magnetic pick-ups, all but the plectra and strings have been eliminated, leaving only the sound of the wire itself. The strings on the Baldwin go from nut to hitchpin without passing over a bridge. The wire must be of steel to respond to the magnetic pick-ups, and this, added to a short bass string (AA = 40 in.) of steel instead of brass, and unaided by bridge or soundboard, results in a dull tone (dull in the sense of "without interest").

The sound the plectra make when plucking, is amplified along with the string itself, and the small increase in pitch which results from a stiff plectrum stretching the string seems especially conducive to amplification. This is the "wow" effect of an electric guitar, and it does very little for the usually crisp music of the harpsichord.

The pinblock, also made from aluminum, has oversized holes into which plastic bushings are inserted, which in turn hold the tuning pins. The reason tuning pins are usually embedded in wood, even in the highly tensioned piano, is that wood is able to keep the pin just tight enough to hold but not too tight for tuning. A metal pin in a metal block (as some makers have tried) is usually disastrous, since metal has no "give" and results in either a rigidly tight fit or a loose one. Even if it were possible to find a size pin which has just the right fit, this would require a more critical tolerance than is possible to manage in production where tuning pins have a plus or minus tolerance of .002 or .003, and those few thousands are enough to eliminate any chance for the precise fit necessary. With metal pinblocks, the answer would seem to be plastic bushings inserted into oversized holes in the pinblock. But plastic is

more rigid than wood and has less give. In the Baldwins, one of the greatest problems is loose tuning pins (something which practically never happens in wooden pinblocks with the comparatively slight tension of a harpsichord); the cause is either wrong bushing dimension or wrong bushing material. Sometimes the pin and bushing turn as a unit in the pinblock hole, and sometimes the pin turns in the bushing itself; occasionally both pin and bushing are so tight that it is difficult to move the pin in tuning.

The jacks and plectra are made of delrin (jacks used to be stainless steel and the plectra brass!) and no attempt is made at voicing. The plectra are just cut to length and left to pluck the string as best as they can. Although no precise figures are available, Caleb Warner estimates that hundreds of these instruments have been made and continue to be made.

Detail of the Baldwin harpsichord showing action and bushed tuning pins.

Harpsichord by Christopher Bannister, with 2 × 8', 1 × 4' disposition and lute stop.

BANNISTER HARPSICHORDS
Spur Rt. 518, Hopewell, New Jersey 08525
Christopher Bannister was born in 1937 in Troy, New York and began study of the harpsichord while a high school student, at the University of Illinois. His interest in harpsichord construction resulted in an apprenticeship, over a period of three years, with Hubbard & Dowd in their partnership days. Concurrently, Bannister attended the Oberlin College Conservatory of Music with a major in harpsichord performance. Following college, in 1959

Bannister established his workshop near Hopewell, New Jersey; harpsichord production began in 1961. Output, as of summer 1969, numbers 46 harpsichords; about one-third are concert doubles, the remainder are mostly large leg-of-mutton spinets.

Early Bannister instruments were patterned on Kirckman and Shudi prototypes. More recent Bannister designs involve eighteenth-century German and French tonal prototypes.

Bannister conceives his instruments on the premise that the final product should need as little tuning and regulation as possible. The instruments are more heavily constructed than classical models. Framing is based on a solid bottom and hardwood I-beam braces from bellyrail to bentside. Just under the soundboard, a plywood "plate" is secured to the entire case rim; this "plate" (a feature now found also in de Angeli instruments) forms a sandwich construction with the other framing and provides lateral bracing. Special hardwood plywoods are used for most construction, and only waterproof adhesives are employed. Bannister uses heavily laminated pin blocks (I counted over 50 layers in one) and reinforces them with aluminum bracing. Metal gap spacers are inserted between the pin block and the bellyrail and these spacers are aligned with the I-beam framework. Jackslides are brass and lower guides are bakelite.

Bannister jacks, developed in conjunction with de Angeli, are moulded from delrin and possess an unusual feature, the anodised aluminum tube which determines the effective length of the jack body; the top plastic portion remains approximately the same length ($2\frac{1}{8}$ in.) for all sizes of jacks. The tube serves to considerably lighten the jack weight and ensures overall jack straightness and rigidity in the great length required in double harpsichords (solid delrin jacks have an annoying habit of warping over their 8-in. length). The tube also guides the jack in the lower guide. Into the bottom of the tube is threaded a delrin endpin. Brass spring-clip dampers fit onto the plastic jack body. Delrin plectra are normally employed.

All Bannister keyboards have a 63 note compass (FF-g^3), and are designed with a key dip of 8.4 mm (about $\frac{5}{16}$ in.) and an octave span of 160 mm (almost $6\frac{5}{16}$ in.), slightly wider than standard harpsichord keyboards. The keys splay out in the back, which allows more space for the jacks and avoids the spacing problems discussed in Chapter III. Bannister double keyboards slightly overlap; the distance between manuals is standardised at 50 mm (about 2 in.).

In line with his desire to produce relatively stable instruments, Bannister undertakes comprehensive scale calculations which predetermine all string tensions, speaking lengths, string materials, and wire diameters. As a further contribution to tuning stability, Bannister arranges his soundboard 8′ bridge so as to equalise the speaking lengths (and thus the tensions) of each pair of 8′ strings. Due to the length of all Bannister harpsichords (doubles are 100 in. long), wrapped strings are never required.

Bannister closely copies eighteenth-century pluck point percentages, and his scales are based on examples in which the extreme treble string lengths have been somewhat increased. String tensions range from 6.7 Kg in the treble to about 8.5 Kg in the extreme bass; in a Bannister concert double with 2 × 8′

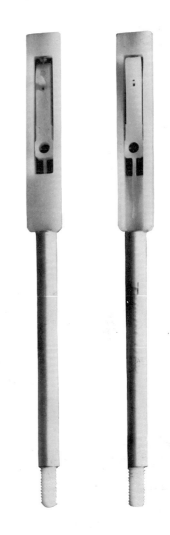

Jack used by Christopher Bannister. De Angeli also used the same jack. Delrin jack body, tongue and spring, and end pin; shaft is anodized aluminum.

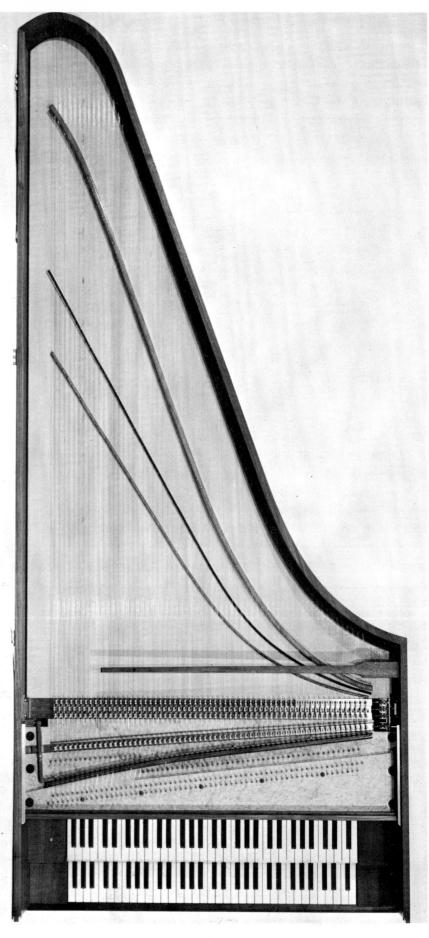

Top view of Bannister harpsichord. Note that key levers fan out at the rear to give more space between strings.

and 1 × 4′, the total string tension is 1317.1 Kg (2903.7 lbs.). (Note: Bannister reports that modern grand pianos generally are designed with a tension of 75 Kg per string; the lowest A_2 on the current 9′ Concert Grand Steinway has a design tension of 182 Kg (398 lbs.). Modern grand pianos have a total design tension of between 20 and 30 tons!)

The strings on all Bannister instruments are hitched, piano fashion, with one wire serving as two strings, going from one tuning pin, around the hitch-pin and then to the next tuning pin. This procedure omits the need for string loops; initial tunings are said to be quickly stabilised, since loops do not "seat"; and string breakage due to wire fatigue at the loop anchor is eliminated. Bannister reports that the two string segments act completely independently.

All Bannister pedal trapwork is mounted with nylon bearings or screw-thread pivots and all trapwork is housed within the body of the instrument so as to prevent accidental trapwork damages. Instruments are finished in various veneers or lacquer colors. As of July 1969, Bannister instruments range in price from about $1391 for Spinets to large Concert Doubles in excess of $5500; his prices in general reflect his meticulous approach to his craft.

Bannister also constructs large clavichords and fortepianos of various types, and restores antiques; the rebuilding of Bechstein and Steinway modern grand pianos is a Bannister specialty.

TREVOR BECKERLEG
54 Bateman Street, Cambridge, England

Trevor Beckerleg has been active since 1964, and has made five instruments. This year he has made three of these, a double, a single, and a spinet, and is planning to continue at that rate.

Beckerleg uses his own design on "historical principles," but would like to dissociate himself from the "modern harpsichord." By this I presume he means the factory harpsichord. However, we have applied the term for purposes of this discussion to any harpsichord made in this century regardless of its style.

Harpsichord and spinet by Trevor Beckerleg.

Beckerleg, who was born in Northumberland in 1941, works by himself, making his own jacks and keyboards. (This would partially account for his slow rate of production.) He uses pearwood for jacks, and solid spruce or cedar for soundboards, and this, plus closed bottoms and square cheeks point to an orientation basically along classical lines. (The shape of the cheek—square or slanted in front—often establishes a neat dividing line between historical and production orientations.)

Beckerleg has not worked with any other makers (this can often be an advantage) but has received many helpful hints from Michael Thomas.

Philip Belt's piano after Johann Andreas Stein, Vienna, 1773.

HUBERT BÉDARD

46, Rue des Batignolles, Paris 17, France

Bédard is a French Canadian, born 1933 in Ottawa, who has had his own shop in Paris for about a year. He collaborated with Frank Hubbard in the restoration of some instruments at the Conservatoire Nationale in Paris, and gives his own total output as 14 instruments.

Bédard copies harpsichords in the Italian, Flemish and French styles, working with a staff of two. He is part of a recent flurry of harpsichord activity in France, a country long dominated exclusively by Pleyel.

PHILIP BELT

Box 173, Center Conway, New Hampshire 03813

Wien, Wien, nur Du allein . . . go the words to a popular Viennese song in ³/₄ time. Well, aside from Schlagobers (whipped cream), Jause (afternoon coffee), and Johann Strauss, Vienna is also responsible for the Viennese piano action, probably the most sensitive and responsive piano action ever designed,

The bass and treble dampers of the Belt piano.

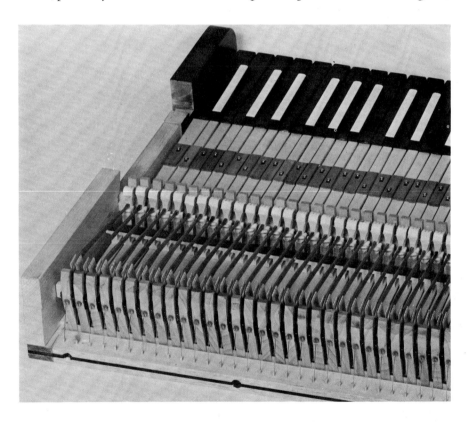

Detail of Belt piano showing escapement mechanism.

The key and hammer assembly of the Belt piano.

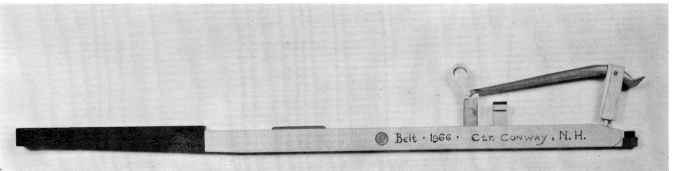

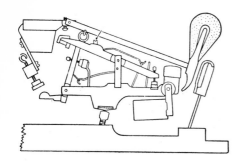

Diagram of modern grand piano action.

and just about perfect for making Mozart runs sound like a string of pearls.

From eighteenth-century Vienna to twentieth-century New Hampshire may seem a giant step in space and time, but it is here, on an isolated farm without a telephone, that we find Philip Belt making exact copies of Viennese pianos.

Belt, who has the look of a farmer about him, worked in Frank Hubbard's shop for two years and has built some harpsichords, but his main interest is early pianos. He concentrates his work on the reproduction of the pianos of Johann Andreas Stein, the eighteenth-century builder whose instruments were praised by Mozart.

In the Stein action, the hammers are tiny, compared to the modern piano, and leather covered. They are attached to thin, flexible shanks, which have enough "spring" to return the hammers with lightening speed. Unlike the modern piano whose hammers rise in the direction towards the player, the fortepiano hammer direction is away from the player. The escapement mechanism is extremely sensitive and seems to favor a light touch. The strings are somewhat heavier than harpsichord strings and are arranged mostly in pairs.

The keyboard and action rest on a "sled" which is shoved under the keyboard once this is in place to allow the hammers close proximity to the strings. Unlike the modern grand action, which can be removed by sliding out the keyboard, the fortepiano action must first be dropped to the level of the instrument's bottom by removal of the sled.

The Stein copy by Philip Belt is $85^1/_2$ in. long, $39^1/_4$ in. wide, and weighs 250 lbs. The range is $5^1/_4$ ocatves, FF–g^3. It is an exact replica of the original of 1773. Belt also is making copies of a Stodart piano of 1812, a Walter of 1815, and a Graf of about 1824, which makes a fairly complete series of fortepianos, since the English Stodart is entirely different (and more akin to the modern piano) than the Viennese type. If history had favored the delicate Viennese type over the more cumbersome English model, the modern piano would have been an entirely different, and one might add, more musical, instrument.

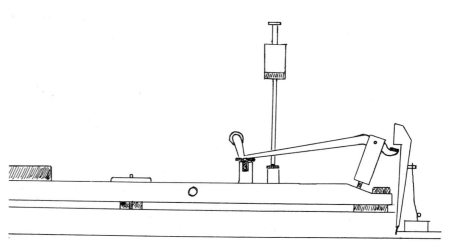

Diagram of Viennese piano action.

JORGEN BENGAARD
Holger Danskesvej 86, 2000, Denmark

Bengaard made harpsichords on a small scale, working by himself, for a number of years, but according to the assistant curator at the Copenhagen Musikhistorisk Museum he has given up his establishment, leaving Denmark without any active harpsichord makers.

A triangular spinet by Jorgen Bengaard.

Detail of the action of the Bengaard spinet.

BRADLEY W. M. BENN
4424 Judson Lane, Minneapolis, Minnesota 55435

Bradley W. M. Benn started his building career at age 28 with a harpsichord kit. In the four years that he has been active, he has made 5 instruments, of which 3 are singles and 2 are clavichords. He works slowly, making his own jacks, keyboards, and quartered spruce soundboards.

Benn uses his own designs but has studied antique instruments and museum collections, as well as worked on restorations. He is currently working on a "utility" model which will feature a "metal frame to better withstand the rigors of our extreme climate." He hopes that a "light, responsive soundboard" will provide "more power and tone than associated with the usual rigid framed instruments."

The harpsichordist Sylvia Marlowe, who was dragged almost bodily to see Benn's instruments (these harpsichord enthusiasts are an insistent lot!) reports that his double-strung clavichord has a big tone.

Beaumont Manor, Hertfordshire, England, where George Braithwaite makes his harpsichords.

Decorated copy of an Italian spinet (ca. 1650) by George Braithwaite.

GEORGE BRAITHWAITE
Beaumont Manor, Wormley, Hertfordshire, England

A glance at this imposing manor house would confirm two hunches about many English makers: (a) they like to work in spacious and gracious surroundings; and (b) harpsichord making is not the sort of activity to produce, through its rewards, surroundings of such magnificence. George Braithwaite and his family work under the name of "Georgian Harpsichords" and "follow the eighteenth-century tradition of semi-professional making of instruments"

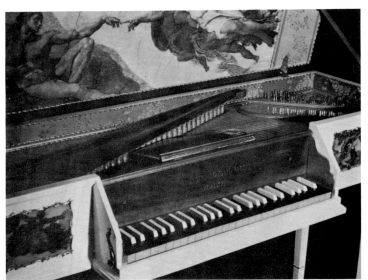

which, it seems to me, is much more of a twentieth-century tradition.

They specialize in supplying small harpsichords to training colleges and county schools whose "budgets will not be sufficient for the excellent instruments by the professional firms in the country." (In America semi-professional makers usually do not charge less than professionals, and often more.) Their standard small harpsichord has $4\frac{1}{4}$ octaves, B–d^3 and is 55 in. long. It has one set of strings and harp stop, and in place of a bentside has a piece running in a straight line from cheek to tail. The construction is of the "English rigid style"; I am not familiar with that style, but the harpsichord certainly bears no relation to classical eighteenth-century English instruments as regards type, style, outline, bass string length, keyboard compass, type of key covering, disposition, bridge shape, or hardware.

Georgian Harpsichords have produced a total of 132 instruments, of which most have been the portables, but they have made some two manual harpsichords and some fairly lavishly decorated virginals, one of which they recently sold to Mrs. Ethel Kennedy.

The jacks, which are made of pear and holly, are supplied by John Barnes who himself has made a few instruments but is now devoting himself to restorations and supervision of the Raymond Russell collection in Edinburgh. The plectra are nylon and the soundboards are made of $\frac{1}{8}$ in. Roumanian pine or spruce. Keyboards come from Pynes in London.

I have not seen the Braithwaite instruments but they undoubtedly fill the need for an inexpensive, portable harpsichord which can introduce the student to the sound of the instrument and lend authenticity to the recorder recitals of the English County School.

JOHN BRUEGGEMAN
10045 Tanager Lane, Cincinnati, Ohio 45215

John Brueggeman, born in Boston 1916, is another former kit builder who has been active as a part-time harpsichord maker for the last seven years. He has made a total of ten instruments and estimates his current yearly output at one double, two singles, and a clavichord.

Brueggeman bases his designs on a "traditional string scale" and a "contemporary style based on Flemish construction."

Brueggeman's price list shows two models, "C" and "D," both built from a Hubbard kit. Putting these kits together seems currently a popular and profitable pastime for the maker starting out; in addition to providing the parts he needs, this excellent though difficult kit teaches the new maker more about the instrument than he could easily learn any other way.

BUECKER AND WHITE
465 West Broadway, New York, N.Y. 10012

With Buecker and White we come to two modern artists who approach harpsichords and clavichords as contemporary pieces of sculpture. Their designs are truly innovative and they have produced startlingly modern constructions. One must keep in mind, however, that they have taken extreme liberties with the scale and geometry to get so far away from traditional design.

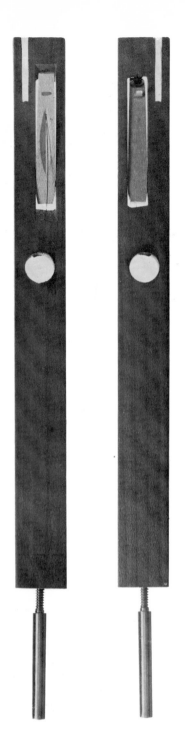

Wooden jack and tongue by John Brueggeman. Steel wire spring, delrin plectrum, top adjustment screw and end pin.

Buecker and White single manual harpsichord with 5 pedals, 62 keys, and 3 legs. Specification: 1 × 8′, 1 × 4′, 1 × 16′, 1 × quint; 38 × 100 in.; and an ottavina virginal: 1 × 4′, 60 keys, 4 legs; 28 × 43 in.

Buecker and White double-strung clavichord with ten separate bridges; and a spinet: 1 × 8′, 60 keys, and 3 legs; 91 × 28 in.

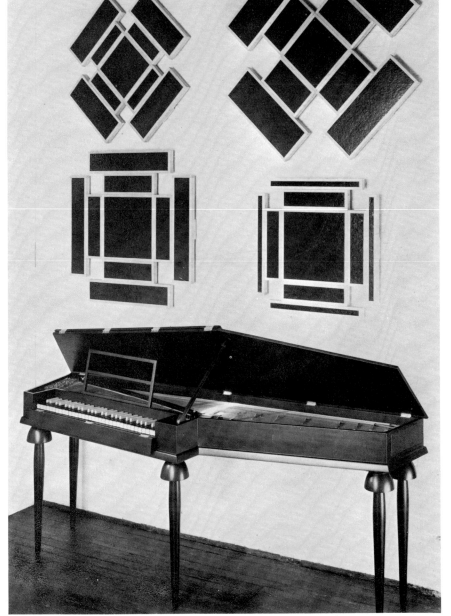

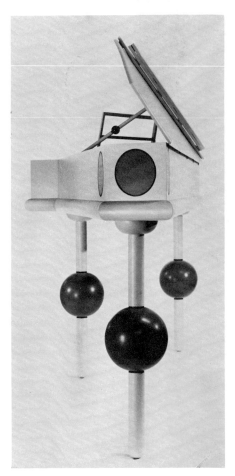

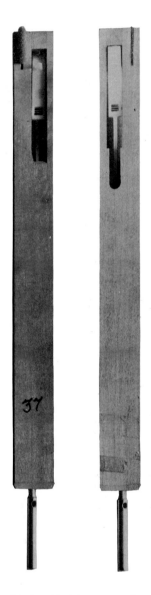

Robert Buecker, born 1935 in Pittsburgh, Pa., has been working part time at Zuckermann Harpsichords for over ten years. He is a painter who has had many shows, but his geometric-abstractionist designs have not had the vogue enjoyed by abstract expressionism, op and pop art. In 1963, Buecker and the sculptor Ralph White embarked on the harpsichord venture.

They have produced about twenty instruments, including some with startling color schemes. One large harpsichord is "done" completely in greens —the case and lid are in different shades of green, and the soundboard and keys are tinted still another delicate shade of green! Most remarkable of all are the legs, both in the number and shape of them. One instrument is listed as possessing fifteen legs. Another has four legs, of which each is a different shape. Still another has legs with an enormous sphere at its center.

Buecker and White approach building instruments from an entirely visual point of view. If Buecker doesn't like the looks of a 4′ bridge, he will do away with it by placing the 8′ bridge in a midway position to serve both 8′ and 4′. The resulting pitch c^2 will measure $9\frac{1}{2}$ in.—too short for the 8′ and too long for the 4′, a Procrustean bed of strings!

For soundboards the two artists use $\frac{1}{8}$ in. mahogany plywood, and this material, combined with the tortured scale, must of necessity result in somewhat less than the ideal tone. However, it should not be impossible for them to improve their internal design to achieve a more conventional sound without sacrificing the look of their instruments.

Buecker, who has an astonishing head of hair and moves around New York on a sleek racing bicycle, shares with White a large and comfortable loft, where they work and live. He recently said: "People ask me why I make these instruments. I don't know why I make them; I just make them."

WALTER BURR
6 Main Street, Hoosick Falls, New York

Walter Burr's first harpsichord was made from a kit while he worked for the organ makers Delaware & Schlicker. He then worked for William Dowd, spending almost two years making keyboards and the remainder of his stay there on casework, leaving Dowd in August 1968.

Aside from Zuckermann and Hubbard kits, Burr has made a 4-octave double, a copy of a 1640 Hans Ruckers. I saw this instrument at Dowd's shop the day it was finished, and it is an impressive beginning. His jacks use Dowd's delrin tongue and integral spring, but are otherwise of pear wood. He makes faithful keyboard copies, putting his two years on that activity to good use.

Burr, who was born in 1944 in Buffalo, is now set up in his own shop, working with his wife. He expects to be making two or three doubles a year, concentrating on the late French double manual. He plans to pattern all his instruments after old ones, feeling there is little he could do to improve upon classical design; he will indulge his creative energies in decorating soundboards.

HERBERT BURTON
917 "O" Street, Lincoln, Nebraska 68508

The Burton story illustrates an attempt to go into the mass-production harpsichord business. Herbert Burton, a businessman of some means who

Pearwood jack with delrin tongue by Walter Burr; spring is molded with tongue; delrin plectrum; flag damper; adjustable tongue screw and end pin.

owned a radio station, became interested in harpsichords some five years ago and asked Frank Hubbard to be his "consultant." Hubbard good-naturedly agreed, and made for Burton a drawing of a simplified classical single manual $2 \times 8'$ harpsichord. Armed with this drawing, for which he was to pay a small royalty fee, Burton, who was born in Wallingford, Conn. in 1916, took himself off to the wilds of Nebraska, relying on his musical daughter for advice.

He next set about making a mould for his jack and applying for a patent. Whether his jack is patentable or not is open to question (after all, what about Ruckers, Kirckman et al, not to speak of the modern makers), but it had two or three features of interest. Made of black delrin, it features a "snap-in" tongue. The tongue has a little moulded-in prong projecting from each side which "snaps" into matching holes in the jack body, eliminating the necessity for an axle pin. The tongue has the plectrum moulded in (if you make a voicing mistake, good-bye tongue—and since the mould makes matching tongue and jack sets, good-bye jack), as well as its spring, which bears against a groove in the jack itself. There are holes for adjustment screws and end screws and the damper slot is located in a short projection at the top of the jack, allowing the main jack body to be slim ($^3/_8 \times {}^5/_{32}$ in.). The damper slot has small bumps on the inside, presumably to keep the damper cloth from moving around after it has been set. This jack, which is very well made, is the result of a sophisticated and expensive mould.

Next, Burton set up shop (1965) proceeding with the manufacture of his simple, classical model. When I first heard about this venture I thought "finally—the expert and the businessman have gotten together; we shall see a classical mass produced harpsichord coming from the heartland of America." (I should have remembered two other famous—and failed—associations of experts, engineers and business men—Hubbard, Dowd, and Charles Fischer for one, and Herz, Jim Cannon, and Caleb Warner, for the other.)

Now Burton assembled a group of four or five part-time college students and a full-time carpenter to start manufacturing. A catalog was issued with headings like "HAND CRAFTED" and "ASTONISHING RESONANCE." Here we read that the bridge and nut were "hand hewn" (an example of a Burton 4' bridge I later saw was, indeed, hand hewn); that the instrument was "crafted" in Lincoln, Nebraska to permit necessary control and supervision (why?); and that the soundboard was placed in the instrument through a "highly skilled procedure" whose "inconsummate [sic] care produces a crowned soundboard, an accoustical wonder of vital resonance." The instrument's weight of 118 lbs. was announced as a "musical coup" notwithstanding the fact that Hubbard, Dowd, Schütze and others had made lighter harpsichords for years. (Schütze's single weighs $93^1/_2$ lbs., and a classical Italian weighs less than 50 lbs.)

The harpsichords were sold through a central Chicago distributor, and went to local dealers from there—a process driving their price up to well over $2000, which compared unfavorably with the average competitor's price of $1200–1500 for a $2 \times 8'$ instrument.

The instruments are not bad; although somewhat crudely made (inside joints showed wide gaps); they are, on the whole, superior to German imports. But a strong guiding force, so necessary in a harpsichord shop, seemed

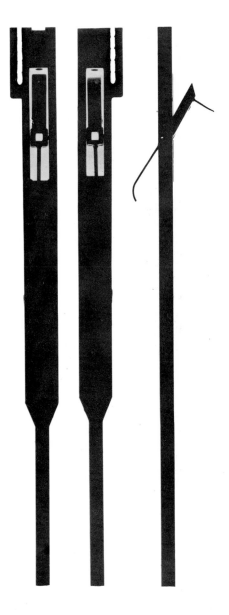

The Burton jack, moulded from black delrin, with plectrum and spring moulded into tongue. There are ridges in the damper slot, and the tongue needs no pivot pin.

The Burton single manual, 2 × 8′ harpsichord.

to be lacking, and there was no distinction technically, musically, or even from a business point of view. Orders, it was announced, were to be shipped by air the day they were received; meanwhile, mere inquiries did not get answered by the Chicago distributor. The design was suddenly changed (without Frank Hubbard's help) from a 2 × 8′ to 1 × 8′, 1 × 4′. The 4′ bridge which normally has a cross section not much bigger than $^1/_4 \times {}^1/_4$ in. at the treble end, grew to $^1/_2$ in. height and $^5/_8$ in. width, making it actually wider than the 8′ bridge, something I have not seen before or since. The 4′ hitch pins were located right next to the 4′ bridge, and because of the bridge height and close proximity, caused an acute string angle downwards. The "highly skilled procedure" of setting in the soundboards turned out to mean leaving them unsupported or totally free for most of the length of belly rail and spine. This was done so they could expand and contract freely. In Burtons that I am familiar with, the customers themselves had to close up these empty spaces.

In four years Burton has made about 180 instruments; when business did not go into mass volumes, he decided to enter the kit business, which is currently the fashionable way for harpsichord makers to turn an extra dollar. His kits are priced at close to $800, and although this included the case completely assembled, it was considerably higher than other kits on the market.

Burton sells his jacks to all comers, and these can be highly recommended.

Detail showing treble end of 4′ and 8′ bridges on Burton harpsichord. Bridges are approximately the same width. The 4′ hitch pins follow close to their bridge throughout, forcing steep down bearing.

JOHN CHALLIS
350 Lafayette Street, New York, New York 10012

John Challis has been called by his friends the "eminent Victorian." He is not just a man but an institution. For years before meeting him I thought of him as an entity or a system, and that name, Challis, fits the harpsichord. (Not all makers have been fortunate enough to possess a name that looks well on a nameboard. Boalch lists names like Assalone, Ban, Bust, Chew, Crang, Daddi, Humbert, Malade, Musch, and Schmutz.)

John Challis was born in South Lyon, Michigan, January 9, 1907. He is the son of a jeweller and watchmaker, and even though modern science frowns upon theories supporting inheritence of acquired characteristics, one would be tempted to say that Challis inherited his passion for getting mechanical systems to work beautifully, smoothly and neatly from his father. His greatest source of unhappiness is something which does not work as it's supposed to. He is Victorian in his tastes, and in his insistence that man, by his own effort, can eradicate mechanical—and social—evils. The chaotic conditions of modern life, in which most mechanical and social systems have broken down, appall him, and his response to our state of near-anarchy is to keep the sidewalk in front of his building swept as often as it gets littered—which is every day. The building, which he owns, is a huge and somewhat spooky former animal hospital in a nondescript section of downtown New York.

In 1926 an American lady travelling in England visited the Dolmetsch workshops and mentioned to Dolmetsch a young man in her home town in Ypsilanti, Michigan who was interested in making and playing harpsichords and had built one or two instruments. Ever eager to spread the gospel of these instruments, Arnold Dolmetsch invited the young man to come and learn the craft in his shop. Challis came and stayed four years.

An early Challis two-manual harpsichord, 2 × 8′, 1 × 4′, 1 × 16′. Except for the stand and decorative stripe on the lid, the appearance of the current Challis instruments remains the same.

The influence of Dolmetsch upon Challis has lasted a long time, perhaps to this day. This illustrates a point which we will encounter again: the master or originator of a school of building has enormous influence on his apprentices and *their* apprentices in turn. For better or worse he sets the tone which may be followed for years to come.

Perhaps three examples of Dolmetsch's influence can be noted in Challis. The first is the appearance of the harpsichord. I was startled the other day when I saw an instrument which I took to be a Challis and it turned out to be a Dolmetsch dating from the 1930's. There is the same thin gold molding, the same slanted cheek in front, the same shape lidstick and jackrail, the same stand (now simplified), and the same style lettering on the nameboard.

Second is the idea of the metal frame. Dolmetsch used a welded metal frame as early as the 30's, which supported the 4′ hitchpin rail. Although Challis' cast aluminum frame is something entirely different, the idea may have originated there.

The third influence of Dolmetsch is negative—Challis learned what not to do. At the time of Challis's apprenticeship, Dolmetsch started his "new" action which became an idée fixe with him. According to Robert Goble, who was also working in the Dolmetsch shop at the time, it was Challis's misfortune to work on the new and hopelessly complicated and inefficient action, and this may have sharpened his determination to develop a harpsichord action that would always work.

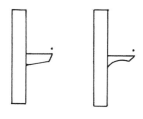

Sketch of typical Challis plectrum at left, contrasted with more usual cut of leather plectrum at right. Dot represents position of string in relation to plectrum.

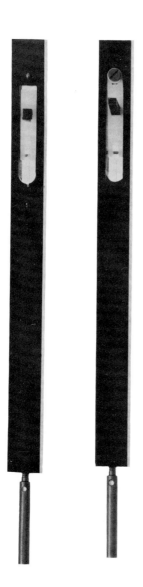

The Challis jack, moulded of black rubber. Tongue is delrin, spring is nylon. Note position of tongue adjustment screw. Plectrum is leather.

When Challis established himself as a harpsichord maker in 1930 he was the only one in America, and was to remain so for many many years. Out of his shop came not only many amateur builders, a few of whom I encountered in the early 50's when I started, but some of our important modern makers like Dowd and Rutkowski. He must be considered the dean of American harpsichord makers.

In the space of 39 years Challis has made 312 instruments of which less than 10 percent have been clavichords and a small number ottavinos. Of the remainder, 80 percent have been single manuals and 20 percent doubles. In all this time Challis has never ceased experimenting.

In his first instruments he used Douglas fir for soundboards, as did Dolmetsch at the time. Challis soon found something strange about this material: glue would not stick to it very well, and bridges and ribs began to come loose. He then went to spruce, but found it insufficiently stable to meet his standards. Next came spruce plywood, which is used by many piano makers (theirs is thicker), and finally, about ten years ago, he went to the controversial metal soundboards he now uses.

The tradition in America and England is for harpsichord makers to have an open shop and to harbor no "trade secrets" which must be shielded from visitors. (This is not so in Germany, as we shall see). Asked about the composition and thickness of his soundboards, Challis replied, "This is my only secret." I suspect the material of being anodized aluminum, and of being very thin—certainly less than $^1/_{16}$ in.

Once Challis had decided to use metal soundboards, in an effort to make the instrument more stable in regard to tuning and regulation, wooden bridges also had to be abandoned and replaced by brass. The brass channel is laboriously drilled out on all sides in an effort to lighten it. There are no ribs at all under the soundboard. (When Challis made wooden soundboards, he used to run many ribs right straight across and under the bridge, sometimes spaced only two to three inches apart.)

Long before the metal soundboard, Challis began his lifelong search for more stability with the development of the aluminum frame which has become his trade mark. He makes a distinction between a metal "plate" (as used by Pleyel) which is screwed on top of a wooden frame and needs that frame for strength, and a true metal frame (used by Challis and Rutkowski), which can support the string tension alone and allows the wooden case to be ornamental. Next followed the aluminum wrest plank, in which tapered tuning pins are set into tapered phenolic bushings, and which is an integral part of the whole frame. Challis considers the wrest plank the number one offender against tuning stability, a judgment with which not many people would agree. (Most of us would put the soundboard and case ahead of the plank.)

The action is also designed with a view toward adjustment, stability, and ease of maintenance. The jacks are made of a hard, black rubber, $^5/_{32}$ in. thick and $^3/_8$ in. wide. They now have plastic tongues, plastic springs and nickel-plated end pins. The tongue-adjusting screw cannot be reached from the top (as in most modern jacks) but is located on the side of the jack. In most cases the jack need not be lifted out for adjustment, since one can get a screwdriver in from the side. The jacks are fabricated rather than cast or moulded, meaning

that Challis receives from his supplier only a rectangular blank, which then has to be machined, drilled, slotted, and filed to size, an enormously painstaking process, which makes these jacks very expensive to produce.

The keyboards are made in his shop as well. (Keyboard- and jack-making are among the most difficult and tedious tasks of the harpsichord maker, and many beginning makers are able to go into business by buying these items elsewhere.) Challis does not use a keyboard coupler; the upper keyboard works the solo 8′ in two positions, loud and soft (no "off" position is necessary for a solo stop), and the lower keyboard works the 8′, 4′, and 16′. Instead of the coupler or dogleg, there is an extra set of 8′ jacks plucking the same string as the upper jacks, so 2 × 8′ 1 × 4′, 1 × 16′ are available on the lower keyboard without coupling. Challis also makes an instrument possessing three sets of strings, 1 × 8′, 1 × 4′, and 1 × 16′, in which there are two rows of jacks both plucking the single set of 8′ strings, one worked from the upper and one from the lower keyboard.

Challis keyboards are more easily serviced than those of anyone else. If a key sticks on the lower keyboard of most harpsichords, the two keyboards

Section of a Challis bridge, the brass extrusion drilled out on all sides to make it lighter.

Detail showing a Challis metal soundboard, 8′ and 4′ bridges, and 4′ hitchpin rail. The 8′ bridge and 4′ hitchpin rail are raised on metal blocks.

must be pulled out as a unit and then disassembled to get at the lower one. With a Challis, it is only necessary to remove the damperless jacks which would fall into the harpsichord (having no keyboard to rest on), and then pull out the upper keyboard alone, exposing the lower for servicing. I have had to do this half an hour before a concert, and blessed Challis for his foresight.

We have described the two different models of two manual harpsichord made by Challis, to which should be added four models of singles. All of these possess beautifully machined pedals. He makes a clavichord, and a "Mozart" piano, which is somewhat misnamed. He used to make the piano with $4^3/_4$ octaves FF–d³ (an odd range, not used in Mozart's day) but now uses $7^1/_3$ octaves AAA–c⁴, the modern piano size. It is a very pleasant instrument, but the Viennese pianos used by Mozart had tiny leather covered hammers on thin flexible shanks and an ingenious escapement, adding up to a totally different feel and sound from the modern action which Challis uses.

The large concert double now costs $8000 (it was $5800 on an earlier price schedule). This price probably reflects the enormous amount of work spent in making one of these instruments. Challis claims that there is nothing enjoyable and easy about working in metal (I believe him!). He does it because he feels he has to. All of his cases are walnut with an oil finish. He has also made pedal harpsichords, and recently made such an instrument for the organist E. Power Biggs with the following specifications: $2 \times 8'$, $1 \times 4'$, $1 \times 16'$ lower manual; $1 \times 8'$ upper manual; $1 \times 8'$, $1 \times 4'$, $1 \times 16'$ pedal.

Early in his career Challis decided to use a long scale, 16 in. for c², in an effort to gain volume and eliminate the shift in pitch of a sustaining tone which occurs right after the pluck. As we have already seen, a shorter and slacker string will stretch upon being plucked, sounding a slightly higher note in its stretched position than immediately afterwards when the string is in its natural position.

The question must now be asked: how successful are Challis instruments both tonally and in regard to stability? Around this question, as around most questions regarding the merit of a certain make, there is considerable controversy. Challis himself tells of many instances in which he has gone to a customer's home after an absence of one or two years to tune his harpsichord. Finding it just a few waves out (not enough to disturb the ordinary ear) he would ask the lady of the house when the tuner had been there last. "Tuner," she would say, "there has been no tuner." These stories are undoubtedly true; I have had similar experiences with Challis instruments. However, what is true in the home is not necessarily true of the concert hall. The New York Philharmonic bought a Challis some years ago. The money for the instrument had been provided by one of their rich patrons, and I happened to be present when Mr. Bernstein and an engineer and harpsichord "bug" from Columbia Records discussed what make of harpsichord to buy. (These decisions are often arrived at quite informally.) I pointed out that tuning stability, although generally desirable, is not the most important value in the concert hall, since an instrument has to be tuned for each performance anyway. (Assuming, of course, that the instrument will hold during the performance, an assumption which is not always warranted.) For a large (and dead) hall like the Philharmonic as it then was, I might have chosen another instrument, but the powers that be got their Challis and later, when it arrived, decided to use a microphone with it. (It is possible that no instrument would fill that hall unmiked, especially when used with orchestra.)

People often say that a metal soundboard produces a "bad" tone and a wooden soundboard a "good" tone. They say this because the first thing that comes to mind in assessing the tone is the soundboard—after all "sound" and "board"—the board making the sound. (Sounding board, incidentally, as it is often called erroneously, is a structure over a pulpit to help the speaker's voice).

I personally can not tell a Challis with a wooden board from a Challis with a metal board. To me they both have the characteristic Challis tone—loud but not particularly singing, and overplucking, causing a slight tearing of the string. Now overplucking can be achieved in two ways—the plectrum can be projected a long way beyond the string, forcing it to bunch up and strain during the pluck; or the plectrum, consisting of hard leather, can be left quite thick, as it is with Challis, so that it will lift and strain the string.

Challis cuts his leather plectra thicker than anyone else, and the only reason they work at all is that the instrument is engineered superbly well. As we have already seen, leather, especially with a stubby cut, will work well in only one precise position—neither overplucking nor failing to pluck, and there can be practically no leeway. The Challis leathers, which are about $1/4$ in. long, measure $3/32$ in. at the base and $1/16$ in. at the tip, with a slant cut at the end (see sketch A). Even under the best of conditions, in my opinion, the tip is going to be stiff enough to overpluck unless it were cut as shown in sketch B.

I once re-cut the leathers on a small Challis (much to his chagrin) more in line with cut B. For all I know these leathers have now given out whereas plectra cut his way continue to work for a long time. But it did seem to me to improve the tone and remove the slightly raucous quality caused by this cut. It is possible, of course, that all the metal in the instrument "kills" the tone or at least prevents it from singing, no matter what cut is used. But there are degrees, and careful voicing with an eye to tone, rather than stability, will often improve an instrument.

Challis is now working with a plastic plectrum which is not flat like the delrin most modern makers use but thick like leather and cut the same way. He has tried the material on his automatic harpsichordist, a machine he designed to put a plectrum through thousands of plucks. The material has stood up well and has been put into two instruments. I have heard the new material and found it quite similar to the Challis leather tone. It seems that a builder's personality is sometimes so strong as to impose itself on his instruments no matter what material he uses.

Does the metal frame "interfere" with the tone? Indirectly it probably does, first by seducing the builder into using greater string tensions and second by preventing the wooden case from resonating to any great extent. But such questions can never be answered very satisfactorily, because of the difficulty of sorting out the different causes bearing on the question. I have seen a metal frame harpsichord, for example (not a Challis) where the entire advantage gained by the frame was lost at the bridge, where the double pinning caused an angle so strong as to prevent a string from being pulled through evenly

A section of a partially completed Challis action, showing two jackslides (without jacks), and separate jack dampers to left and right.

The cast aluminum frame of a Challis harpsichord, with braced wrestplank at left.

when tuning. A casual observer, finding the instrument constantly out of tune, would draw the conclusion that the metal frame is not helping, when in reality the metal frame has no chance to do its job since what is called "frictional retardation" is keeping the strings out of tune no matter what the frame might do. Sometimes not even the experts (if such there be) can separate the different factors.

It does seem that the builder often has to make a choice whether to go for the best tone or the greatest amount of stability. That choice is not easily made, since an instrument with the most ideal tone will never get the chance to be heard at all if it is constantly out of tune and regulation. One can easily learn to live with a tone somewhat below the ideal (especially when no means of comparison is at hand), but it is hard to live with an instrument needing constant attention. In his brochure, Challis restates the traditional problems of the harpsichord: "How long will it endure? How long will it keep in tune? Will repairs be frequent and costly?" Challis has solved these problems just as he has promised in his brochure, and solved them better than anyone else.

INSTRUMENTS BY JOHN CHALLIS (Waiting time 1 to 3 years)

1. Clavichord: 4⅞ octaves GG–f3; length 58 in.
2. Portable harpsichord: 4¾ octaves AA–f3; 1 × 8′, half and buff stops. Available with hand stops or two pedals.
3. Single manual harpsichord: 5 octaves GG–g3; 2 × 8′, buff; 78 in. Three pedals.
4. Single manual harpsichord: 5 octaves GG–g3; 1 × 16′, 1 × 8′, buff, 1 × 4′; 78 in. Four pedals.
5. Double manual harpsichord: 5 octaves GG–g3; three sets of strings, four sets of jacks, 2 × 8′, buff, 1 × 4′, 1 × 16′; 84 in. Five pedals.
6. Double harpsichord for concert use: 5¼ octaves FF–g3; upper manual, 1 × 8′, buff and half stops; lower manual, 1 × 16′, 2 × 8′, buff, 1 × 4′; 96 in. Seven pedals.
7. Mozart Pianoforte: 7⅓ octaves AAA–c4; 96 in. Damper and Una Corde Pedals.

CLAUDE CHIASSON
West Caldwell, New Jersey

When I started making harpsichords in 1955, Chiasson's name was better known than it is now; he was then one of the few makers in America producing double manual instruments. I went to see him, and remember having

98

been enormously impressed; all those hundreds of jacks going up and down, all those multi-level string sets, and the—to me—hopeless complexity of it all! And here was Chiasson himself, in casual slacks and tennis shoes, sitting down and playing quite beautifully.

Only later, when used Chiassons turned up quite regularly (their owners had gone on to smaller and better things), did I begin to realize that this instrument, so much admired by me, was in fact astonishingly crude. The keyboards showed wide, irregular gaps between keys; the soundboard was hopelessly thick and unresponsive; the case had that massive simplicity which, as one player remarked, would look at home in a Lutheran Church; but worst of all, the jacks were crudely made and nearly unworkable.

A Chiasson still turns up now and then, usually for one tenth of current double manual prices; and some enthusiast will snap it up, only to pass it on.

RICHARD CLAYSON AND ANDREW GARRETT
(Early Keyboard Instruments)
Lyminge, Kent, England

Located in a sleepy English village in rural Kent, Messrs. Clayson and Garrett have an enormous shop, somewhat suggestive of a cavernous, disused railway station. Here they work, with one assistant, in almost ideal shop conditions.

Both are ex-Oxford students, and of a breed of educated young devotees to the craft which, though common in America, is still relatively rare in Europe. They somewhat resemble, in fact, the Hubbard and Dowd of the early days, except that they seem to be more relaxed and less knowledgeable.

Richard Clayson and Andrew Garrett have been in business for six years, and in this time they have produced 4 doubles, 12 singles, 6 spinets, and some 3 dozen clavichords, including tiny portables. They gave their yearly average output as only six instruments, which seems a low figure for so large a shop. While they don't make exact copies of classical harpsichords (few English makers do), they are going in that direction, and I saw fairly reasonable Italian copies under construction.

Their prices are remarkably low—a double manual 2 × 8′, 1 × 4′ costs the equivalent of $1620, the double with 16′ is under $3000, and the little portable clavichord is about $300.

Clayson and Garrett's clavichords are mostly polygonal in shape, an idea they borrowed from the English maker Michael Thomas. Almost any instrument in rectangular shape, from clavichord to square piano, shows a "whip" or warp after a few years; this is caused by the string tension being concentrated in the right front corner rather than distributed evenly as in a harpsichord. The polygonal shape distributes the string tension over a greater area and prevents the right front corner from whipping up. It makes, however, for an awkward looking lid. Clayson and Garrett's jacks are made from an English plastic called tufnel, also used by other English makers. Since this is not moulded but fabricated it entails almost as much work as wooden jacks. Delrin is the plectrum material, and their soundboards are Sitka spruce, 1/8 in. or thinner, and barred the classical way. The case thicknesses also hold to classical dimensions and the resulting tone is excellent.

A polygonal clavichord by Clayson and Garrett, five octaves, double strung.

One manual Clayson and Garrett harpsichord, with $2 \times 8'$, $1 \times 4'$, buff stop.

Soundboard view of the Clayson and Garrett polygonal clavichord. The odd shape is to overcome the usual problem of clavichords, the tendency of the right front corner to pull up and whip out of shape.

An instrument in playing condition in their shop had a big and silky tone, proving that you don't have to be an old master to make a good harpsichord. It seems, in fact, that one has to go out of one's way to make a bad one; in view of which it is surprising to see how many builders are willing to go to the trouble of making bad instruments.

INSTRUMENTS BY CLAYSON & GARRETT:

Clavichords:
1. Polygonal, C–d3, 55 × 22 in., double strung
2. Square, 5 octaves FF–f3, 68 × 22 in., double strung
3. Polygonal, 5 octaves FF–f3, 68 × 22 in., double strung
4. Portable, C–d3, 40 × 11 × 4 in.

Virginals:
1. Square, 5 octaves FF–f3, 78 × 24 in.
2. Square 4½ octaves, GG–d3, 60 × 22 in.

Spinet:
1. Polygonal, 5 octaves GG–g3, 74 × 30 in.

Harpsichords:
1. Single manual, 2 × 8′, buff, 84 in.
2. Single manual, 2 × 8′, 1 × 4′, buff on 8′, 86 in.
3. Double manual, 2 × 8′, 1 × 4′, buff on 8′, 94 in.
4. As above, but with additional 8′ soft leather *(peau de buffle)*
5. Double manual, 2 × 8′, 1 × 4′, 1 × lute, buff on 8′, 94 in.
6. Double manual, 2 × 8′, 1 × 4′, 1 × lute, 1 × 16′, buff on 8′, 111″ in. Compass on all harpsichords is 5 octaves FF–f3; plucking material is delrin.

PETER COUTTS

43 Perryn Road, Acton W3, London, England

Peter Coutts is something of rarity—neither an aristocrat with a hankering for meaningful work, nor yet an old time piano man—but an honest-to-goodness English workman. Coutts was a toolmaker until 1963, and then decided to make harpsichords in a room of the little suburban house he occupies with his wife. Since then he has made 24 of them, mostly small singles. Since he makes a single 8′ model for a fairly low price, he has no trouble finding customers even in England, where people have much less spending money than in America.

Coutts was born in London in 1923, and has played the cello for many years. Because of his toolmaking background his instruments are well engineered, but he works pretty much in isolation from the harpsichord world (few of the other English makers have ever met him), and is not very familiar with instrument building theory or classical harpsichords.

Coutts' jacks are made of bakelite (a rather brittle and early plastic, not much used by other makers) with a hornbeam wood tongue. His pinblock is laminated beech, the slide and guide are aluminum, the soundboard $1/8$ in. spruce ribbed straight across, and the keyboards, which he buys ready-made from a "bloke in London," are standard piano width, $6^3/8$ in. to the octave. His cases are just over $1/2$ in. in thickness, of a simple and pleasant design with square cheeks, and panels of inlay or gold striping. The instruments are set on a modified stand, in which the rear leg is independent, but the front two legs are connected by a low crossbrace which also holds the pedals, as simple a system for holding pedals as I have seen. (Both full stands and pedal lyres necessitated by individual legs are time-consuming to make, but Coutts' system gets around these chores.)

HUGH CRAIG
18 French Street, Croydon, Victoria 3136, Australia

Leafing through the pink (not yellow) pages of Melbourne, Australia, under the heading "Musical Instruments," one is somewhat startled to discover "Hugh Craig, harpsichord manufacturers." It would have been nice to report that the harpsichord was brought over in the nineteenth century along with the rabbit, and became the cottage industry of out back villages, but such, alas, is not the case; Hugh Craig was born in 1942 in Haslemere, Surrey, England, a neighbor of the Dolmetsches to whom he was apprenticed at the age of 16 after having already made some instruments on his own.

After being "honorably discharged" from Dolmetsch with an official certificate signed by Carl Dolmetsch, Leslie Ward, and Jan Karporvicz (all of whom we shall meet shortly), Craig went to Feldberg, and from there to de Blaise. Wanting to set up on his own and realizing that England contains almost as many harpsichord makers as Elizabethan manor houses, Craig set sail for greener pastures and landed in Australia in 1965.

In his three years there, Craig—in partnership with his wife—has produced some 25 instruments, consisting of one double, ten singles, eight spinets, and six clavichords. His current yearly output stands at eight. He uses a conventional wooden jack and leather plectra and has taken over some of the bad habits learned from his masters, such as open bottoms and $1/4$ in. thick soundboards (on doubles).

A faint newspaper clipping containing the usual journalistic fictions ("reminiscent of lavender and old lace," "vitality and volume unrelated to its past," "popular with the Beatles") shows Mr. Craig seated at his harpsichord looking like a youthful version of Chopin and Mendelsohn rolled into one.

MAURICE DE ANGELI
Box 190, Upper Ridge Road, R. D. 1, Pennsburg, Pennsylvania 18073

Maurice de Angeli has been making harpsichords and clavichords since October 1967, and has now acquired a little farm building across from his house which is just the right size for a shop. In this pleasantly rural surrounding he makes six instruments at once in a sort of one-man mass production.

He is now set up to make about 10 instruments a year, and he keeps going whether he has orders or not. If they are not sold by the time they are finished, he may put them in a piano store. His instruments have a "hidden" tubular steel frame and are, on the whole, fairly heavily made (his large harpsichord

Backyard snapshot of a clavichord built by Hugh Craig of Australia in 1969.

weighs 350 lbs.). Like Bannister, with whom he shares his jacks, he uses one continuous wire for two strings, piano-style, eliminating any hitchpin loops.

De Angeli's c^2 string is $15^3/_4$ in. long, suggesting a rather long scale and great tension, but his metal frame which goes right into the laminated pin-block presumably prevents any noticeable "give" of the case. His soundboards are glued to "flexible" liners to prevent warping or cracking. These consist of a strip of $1/_8$ in. plywood attached to the inside of the case by means of blocks. Most of the strip is floating, and the soundboard is glued to its top edge, thus being able to expand sideways, since the thin strip will give in either direction. De Angeli uses solid spruce soundboards somewhat thicker than $1/_8$ in.

De Angeli, who was born in 1928 near Philadelphia, worked for a furniture maker before he got interested in baroque instruments. He makes his key-boards in a rather unorthodox fashion, cutting out all the C's, all the D's, all the E's etc., and just pulling the right key out of a box when the time comes to put the keyboards together. This is something of a feat, since keyboards are so irregular that often no two C's or D's or others are interchangeable. Most builders cut their keyboards from a plank which has been glued up to the right thickness, width and length; this plank is marked out with all the keys shown on it, and their balance and front pin holes are marked and drilled before cutting the keys apart. The plank is often set on the keyframe and the location of the balance and front pin holes are marked on the frame so that these pins will later fit through their matching holes and be spaced correctly.

A De Angeli clavichord which I played was over 6′ long and this size produced a rather large tone when played with a certain amount of force, but it had the fault of "chucking" or spitting when played with a light and staccato touch. This is a fault common to many clavichords, including some very good ones (the old Dolmetsch-Chickerings had it), but makes playing triple pianissimo a trying experience. The cause of chucking in a clavichord seems to be related to how quickly the string can be set in motion by the strik-ing tangent. On a very responsive clavichord even a quick touch of tangent to string will still transmit the vibrating energy of the string to the bridge and soundboard and produce a viable sound. A combination of factors may inhibit the string from responding to the tangent's touch, unless this touch is firm and legato—these may include thick cases, bridges and soundboards; also great string tension, resulting in a hard springy surface from which the tangent bounces back after impact, thus returning instantly rather than permitting a split second of string contact even if the player has released the key. It is per-haps something like hammering a nail into a brick wall rather than hammer-ing it into wood, the hammer representing the tangent.

A harpsichord of de Angeli which I saw in a New York piano store had a rather strong, gutsy tone, but its appearance was somewhat bulky and not very elegant. This was due partly to an unfortunate choice of veneer and stain, and does not necessarily apply to his other instruments.

WILLIAM DE BLAISE
60 North End Road, London N.W. 11, England

William de Blaise is one of the most prolific of the makers, and his instru-ments are scattered all over the world. De Blaise was born in Latvia in 1907

The reinforcing plate of plywood with cutouts used by de Angeli; this lies about 3 in. below the soundboard.

Detail of a de Angeli harpsichord showing dogs pivoted to lower key levers which rise to vertical position when lower keyboard is pushed in, engaging buttons on underside of upper manual key shanks.

and has lived in many different countries, becoming easily fluent in their respective languages. In the 40's and early 50's he was in Israel as flutist for the Israel Philharmonic. Playing next to him was another future harpsichord maker, the American builder Eric Herz.

In 1952 de Blaise came to London and started making harpsichords. While in Israel, he had seen and admired some pre-war Neuperts (which are said to have been considerably better than their post-war products), and it was probably then that he formed his conception of the harpsichord as a modern, mass production instrument, perhaps a modified piano. De Blaise, who defends his views with great gusto, proudly admits that he is not the artist-craftsman, or *Kunsthandwerker*, who piddles around in his little shop making a few copies.

De Blaise vigorously defends the Bach disposition used by Neupert and many others, in which the lower manual has $1 \times 8'$, $1 \times 16'$, and the upper has $1 \times 8'$, $1 \times 4'$. The argument that the old harpsichords were never disposed that way, and that the Bach instrument is of dubious authenticity and has had its registration altered, does not impress him. He argues that it makes no sense to put the $16'$, $8'$, and $4'$ all on the lower keyboard, thereby hopelessly outbalancing the single $8'$ on the upper manual. He cites the organ as an example of a two manual instrument, in which the manuals are evenly balanced. Since most old harpsichords had no $16'$, their registration of $1 \times 8'$, $1 \times 4'$ on the lower keyboard and $1 \times 8'$ solo stop on the upper made sense; but, claims de Blaise, when the $16'$ was added, the $4'$ needed to be shifted to the upper

Jacks by de Blaise. Wooden jack and tongue, leather plectrum, tongue adjustment in center of jack.

Three-manual harpsichord by de Blaise: upper manual $2 \times 8'$, middle manual $2 \times 8'$, $1 \times 4'$, lower manual $1 \times 8'$, $1 \times 4'$, $1 \times 16'$. Six rows of jacks, with two of the $8'$ and two of the $4'$ doglegged. The middle and lower manual are permanently coupled.

manual. The fact that the old Hass harpsichords *did* have a 16′, 8′ and 4′ on the lower keyboard is not important to him. He frankly admits not being terribly interested in the old harpsichords.

De Blaise has solved a vexing problem of the harpsichord maker—whether to have a small shop allowing him active participation, or a production set-up putting him into the front office—by associating himself with the medium-sized firm of Welmar pianos. Welmar makes some 800 pianos a year, and average a yearly harpsichord output of 60 instruments. Of this number there will be one or two fancy ones, eight very large doubles, twenty smaller doubles, and thirty singles.

All the cabinet and woodwork is done in the Welmar shop by the crew that makes pianos. The final steps of stringing, action adjustment and voicing is done by de Blaise personally. Since his production of over one instrument weekly is too much for one person to finish up, he depends on trained assistants, of which there seems to be a shortage in England as in the rest of the world. In England an apprentice, after a few months of try-out, signs a five year contract with his employer which cannot be legally broken by either side. This leads to unhappy situations, and most English makers complain of being stuck with incompetent or surly workers. It is said that in Germany, where a similar system is in effect, the makers would rather fall behind in production than hire new workers, or take on new apprentices.

If you are unlucky, as de Blaise has been, you may find yourself stringing your harpsichord one day, as de Blaise in fact has done, and breaking all the strings. Upon investigation, you would discover that your workman had glued the 8′ bridge 2 in. further back than your drawing indicated. "What's this" you would say, "can't you read the drawing?" "Well," he would reply, "I decided the bridge really belongs further back, so I just went ahead and put it there." Can you fire him? No. Can you at least get mad at him? No, or he would make your life miserable for the next five years.

The jacks de Blaise uses are made of hornbeam wood (the German Weiss-buche) which is used in oxen yokes. The jacks are made by a Polish workman who used to be with Hugh Gough in the days of Gough's English activities, but who is now set up on his own. The old world craftsmen not being what they used to be, this jack maker now puts a high price on his skills, making the jacks considerably more expensive than plastic ones. The jack slides are made of brass channel with the channel sides sticking up, and the lower guides are wood, the guide holes being bushed with leather.

Soundboards in de Blaise instruments are made from Roumanian pine, a sort of spruce popular in England till recently when the source dried up. The soundboards are over $1/8$ in. thick and barred straight across with many ribs.

His cases, which are made of $5/8$ in. birch plywood, are always veneered with the grain running vertically; this way of veneering, claims de Blaise, wastes less veneer than the horizontal graining, where the necessary width is hard to find. His keyboards are piano-size in the octave span, and usually have black naturals and white sharps. (There are several keyboard traditions, and "reverse color keyboards," as they are popularly called, do not necessarily denote the "true" harpsichord. Some of the finest old instruments, like Ruckers and Kirckman, had bone or ivory naturals and ebony sharps, and the

William de Blaise

A de Blaise "Cembalo Traverso," with reverse straight bentside going north.

Underside of a de Blaise harpsichord, showing piano-style framing and ribs crossing soundboard.

Soundboard, bridges and hitchpin rails of de Blaise "Cembalo Traverso."

modern piano keyboard derives, in fact, from Kirckman and from Shudi.)

De Blaise, who has personally voiced nearly all of the 800 harpsichords to come out of the Welmar shop, uses a tool no more sophisticated than a razor blade. He uses leather for plectra, and cuts it to size with a couple of deft strokes, cutting back toward the tongue from the point of the plectrum. His leathers are stiff and produce a loud, full tone, which is repeatedly mentioned in his many testimonials from well known performers like Veyron-Lacroix and Picht-Axenfeld. The problem with testimonials in general is that the pronouncement represents an enthusiastic moment which is frozen on paper forever, while the performer may have changed his mind, his harpsichord or his profession years ago.

On receiving one of my own harpsichords, a lady wrote me an enthusiastic letter, telling me how her husband would pray for something to go wrong on the instrument so that he might have a chance to work on it. It was not long before his prayer was answered and he not only had the chance but muffed it, calling me instead. By that time the couple's enthusiasm had cooled down considerably. This sort of thing happens, of course, to all the makers. One of the performers mentioned in the de Blaise brochure is Stewart Robb who is quoted as saying: "it holds up very well, considering the fact that we live right on the water." Evidently that fact finally caught up with the harpsichord, for when I saw the same instrument, not one single note was playing! The lower guide had swelled, "freezing" all the end pins. Another de Blaise I used to service was also hard hit by the American climate of extreme steam heat in winter and extreme humidity in summer. It did, however, not lose its strong and perhaps somewhat crude tone, which worked out fine for this particular instrument; it belonged to jazz pianist John Lewis.

De Blaise makes an oddly shaped triangular instrument he calls a "cembalo traverso" which looks something like a mirror image of a regular harpsichord. The right cheek continues in a straight line to the tail, and the normally straight spine becomes the bent or angled side. The strings, running parallel to the spine, naturally cross the jack slides at an angle, since the spine is angled with respect to the pinblock. This means that there is less space between strings, since a string band swung from a straight to an angled position reduces the width of the band. The space between strings lost in the string angle is gained nowhere else (except for allowing the bass strings to be slightly longer) and the net effect of the angle is to make jack spacing tighter and more critical.

De Blaise had a double out in this shape, with the odd registration of 1 × 16′, 1 × 4′ on the lower manual, and 1 × 8′ on the upper. This double was something of a technician's nightmare and has mercifully been discontinued. When I asked him why he makes instruments in that shape he mentioned something about the width of the doors in Jerusalem. But he wasn't making harpsichords in Jerusalem, and moreover any harpsichord can be carried, tipped on its side, through even the narrowest door of a New York tenement apartment.

De Blaise lives with his wife, also a flutist, in a cozy, tastefully furnished house in a London suburb. Both of them are unhappy about the English climate and flee to sunny France and Italy every summer. De Blaise travels a lot, servicing his instruments, attending trade fairs, and exchanging pleasantries with other makers. He still has time to play the flute, though he puts in a full day at the shop.

Detail of a large de Blaise harpsichord, showing jackslides (one with jacks), and buff stop.

Detail of de Blaise "Cembalo Traverso," showing angle of strings to pinblock, jackslides, bridges, 4′ hitchpin rail, and hand stop.

INSTRUMENTS BY WILLIAM DE BLAISE

1. Single manual Cembalo Traverso, Model A: 5 octaves FF–f3; 1 × 8′, 1 × 4′, buff and half on 8′; 56½ × 41½ in., 141 lbs. Three pedals, one hand stop.
2. Double manual harpsichord Model B3: 5 octaves FF–f3; upper manual 1 × 8′, 1 × 4′, lute, buff to 8′ and lute; lower manual 1 × 8′, 1 × 16′, buff and half on 8′, buff on 16′; 93 × 41½ in., 356 lbs. Seven pedals, three hand stops.
3. Double manual harpsichord Model B4: 5 octaves FF–f3; upper manual 1 × 8′, lute, buff to 8′ and lute; lower manual 1 × 8′, 1 × 4′, 1 × 16′, half and buff to 8′, buff to 16′; 93 × 41½ in., 356 lbs. Seven pedals, three hand stops.
4. Double manual harpsichord Model C1: FF–g3; upper manual 1 × 8′, 1 × 4′, lute, buff to 8′ and lute; lower manual 1 × 8′, 1 × 4′, 1 × 16′, half and buff to 8′, buff to 16′; 93 × 41½ in., 403 lbs. Seven pedals, three hand stops.
5. Double manual harpsichord Model C2: FF–g3; upper manual 1 × 8′, lute, buff to 8′ and lute; lower manual 1 × 8′, 1 × 4, 1 × 16′, buff and half to 8′, buff to 16′; 104 × 44 in., 403 lbs. Seven pedals, three hand stops.
6. Double or triple manual harpsichord Model C3: FF–g3; upper manual 1 × 8′, lute, buff to 8′ and lute; middle manual 2 × 8′, 1 × 4′, buff to 8′ and 4′; lower manual 1 × 8′, 1 × 4′, 1 × 16′, buff to 8′, 4′, and 16′; 109 × 44 in., 440 lbs. Seven pedals, three hand stops.
7. Double manual harpsichord Model K 1 and 2: 5 octaves GG–g3; upper manual 2 × 8′, or 1 × 8′ and 1 × 4′; lower manual 1 × 8′, 1 × 4′, 1 × 16′, or 2 × 8′, 1 × 16′; 78 × 41½ in., 308 lbs.

G. A. C. DE GRAAF
Amsterdam, Koggestraat 11, Holland

De Graaf is an organ maker who has been active since 1957 building harpsichords and clavichords. He has produced a total of fifteen instruments, but his main line continues to be pipe organs. The harpsichords made by de Graaf are of his own design. He also has a shop in Plasencia de Jalon, Zaragoza, Spain, where he works part of the time.

ARNOLD DOLMETSCH, LTD.
"Beechside," Haslemere, Surrey, England

We have already mentioned Arnold Dolmetsch, one of the most important figures in the modern harpsichord revival. Dolmetsch was born in 1858 in Le Mans, France, of Swiss and French parentage. His father was an organ builder and piano dealer who was responsible for the dismemberment of many an old square piano. Young Dolmetsch had his first violin lessons from a gypsy fiddler, who disappeared one day for good with a violin which Dolmetsch père had lent him. In his early teens, Dolmetsch formed a trio whose startling outcome was Dolmetsch's elopement with the trio's pianist to, of all places, Louisville, Kentucky.

Dolmetsch, who was restless all his life, soon returned to France and from there to England to study music. He got interested in early English music and found a viola d'amore. Going to the British museum to look for viola d'amore music, he found none but came across music for viols which lay there waiting to be discovered. Next Dolmetsch gathered and restored a chest of viols and some lutes.

He divorced his first wife, who approved neither of his Bohemian pre-Raphaelite friends nor of his consuming interest in old music. His next wife was Elodie Desirée who was a fine pianist, but this marriage, too, ended in divorce. He finally married one of his students, Mabel Johnston, who later wrote a charming biography of her husband, now unfortunately out of print. (*Personal Recollections of Arnold Dolmetsch*, New York 1958).

In all this time Dolmetsch played, lectured, toured, and made reproductions of the old instruments. In 1905 he came to America to tour, but stayed on in Boston when the piano firm of Chickering & Sons put him in charge of a specially created harpsichord department. For the next few years Dolmetsch, with the aid of the Chickering workshop, produced a series of harpsichords and clavichords, many of which are still in use. I have tuned and adjusted a number of them, and while they are impressive, they are by no means free of faults.

It must be remembered that Arnold Dolmetsch did not have the easy access to the body of research on old instruments that we have today. He had to ferret the information out painstakingly by himself, and during restorations and the building of new instruments he would often make mistakes, for instance stringing too heavily. (The Dolmetsch firm is very conservative and tends to perpetuate these mistakes—a recent spinet of theirs started with .012 steel wire in the treble instead of the usual .009.)

Moreover, Dolmetsch was by no means a believer in copying what the old boys had done. He was always on the look-out for innovations, culminating in the welded steel frame and the disastrous "new" action with sustaining pedal. When Chickering was hit hard by the depression of 1910, Dolmetsch returned to England and soon after tried another stint of production work by associating himself with the French piano firm of Gaveau. This lasted from 1911 to 1914, and was perhaps an attempt by Gaveau to capture the harpsichord market, such as it was, from its rival, Pleyel.

Pleyel had the lead because of its association with Wanda Landowska. Landowska did come to see Dolmetsch and liked his instruments, but accord-

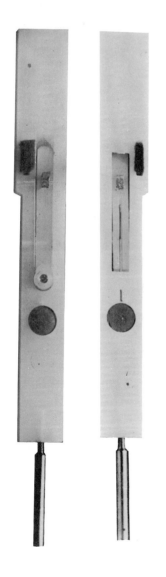

The Dolmetsch jack, plastic with leather plectrum. The adjustment screw is on the tongue itself; end pin and spring are brass.

ing to Carl Dolmetsch who was present at that meeting, expected Arnold to "donate" one of his harpsichords to her. According to Denise Restout, Landowska's long-time companion, the relationship between maker and player was rather different. Landowska had the free use of Pleyels and played them in, "test-driving" them so to speak, and returning them for a new one off the assembly line. It is probable that she had this arrangement in mind with Dolmetsch, but Arnold could neither afford it nor would he have had a taste for such an arrangement.

In 1918, the Dolmetsches settled in Haslemere, Surrey, one of the prettiest towns in England, where they still are today. Arnold Dolmetsch's old workshop, which was located in a beautiful Elizabethan house has now been vacated, the shop having moved to a red brick factory building, and I learned only recently that the Elizabethan house is to be torn down to make way for luxury flats. (Haslemere is in the "stockbrokers belt" within easy commuting distance of London.) I have nostalgically walked around the empty rooms of his old shop trying to imagine the way it was set up.

From the old Dolmetsch, who was friendly with the pre-Raphaelites, D'Annunzio, Yeats, Shaw, William Morris, Isadora Duncan, and Swinburne, it is something of a let-down to discuss the modern Dolmetsch factory. Since 1940, when Arnold Dolmetsch died, the production of keyboard instruments

Carl Dolmetsch

A Dolmetsch spinet harpsichord.

109

A Dolmetsch clavichord, showing the pretty casework for which these instruments are famous. Note arcaded fronts of keys.

The carved key levers of a Dolmetsch clavichord.

has occupied a position of minor importance in the interests of the family, who concentrate on recorders, viols and lutes. Since 1948, the workshop has produced some 600 keyboard instruments, which comes to no more than 30 yearly. Their current yearly average is given as four large doubles, six small doubles, six clavichords, twelve to fourteen large triangular spinets, and twenty-five to thirty small spinets and ottavinos. (This adds up to almost 60, and is in line with most makers' tendency to overestimate their current production; when their entire previous production is added up and divided by the number of years in business, the result is always a smaller figure than the current yearly production.)

This should be contrasted to Dolmetsch's current yearly production of 200,000 plastic recorders. Arnold's son Carl, who is the present head of the family, is a fine recorder player himself and concerns himself mostly with the recorder production. Until recently, Arnold's son-in-law Leslie Ward was head of the keyboard department, which employs some 8 workers, but with his retirement the shop is run by the works manager, Jan Karpowicz, who has been with the Dolmetsches for 21 years.

Since 1960 the Dolmetsch jacks have been made of a plastic called Diokon, but the plectrum continues to be made of stiff leather, except for one stop in the large doubles, and other materials supplied at customer's request. Their keyboards have piano octave spans. (Harpsichords in general are divided just about evenly between the wider piano octave and the narrower octave span used by the old French builders. The difference is about $1/4$ in. to the octave C–B, and most players seem to adjust to that difference easily.)

In some of the older Dolmetsches the keyboard would come out only by

dropping it straight down, and the instrument had to be turned sideways during this cumbersome operation. Keyboard removal sometimes became necessary because sticking keys could not be removed individually due to lack of space between keyboards and pinblock. Keys had a tendency to stick because of a thick felt bushing set into the bottom of the key around the balance pin hole. We know from the keyboards on old instruments that completely unbushed keys work silently and rarely stick, but Dolmetsch continues to use this bushing.

English instruments in general, and Dolmetsches in particular, are made with very close tolerances; moving parts are allowed a minimum of play for expansion, and this works in England with almost constant humidity but not elsewhere. The harp stop on one type of Dolmetsch spinet used to consist of tiny dowels with felt pads, which would ride through holes in the pinblock and press against the strings from underneath. (In paired spinet stringing, the harp cannot be put on a sliding rail, since only half of the strings would be contacted that way.) What invariably happened was that these dowels, which were just a shade thinner than the holes in which they rode, would swell and stick in their holes. They would "freeze" in this position, resulting in a permanent harp stop to the exclusion of all else. It would have been easy to make the dowels really undersized, since a sloppy fit here would not have mattered.

The question of play becomes critical in a popular Dolmetsch model, the larger triangular spinet with pedals (they refer to it as a harpsichord). Here the strings are not paired to save space, but left evenly spaced, probably in order to take advantage of a "half" stop. The half stop is the slight movement of the jackslide away from the strings which forces the jacks to pluck at the very tip of the plectrum, resulting in a softer tone. This stop rarely works well since it depends on a minute amount of travel and rigidly precise adjustment of the jacks. The half stop demands more room between strings than would be required without it in a single set of strings, since the jacks must be able to move backwards without touching the strings. In a spinet in which the string band is angled, the space between strings is reduced anyway, so the half stop in a spinet becomes a precarious undertaking, not tried by anyone else. Add to this the tendency for the jacks to stick in the slide, forcing an enlargement of the jack slots which will make the half stop unreliable as well as further reduce the space available to the jack, and you will see that the triangular Dolmetsch is

Soundboard of a Dolmetsch triangular harpsichord showing 8′ and 4′ bridges, and 4′ hitchpin rail.

Framing of a Dolmetsch triangular harpsichord.

A detail of the "new" Dolmetsch action which eliminated the plectrum's touching the string on its return.

113

Jacks being fitted to a large single-manual Dolmetsch.

Framing and soundboard of a Dolmetsch double-manual harpsichord.

not popular with technicians in America. Needless to say, the problem is further compounded by an addition of the 4′ in the triangle.

This instrument has, or at least had, an excellent tone when it was voiced carefully. I have not seen a recent example with the triple laminated pine soundboard which the Dolmetsches are now using. They have always ribbed straight across the soundboard, but with this new material most of the ribs have been eliminated. The cases are rather heavily constructed and framed and despite Arnold's concern for the old instruments, the Dolmetsch harpsichord has few similarities to the old ones. This is due partly to the dearth of published material about old instruments in his day, partly to his tendency to innovate, partly to the family's perpetuation of whatever Arnold did, and partly to the whole state of harpsichord making in England, where the current tendency to go back to historical models has only begun to make any headway.

Carl Dolmetsch now resides in his father's house, not far from the old shop. Next to this house is a large studio filled with instruments related to the Dolmetsch family in some way. The Dolmetsches are also engaged in producing the Haslemere Festival, which was founded by Arnold in 1925 and which is now one of the oldest festivals in England and is devoted to performances of early instrumental and vocal chamber music played on the old instruments and interpreted in the style of the period. Among the composers to be performed this year are Blow, Wagenseil, Breval, Merci, Vecchi, Avison, Locke, Leclair, Guedron, Paisible, Lawes, Eccles, Easte, and Porpora. While some of these unfamiliar names are modern composers, most of them are obscure early composers who are being resurrected in the spirit of the old Arnold Dolmetsch, a spirit so strong that its presence is still felt everywhere.

INSTRUMENTS BY DOLMETSCH

1. Clavichord, double strung: 4¼ octaves C–d3, 44½ × 15 in.
2. Portable Virginal: 4 octaves C–c3; 1 × 8′ (buff stop extra); length 30 in.
3. Small Spinet: 4½ octaves C–f3; 1 × 8′ (buff stop extra); length 43 in.
4. Triangular Harpsichord: 5 octaves FF–f3; 1 × 8, buff stop. Two pedals.
5. Triangular Harpsichord: 5 octaves FF–f3; 1 × 8′, 1 × 4′, buff to 8′. Three pedals.
6. Single manual harpsichord: 5 octaves FF–f3; 2 × 8′, 1 × 4′, buff to 8′; 72 × 36 in. Four pedals.
7. Small double manual harpsichord: 5 octaves FF–f3; upper manual 1 × 8′, buff; lower manual 1 × 8′ leather, 1 × 8′ quill, 1 × 4′, buff to 8′; 63 × 40 in. Six pedals.
8. Concert double manual harpsichord: upper manual 1 × 8′ leather, 1 × 8′ lute (quill), buff to 8′; lower manual 1 × 8′, 1 × 4′, 1 × 16′, buff to 8′. Eight pedals.

WILLIAM DOWD
25 Thorndyke Street, Cambridge 41, Massachusetts

If Boston can be said to be the Antwerp of the modern harpsichord, then Frank Hubbard and William Dowd are the Ruckers of the twentieth century. They deserve this distinction not only because of the quality of their work, but the quantity as well; and chiefly because they have had a profound influence on harpsichord making not only in America but all over the world.

William Dowd was born in 1922 in Newark, N.J. He became interested in harpsichords while at school, and after graduating from Harvard where his field was English literature, he apprenticed himself to John Challis, who himself had earlier been apprenticed to Arnold Dolmetsch. In 1949, after 18 months with Challis, Dowd and Frank Hubbard went into business under the name of Hubbard and Dowd, and this famous association lasted until 1958, when Dowd established his own business. Their first shop was on Tremont Street in Boston, and thus the "Boston School" was born.

The firm of Hubbard and Dowd must be credited with the first serious and systematic attempt in modern times to build production harpsichords based entirely on historical models. Both Hubbard and Dowd were scholarly, devoted and skilled and they began turning out a series of instruments which have few equals among modern harpsichords. Towards the end of the association, when personality differences began to assert themselves, they took in a third partner, Charles Fischer, who was an engineer and presumably was to supervise production and perhaps attend to business administration. But the three partners did not work toward a common purpose. Frank Hubbard was mainly interested in the theory of the old harpsichords and was then already spending a lot of time studying and writing; Dowd was interested in the practical production of the instruments, and Charlie Fischer was absorbed in gadgetry and improvements. (One of Fischer's gadgets which is still being used is the so-called "happiness bar." This is a post set under a sagging soundboard to bring it level. On top of the post is a coil spring, pushing against the underside of the soundboard and allowing it to move up and down, thus presumably not interfering with the tone.)

Since 1958 Dowd has produced about 180 instruments, of which 40 have been singles in the Italian style, and the rest have been mostly French and some Flemish doubles. His current production with a staff of 6 co-workers is 30 instruments per year, and Dowd does not want to increase the size of his business since he does not want to be condemned to be his own office manager. Life for him now is probably more hectic than suits his taste, since he is in demand as lecturer and restorer, as well as being a popular tourist attraction around Cambridge. (Visitors to harpsichord shops treat the workshops as a combination of museum and university extension course. Time for the visitor stands still, but not so for the harpsichord maker who may be in the middle of a voicing job that must be completed that day.)

Dowd uses a delrin jack of simple design which has a tongue with a moulded-in spring as its tail. The spring of a jack usually presents a problem, since there is no simple way to attach spring to body of jack. The moulded tongue tail, bearing against a matching recess in the jack body, would seem to be the best solution to the problem. Since the tension of this spring is critical (it must

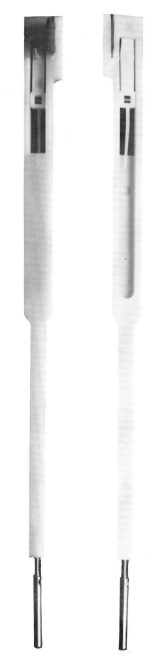

The Dowd jack: delrin, with spring and plectrum moulded to tongue. Top adjustment screw.

Detail of Dowd action showing coupler dogs. Upper manual is in forward position, allowings dogs to miss upper keys.

Upper manual is here moved to the rear, to allow dogs on lower key levers to engage adjustable buttons on upper key levers; lower manual will now play all jacks.

not be weak enough to prevent fast repetition nor strong enough to foil the plectrum's return) one might assume that a plastic spring moulded in production would not have a dependable amount of tension. However, according to Dowd, the spring is responsive to manipulation with tweezers to increase or decrease its tension. The plectra are delrin as well, but are not moulded into the jack, to permit change of plectra without discarding the tongue. The Dowd jack is $5/_{32}$ in. thick and $3/_8$ in. wide and works extremely well for such a slim and narrow jack. At the top it widens out to provide a slit for the "flag" damper.

The jackslides are made of channel brass but Dowd is now thinking of going back to wooden slides with slightly oversized slots and a covering of thin leather into which is punched the exact slot to fit the jack. Although the brass worked well, Dowd now feels that the wooden slide would keep pace in expansion with the case itself and thus help match the strings more accurately. In this Dowd is coming around to a view held by Hubbard for a long time. The end pins go through a thick plexiglass lower guide.

Dowd, who sometimes looks and talks like a scoutmaster addressing his boys on a Sunday afternoon, is several years behind in orders. His shop, in a solid old building, is large, light, and airy. It is as close to the ideal harpsichord shop as could be imagined, being equipped with the latest wood-working machinery, ample racks for storage, and the customary go-bar deck found in every Boston shop. (A go-bar deck is a large structure, the size of a small low-ceilinged room with a high platform. Work to be glued which cannot be held with conventional clamps like soundboard ribs, is placed on the platform, and thin flexible sticks of wood, the go-bars, are jammed between the work and the ceiling of the structure.)

Dowd still personally voices almost all his instruments. On weekends he will often cart a harpsichord to his summer house in the country where he can voice in quiet without being distracted by visitors, phones, and the demands of the shop.

For a period Dowd made a French harpsichord to which he added a 16′ stop at the request of some players. Since he rightly did not want to encumber

A double manual harpsichord by William Dowd, based on a Taskin: 2×8′, 1×4′, 38×93 in.

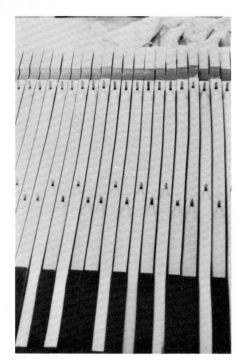

Lower manual of a Dowd two-manual action, showing slots in rear of key levers to receive dogs.

Model of the Dowd action, showing cross section of bridges, nuts, slides and guides.

A single manual harpsichord by William Dowd.

the 8′ bridge with the addition of 16′ strings, he squeezed a separate 16′ bridge into the space between 8′ bridge and hitch pins. In order not to crowd the 8′ bridge, Dowd moved the 16′ bridge practically to the edge of the harpsichord, only about ³/₄ in. away from the hitchpin rail. The resulting 16′ sound was almost worthless and it has taught some players that a poor 16′ is worse than none at all, especially if the 8′ bass is sonorous and resonant, as it usually is in Dowds. Sylvia Marlowe, who was practically brought up on Pleyels with 16′ strings, and who owned a Dowd with 16′, has now reached the conclusion, like many other players, that a 16′ is not all that important. Her new Dowd has no 16′.

The Dowd is by far the most popular instrument with concert performers in America. They like its easy action, its crisp tone, its carrying power, and its relative stability. In spite of his success, Dowd is looking forward to the day that he again can work all alone, making two instruments a year, and who can blame him? When that day comes, he will not take orders, so as not to be pressured by his customers, but just sell the instruments to the first person who appears the day they are ready.

INSTRUMENTS OFFERED BY WILLIAM DOWD

1. Single manual Italian harpsichord: FF–g3; 2 × 8′, buff; 38 × 90 in.; case thickness ½ in. Hand stops or knee levers. Or with 4-octave compass and traditional Italian inner–outer case construction, inner case ³/₁₆ in. thick.
2. Double manual Flemish harpsichord: 4 octaves BB–b2, tuned short octave to GG; 2 × 8′, 1 × 4′; 88 × 32 in.; Hand stops.
3. Double manual French harpsichord: FF–g3; upper manual 1 × 8′; lower manual 1 × 8′, 1 × 4′, buff to 8′; 93 × 38 in. Coupler.

EBELOE
Hamburg, Germany

This firm made harpsichords and clavichords for a time, but there is no evidence of its present existence. I've seen an example of both a harpsichord and a clavichord made by Ebeloe and there was little to distinguish them from the run-of-the-mill German production instrument.

HOWARD EVERNGAM
210 East 96th Street, New York, New York 10028

Howard Everngam started making harpsichords the same year I did, 1955. In fact, our first instrument was a joint effort—a clavichord made out of a practice clavier. This instrument has gone through a number of hands, ending up with a descendant of Count Tolstoy who, when last heard from, had dropped it on the floor during shipment somewhere in Africa.

Everngam works in a tiny room of his three room apartment on New York's upper East Side. In these cramped quarters he has made some 41 instruments of which 6 or 7 have been doubles. His scale is long in the treble, short in the tenor, and shorter in the bass. He makes his own wooden jacks but buys factory keyboards with piano octave spans. The soundboards are ¹/₈ in. spruce barred the classical way.

Everngam, who was born in New York in 1928, devotes himself to harpsichord making only part-time. His many other interests include photography, film-making, electronics, pacifism, and bicycle racing.

A double-manual harpsichord by Howard Everngam.

1. Small triangular spinet: 4½ octaves C–f3; 1 × 8′, buff stop; 48 × 23 in.
2. Wing-shaped spinet: 4¾ octaves AA–f3; 1 × 8′, buff stop; 60 × 23 in.
3. Small harpsichord: 4¾ octaves AA–f3; 2 × 8′, half and buff stops; 35 × 60 in. Handstops or three pedals.
4. Medium harpsichord: GG–f3; 2 × 8′, 1 × 4′, buff on 8′; 63 × 36 in.
5. Double manual harpsichord: GG–f3; 1 × 8′; 1 × 8′, 1 × 4′, buff on 8′; 80 × 36 in. Extra row of jacks optional.
6. Large double manual harpsichord: FF–g3; 1 × 8′; 1 × 8′, 1 × 4′; optional 1 × 16′; 37 × 92 in.

— JOHN FELDBERG

24 Pembroke Road, Sevenoaks, Kent, England

John Feldberg was, according to some who knew him then, an "angry young man" in the late 1950's, who wanted to build harpsichords. Not finding an English maker who could take him on at that time, he was referred by William de Blaise to the German firm of Neupert where he promptly started as an apprentice.

In 1958, after 18 months at Neupert, he returned to England to set up his own shop. There he began assembling Neupert harpsichords with parts imported from Bamberg, and to make his own harpsichords in a style almost indistinguishable from Neupert's. After a number of years in this activity, John Feldberg died suddenly, at night alone in his shop.

The work has since been carried on by his widow, Mrs. Ann Feldberg, who employs 4 workers and now makes an average of 20 instruments a year. In the last 12 months they have made 3 clavichords, 4 spinets, 3 singles, 6 doubles, and 3 large doubles. They have made a total of 150 instruments.

In his brochure Feldberg states that pitch instability was one of the factors contributing to the eclipse of the historical harpsichord. But if tuning instability were truly a factor leading to eclipse, most modern harpsichords, certainly including the Neuperts on which Feldbergs are modelled, would soon be on their way to oblivion.

He further holds that since the tradition of harpsichord making was broken, we have no sure way of knowing how they were made, but can guide ourselves by the tradition of organ building, which has been continuous. The relationship between the organ and harpsichord tone is "much closer than is generally realized." This statement illustrates well the philosophy of the Neuperts, whose registration and conception of tone is heavily influenced by the organ. Looking at the modern harpsichord, one would be tempted to assign to the organ a place right next to the piano as a prime source of unfortunate building practices. The harpsichord, it should be apparent from a study of the historical instruments, resembles nothing but itself.

Although similar to their Neupert models, Feldberg cases are on the whole more handsome, showing horizontal graining and inlays. Mrs. Ann Feldberg shares with Mars MacMillan of Australia and Frau Schulz-Ammer of East Germany the distinction of being one of the few female proprietors in an otherwise male occupation.

The F3 double-manual harpsichord by John Feldberg.

1. Clavichord F 54: 4½ octaves C–f3; single strung except for top octave; 15 × 46 in., 75 lbs.
2. Clavichord F 61: 5 octaves FF–f3; single strung except for top octave; 20 × 53 in., 82 lbs.

3. Harpsichord FW 57: 4¾ octaves AA–f3; 1 × 8′, 1 × 4′, buff and half stops; 64½ × 38 in., 165 lbs. Three pedals, straight bentside.
4. Double manual harpsichord FW 2.57: 4¾ octaves AA–f3; upper manual 1 × 8′; lower manual 1 × 8′, 1 × 4′, half and buff stops on 8′; 72 × 38 in., 235 lbs. Coupler and four pedals; straight bentside.
5. Double manual harpsichord F 1: 5 octaves GG–g3; upper manual 1 × 8′, 1 × 4′, half to 8′; lower manual 1 × 8′, 1 × 16′, half to 8′, buff to 16′; 84 × 41 in., 308 lbs. Coupler, five pedals.
6. Concert harpsichord F 2: FF–g3; upper manual 1 × 8′, 1 × 4′, half to 8′; lower manual 1 × 8′, 1 × 16′, half to 8′, buff to 16′; 102 × 41 in., 396 lbs. Coupler, five pedals, four hand stops.
7. Concert harpsichord F3: upper manual 1 × 8′, 1 × 4′, half and buff on 8′; lower manual 1 × 8′, 1 × 4′, 1 × 16′, half to 8′, harp to 16′; 102 × 41 in., 418 lbs.
8. Pedal harpsichord: C–f, 30 notes (also available with 27 and 32 notes); 1 × 8′, 1 × 4′, 1 × 16′; swell; 89 × 49 in., 297 lbs.

BERNARD FLEIG

4107 Ettingen, Basel, Switzerland

Fleig has had his own shop since 1966, starting out as an organ maker. He has so far made 1 double, 2 singles, 1 virginal, 2 clavichords, and a pedal harpsichord. The 33-year old maker works strictly to order, one at a time, and has no standard models.

GERARD FONVIEILLE

Place au Bois, Lezoux 63, France

Fonvieille is another example of the recent flurry of harpsichord activities in France, a country long under the domination of Pleyel. He has been active since 1963, but started full time production only in 1967. Since then he has made 4 doubles, 3 singles, 5 spinets, and 3 virginals, using both open and closed bottoms. The 42-year-old maker works alone, making his own keyboards and jacks. He uses delrin plectra.

Two-manual harpsichord by Gerard Fonvieille: 5 octaves; upper manual 8′ and 8′ lute (both plucking the same string; lower manual 8′ and 4′; buff on both 8′ choirs.

The long harpsichord by Carl Fudge, after a Baffo of 1579, but with wider compass.

CARL FUDGE

208 Ridge Street, Winchester, Massachusetts 01890

Carl Fudge has been active for about three years. He studied the harpsichord with Fernando Valenti and Gustav Leonhardt and was apprenticed to an organ maker for two years. Since then he has worked under Frank Hubbard's guidance, putting together some Hubbard kits and making his own drawings. In addition to many restorations, he has made 4 harpsichords.

Fudge started his playing career with a Sperrhake, but is gradually leaning towards historically oriented harpsichords. The Italian copy illustrated here is based on the Baffo harpsichord (1579), but the original had a compass of only AA–f³. It is interesting that practically all the historical makers had a sure feeling for the aesthetic proportions of a harpsichord, and few of the old harpsichords have other than graceful outlines. In this case Fudge extended the compass to FF in the bass and g³ in the treble; the bass extension necessitated a much longer case to accomodate the longer string lengths, and the additional keys give a wider front and deeper curve. The result is something reminiscent of Alice in Wonderland after she nibbled the mushroom; her neck just grew and grew.

When I examined the instrument it was overplucking, and had a $^1/_2$ in. key dip which is deeper than that of the modern piano and unheard of in an Italian harpsichord. But these faults have since been corrected. His work was otherwise meticulous.

Fudge continues his activities as organist and choirmaster, and plans to restrict his harpsichord workshop to a size enabling him to work on the instruments themselves rather than in a managerial capacity.

CHARLES GANNON
Ireland

Charles Gannon has made seven double harpsichords, exact copies of a Kirckman of 1772, in the course of 15 years. In 1967 he ceased his building activities and is not now planning to resume them.

ROBERT GOBLE AND SONS LIMITED
Greatstones, Kiln Lane, Headington, Oxford, England

The Gobles live and make harpsichords in a former brick kiln, which has been converted into an elaborate estate consisting of a beautiful house and a number of workshop outbuildings. It is just the sort of place one would expect to find a harpsichord maker in; one admires the aesthetic sense of the many English makers who live this graciously; it is in sharp contrast to the American makers, many of whom live and work in small, undistinguished suburban dwellings.

A Goble clavichord.

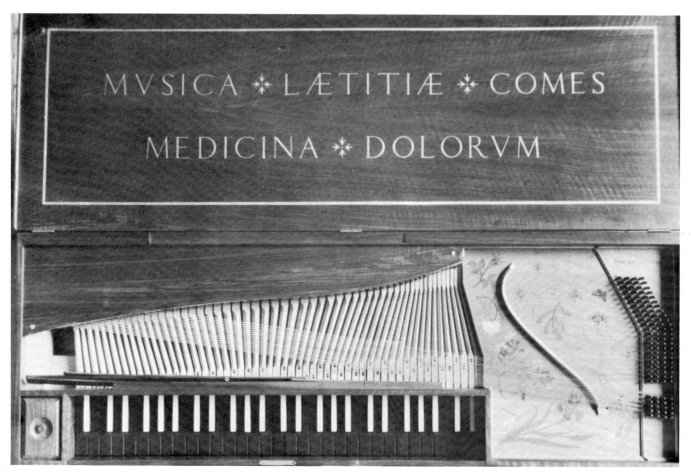

Goble is another family enterprise consisting of Robert, born in Haslemere in 1903; Mrs. Elizabeth Goble, a concertising gama player; and a son appropriately named Andreas who now manages the shop. Robert Goble worked for Arnold Dolmetsch for 12 years starting in 1925, mostly on recorders, and set up his own shop in 1937. His is, by general consensus, the most respected harpsichord shop in Britain. Aside from the three owners, there is now a staff of seven workers.

The Gobles have made a total of 500 instruments, and their current yearly average runs to 10 doubles, 5 singles, 10 spinets, and 10 to 15 clavichords. The jacks which they now use are based on the design of Eric Herz, the American maker, but are manufactured in England. They have a short spring of delrin moulded into the jack body. Unlike Herz, the Gobles use leather plectra but are now experimenting with delrin. The slides and guides are made of aluminum.

Andreas Goble setting a pin.

George Goble with one of his two instruments.

The soundboard material is sitka spruce, $^1/_8$ in. to $^3/_{16}$ in. in thickness; surprisingly for such an established shop, they have no firm theory on soundboard barring. The illustration shows ribbing straight across under the bridge, with a 4′ hitchpin rail $^1/_2$ in. wide and $^3/_{16}$ in. thick, but they have also ribbed soundboards in the classical manner, with a cut-off bar and small ribs extending to the spine, leaving the bridge underside clear. Their bottoms are an afterthought added when the instrument is all done. (To take full advantage of the strength the bottom can provide, the framing must be integral with it, as it is on most classical harpsichords.)

The cases are considerably heavier than historical ones, the bentside measuring $1^5/_8$ in. and the straight sides $1^3/_8$ in. in thickness. (There is no evidence that thicker cases and heavier framing increases the stability of a harpsichord; thus the Gobles, for example, are no more stable than, say, Dowds with cases of about half the thickness.)

The tone of their instruments is very satisfactory, but the Gobles are fussy about their product and always strive for improvement. A long roster of performers and universities use Gobles, and they now work with a two-year backlog.

INSTRUMENTS OFFERED BY ROBERT GOBLE AND SONS LIMITED

1. Clavichord: $4^1/_2$ octaves AA–e3; double strung; 48 × 16 in., 62 lbs.
2. Wing-shaped spinet: 5 octaves FF–f3; 1 × 8′, buff and half stops; 56 in. long, 85 lbs. Two pedals.
3. Single manual harpsichord: 5 octaves FF–f3; 2 × 8′, 1 × 4′, buff to 8′; 70 × 37 in., 102 lbs. Four pedals.
4. Double manual harpsichord: upper manual 1 × 8′; lower manual 1 × 8′, 1 × 4′, buff to 8′; 78 × 38 in., 230 lbs. Coupler, five pedals.
5. Double manual concert harpsichord: upper manual 1 × 8′, buff stop; lower manual 1 × 8′, 1 × 4′, 1 × 16′, buff to 8′; 84 × 39 in. Coupler, seven pedals.
6. Double manual concert harpsichord: upper manual 1 × 8′, lute course, buff; lower manual 1 × 8′, 1 × 4′, 1 × 16′, buff to 8′; 96 × 39 in., 274 lbs. Coupler, eight pedals.

Detail of a Goble keyboard. The balance pin bushing is a smooth, unfelted plastic insert. Two balance pin felts on which the key rides are seen at left.

Underside of a Goble harpsichord. Ribs crossing under the bridge are $^3/_8 × ^3/_4$ in.

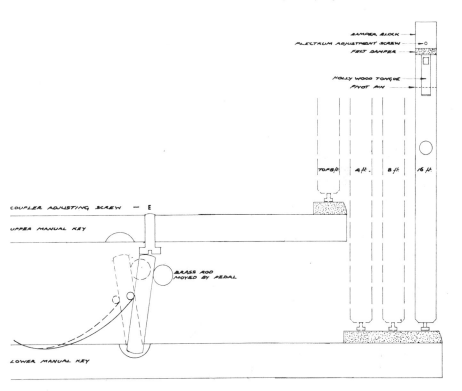

Diagram of Goble coupler action. Dogs pivoted in lower manual keys are moved against spring tension to "off" position by pedal. In "off" position, dogs ride up into cutout in upper key lever.

Double-manual harpsichord by Thomas Goff in the English style.

—THOMAS GOFF

46 Pont Street, London S.W. 1, England

Thomas Goff has been a fixture on the London harpsichord scene for 35 years. Residing in a large, comfortable house in a fashionable section of London, Goff has his workshop in the attic of his house, in somewhat cramped quarters. He has one cabinet maker who has been with him almost the entire time.

Although he has produced a total of some 125 instruments, the great majority of these have been small clavichords. He makes a few large double harpsichords, and keeps most of them for rental purposes. Many of his cases are veneered and inlaid in a fairly elaborate way.

His harpsichords have aluminum frames, with $2 \times 8'$, $1 \times 4'$, $1 \times 16'$, plus a lute stop. The Goff harpsichords record well, but those I have heard in the flesh have lacked a certain amount of punch in their tone; this may have been due to rough treatment of leather plectra during frequent rentals. It is at least conceivable that the tone would pick up brightness, clarity, and volume with a proper revoicing job.

Some of the small Goff clavichords which have come to the U.S. have not fared very well under American climate conditions. A Goff clavichord owned by pianist Claudio Arrau had keys sticking to such an extent that the instrument was unplayable. (I repaired it some years ago and have heard no more about it.) Another small Goff owned by Sylvia Marlowe showed the twist that is so common in rectangular instruments of any kind and any make, since the string tension is concentrated in a small area. In this case, the area was even smaller, and the twist greater, than usual. This instrument, like most small

Goff clavichords, was strung entirely in brass, which demands a shorter scale because it breaks more easily than steels. (Italian harpsichords with their extremely short scale are often successfully re-strung in brass.) The short scale demanded by brass should ordinarily exert less tension, so an undue amount of twist in a brass strung clavichord is somewhat puzzling.

Tom Goff, who is related to English royalty in a roundabout way, is another English maker who lives in a leisurely style and does not have to depend on the income from his workshop. He is (as are all the English makers without exception) charming, gracious, and interesting.

INSTRUMENTS BY THOMAS GOFF

1. Clavichords: There are four varieties of Goff clavichords: the smaller ones are single strung. Some are veneered and inlaid, others painted or lacquered.
2. Double manual harpsichord: 5 octaves FF–f3: upper manual 1 × 8′, lute course; lower manual 1 × 8′, 1 × 4′, 1 × 16′, buff to 8′; 90 × 40 in., 341 lbs. Coupler, seven pedals.

HUGH GOUGH

43 Bond Street, New York, New York 10012

Hugh Gough has been involved with historical keyboard instruments longer than most people in the field, being one of the first (perhaps *the* first) to work in a classical style. Gough studied clavichord playing with Arnold

Hugh Gough tuning his cembal d'amour. *This instrument is a clavichord in which the tangents hit the center of the string, setting both halves of the string vibrating at the same pitch. When the tangent is released, the string settles onto an individual damper felt.*

A clavichord made by Hugh Gough in 1938. Note the curve of the bridge, which follows very closely the mathematical scale points. In later instruments, Gough smoothed out the curve into a more graceful line; the slight deviations from exact theoretical string lengths do not seriously affect the tone.

Clavichord by Hugh Gough, 1946, with elegant bridge curve. The instrument is scaled for all brass strings.

A fortepiano made by Hugh Gough, 1957.

126

Dolmetsch in the late 30's. He began spending time at the Dolmetsch work-shop on weekends, and making some instruments.

But it wasn't until 1946, immediately after the war, that Gough, then 30 years old and living in England, embarked on a professional career. At that time only a handful of people were making instruments, and Gough had to rely on his own resources to find out what he wanted to know. He never made "standard" models, and has produced a great variety of all types and sizes of instruments in his long career. His output includes 8 doubles, 10 singles, 5 fortepianos, 25 virginals and spinets, 2 cembali d'amore (see illustration) and some 65 clavichords, the instruments he tended to specialize in.

In 1958 Gough came to the U.S. for a visit and stayed to work at Hubbard and Dowd's for 6 months. (Hubbard had previously worked at Gough's in London.) He returned to England for a brief period and then came back to America for a permanent stay, this time in New York. For the next two or three years he took some space in my workshop and, in return for the space, helped me with my own work. He greatly improved the quality of my instruments and steered me in the direction of a more classical design.

For all the years he has been in business and all the instruments he has made, Hugh Gough is an elusive figure. He does not advertise, nor issue a catalogue or even a price list, and the average harpsichord enthusiast has only a dim awareness of his existence, thinking him perhaps a figure out of the past. In the flesh he looks considerably younger than his 53 years; in fact Gough, who often forgets his age, has finally resorted to looking himself up in Groves dictionary to discover his birthday; not only is he the subject of an entry, but he wrote the articles on harpsichords—also the article on clavichords. In addition to building his own instruments, he has made a large number of restorations.

At present Gough is devoting himself to his beautifully designed five octave double strung clavichords, and to lutes ("the last instrument fit for a gentleman to play"), as well as to writing about these instruments. He recently said to me: "I've been purified; I have nothing whatever to do with harpsichords. When are you going to be purified?"

ERIC HERZ HARPSICHORDS
5 Howard Street, Cambridge, Massachusetts

The Herz workshop is one of the very few venerable and solid harpsichord establishments in America. The sudden bursting forth of harpsichord makers in this country is a rather recent phenomenon, and fifteen years ago there were only Challis, Hubbard and Dowd, Herz, and perhaps one or two others.

Eric Herz was born in Cologne, Germany in 1919. He spent the war years in Israel playing the flute in the Israel Philmarmonic and went on to America, where he spent two years with Hubbard and Dowd. In 1953 he set up his own shop in Harvard, Massachusetts, and later moved to Cambridge.

Herz has made a total of 150 instruments and is currently producing 15 large and 25 smaller harpsichords yearly in a large and well organized shop with five employees. Some years ago he teamed up with an industrialist named Jim Cannon and engineer Caleb Warner whom we have already encountered in discussing the Baldwin harpsichord, in one of those attempts at commercial

Eric Herz

Framing of a large Herz double with 16′ choir.

Herz keyboard coupler. Dogs are individually sprung to enable coupler to be moved while some keys are still in use.

Anthony Newman at a Herz pedal harpsichord.

harpsichord production which look better on paper than in reality. After inflicting the Warner-Baldwin on the world, the venture quietly folded and Herz went back to making his own instruments.

Herz bases his instruments loosely on the North European harpsichords, and his pitch c^2 is 14$\frac{1}{2}$ in. to 14$\frac{3}{4}$ in. which suggests perhaps a longer scale than the Ruckers and French makers used. His framing, as can be seen in the illustration, is considerably heavier than that of classical harpsichords, and the

Laminated pinblock for a Herz harpsichord. Note metal plates on fore edge of pinblock which will receive struts connecting belly rail (and framing members) to pinblock.

4′ hitchpin rail is attached solidly to the frame members, thereby making the soundboard quite rigid since it, in turn, is glued to the rail. In the old harpsichords the rail was glued to the soundboard underside, but was free to move up and down with the soundboard.

Herz has introduced a lamination of fiberglass and wood which he claims makes the instrument considerably more stable, but no other makers have followed suit. For soundboards he uses two sheets of $^1/_{16}$ in. spruce, laminated with a thin sheet of fiberglass in between. The plywood used in his cases and frame members is laminated from $^1/_8$ in. sheets, also with fiberglass at the center. The fiberglass is supposed to act as a shield against outside conditions and I have indeed heard that Herz instruments are more stable than the average harpsichord. However, Herz himself admits that the fiberglass sandwich may affect the resonance of the instrument. Perhaps what really affects the tone is not the fiberglass but his heavy framing.

The Herz jack, which is now also used by Goble, is well designed; both jack and plectra are delrin. The slide is brass channel; the lower guide is plexiglass. Herz sometimes makes his own keyboards and sometimes gets them from Kluge in Germany where it is possible to get a keyboard with a $6^1/_4$-in. octave span. American keyboard makers refuse to make the narrower octave.

With harpsichords becoming constantly more expensive, Herz decided to put out a small all-around instrument with either $2 \times 8'$, or $1 \times 8'$ and $1 \times 4'$, for about $1500. This must be considered fairly low for a reasonable looking and sounding instrument by a reputable maker.

INSTRUMENTS BY ERIC HERZ

1. Clavichord: FF–g3, double strung; 62 × 19 in.
2. Virginal: 4¾ octaves AA–f3; 1 × 8′, buff; 66 × 21 in.
3. Single manual harpsichord, Model S: 4¾ octaves AA–f3; 2 × 8′, buff; or 1 × 8′, 1 × 4′, buff; 72 × 33 in.
4. Single manual harpsichord, Model A: 5 octaves FF–f3; 2 × 8′, buff; 86 × 36 in.
5. Single manual harpsichord, Model B: 5 octaves FF–f3; 2 × 8′, 1 × 4′, harp; 86 × 36 in.
6. Double manual harpsichord, Model C: FF–g3; upper manual 1 × 8′; lower manual 1 × 8′, 1 × 4′, buff; 93 × 37 in. Coupler, four pedals.
7. Double manual harpsichord, Model D: FF–g3; upper manual 1 × 8, lute course; lower manual 1 × 8′, 1 × 4′, buff; 96 × 37 in. Coupler, 5 pedals.
8. Double manual harpsichord, Model E: upper manual 1 × 8′; lower manual: 1 × 8′, 1 × 4′, 1 × 16′, buff to 8′; 99 × 37 in. Coupler, 5 pedals.
9. Double manual harpsichord, Model F: FF–g3; upper manual 1 × 8′, lute course; lower manual 1 × 8′, 1 × 4′, 1 × 16′, buff; 108 × 37 in. Coupler, six pedals. Separate soundboard and bridge for 16′.
10. Pedal Harpsichord: 32 notes, C–g; 1 × 4′, 2 × 8′, 1 × 16′ (1 × 2′ optional); 115 × 52 in.

Jack by Eric Herz: delrin jack with moulded attached spring, delrin tongue; removable delrin plectrum; steel adjustment screw and end pin.

ALEC HODSDON

Lavenham, Suffolk, England

Alec Hodsdon, who is located in the picturesque town of Lavenham, has been making instruments for 40 years, which is some sort of record. During that time he has made about 700 instruments, of which the majority have been spinets, virginals and clavichords.

Hodsdon harpsichords are not very well thought of in America, since they will generally respond in drastic ways to any severe weather changes. A two-manual instrument of his which I once saw in the basement of a church had undergone a gruesome transformation: the wrestplank had pulled up, there were huge cracks in the soundboard, the case sides had opened up, and the action was thoroughly unplayable. It was beyond redemption. There is, of course, no truth in what another English maker says about him: "Hodsdon pulls his wood out of the rivah!"

However, a spinet of Hodsdon's which I repaired needed some work but was basically in reasonable condition. Hodsdon makes his own keyboards and uses pearwood jacks and solid spruce soundboards. His prices seem lower than those of other English makers.

In 1946 the BBC commissioned Hodsdon to make, according to him, the biggest harpsichord ever constructed; 1 × 8′, 1 × 4′, 1 × 16′ on the lower manual, and 1 × 8′, 1 × 4′ on the upper, plus two harp stops and coupler. Lately, Hodsdon has gotten away from the 16′ and into a more classical mode of construction. A leaflet issued by him cites a number of authorities all railing against the use of the 16′ stop.

According to many reports, Hodsdon is not very active in harpsichord production at the present time. In what may be an apocryphal story, a couple who left a square piano with him for repair report calling for the instrument a year and a half later. When they got to the house, Mrs. Hodsdon opened the door and advised them that Hodsdon was out. After a while she exclaimed: "Hark, I hear my husband coming." Hodsdon promptly arrived in an early twentieth-century steam car, the product of a hobby which for him seems to have taken the place of harpsichords. (The square piano, as reported by the owners, was unchanged after its long stay in Lavenham.)

FRANK HUBBARD

185A Lyman Street, Waltham, Massachusetts 02154

By this time the reader has encountered Frank Hubbard, the authority, so often that he may be interested in the man behind the name. A visit to Frank Hubbard's shop is always an unalloyed pleasure, as I discovered the first time I went there in the days of the now famous firm of Hubbard and Dowd on Tremont Street in Boston.

I arrived on a Sunday morning and got Frank Hubbard out of bed. He took me over to the shop and patiently gave me the guided tour, although I was a total stranger, one of a growing group of "harpsichord bugs."

We have called these two pioneers the "Ruckers of the modern harpsichord," and I was thinking of this and my first visit when I went to see Frank Hubbard again recently. It was a brilliant day in May; the sky was the bluest of blues, the trees and lawns of the estate on which the Hubbards live (under some

The Hubbard jack of moulded delrin; spring moulded with tongue; adjustable delrin damper block.

A 5-octave Flemish single, and a 5-octave
Flemish double by Frank Hubbard.

arrangement with the property's antiquarian society owners) were the
greenest of greens. The entire Hubbard clan, Frank and charming wife Diane,
little Polly and a baby (but, alas, without the dachshund Schnittger who had
died of old age), plus the work force of some 7 or 8 assorted employees, were
gathered in the annual shop picnic in honor of Frank's birthday. He was 49
that day, having been born in 1920 in New York City, a town he avoids
whenever he can.

As we sipped red wine, ate French bread and salami, and talked about harpsichords, the impression was strong that here was the best of all possible harpsichord worlds; a fairy-tale house to live in, and nearby, past the greenhouses,
the old barn-shop to work in. In this environment Frank Hubbard lives, works,
studies, writes, plays chamber music, makes violin and gamba bows, produces
harpsichord kits, designs new models, and supervises his workforce. The
shop, with its barn floor boards and rough beams, conveys the feeling of one
of those antique workshops portrayed in marvellous drawings in Hubbard's
book. The workers are, as is usual in American harpsichord shops, an assort-
ment of college drop-outs, Sicilian cabinet makers, semi-hippies, harpsichord
"nuts" and deaf-mutes. (Deaf mutes seem to be peculiarly adept as harpsichord
and piano makers; Hugh Gough had one who did everything but answer the
phone and voice plectra.)

Hubbard, who worked both with Dolmetsch and Hugh Gough in England, got his masters degree from Harvard in 1947, and went into business with
Dowd two years later. They produced some 50 instruments during their
partnership. Since 1958 Hubbard has turned out 80 harpsichords plus about 200
elaborate single and double manual kits.

131

Case of a harpsichord in the Italian style by Frank Hubbard, showing typical framing with knees.

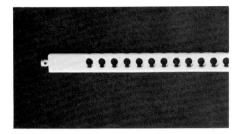

Section of Hubbard wooden jackslide with capstan.

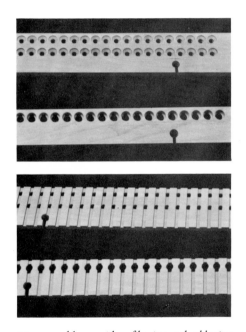

Upper and lower sides of boring and rabbeting of Hubbard slides and guides.

Hubbard wooden guides (double and single), showing boring on top of guide and rabbeting of underside.

Hubbard harpsichords are essentially copies of classical types. Thus one model is based on a French harpsichord by Hemsch (1756), another one on a Flemish instrument enlarged in eighteenth-century France. Smaller instruments are based on earlier Flemish and Italian prototypes, and a virginal is a copy of a seventeenth-century Italian original. Hubbard's jacks and plectra are of delrin plastic, and the damper is glued to an adjustable delrin block. (Delrin is very slippery and does not accept glue readily. Hubbard uses a special glue not commercially available, but we have found that pliobond, a common glue available in hardware stores, will work on delrin.)

The jacks have a long, square extension which slides through a round lower guide hole. The height adjustment of the jack is regulated by Phillips-head (cross-slotted) screws which are mounted on the key ends. Felt washers are glued to the screw heads and the jack rests on these. To adjust the jack height, the jack is removed and a long Phillips-head screwdriver is dropped through slide and guide, seating itself in the screw head through a hole in the felt washer. The system has the advantage of not adding to the jacks's weight with an end pin.

The soundboard in Hubbard's instruments is made of solid spruce barred in the traditional way. The soundboard is arched slightly upwards to get the board started in an upward direction, if it is to go anywhere due to expansion. A sinking soundboard could result in loss of bearing on the bridge, but a board arched upwards will usually be safe. Piano men are forever carrying on about arched soundboards, and there may be something to it for the piano; on harpsichords there is little evidence that soundboards were ever arched, or that the arching improves the tone.

Hubbard's keyboards, which are made in his shop (except for the kit keyboards which are imported from Germany), make use of the old Italian rack system guiding the keys in the back. Instead of wood or ivory slips, Hubbard's keys have pins extending in back. The rack has thin slits ending in large vertical holes, thus lessening the chance for sticking keys. The keyboards are covered with ivory, ebony, or other woods as the style demands. In keys which show scorings of double lines and tiny scallops between them, Hubbard will occasionally omit just a single scallop per keyboard, giving the appearance of having been overlooked by the maker. In the old days this was sometimes done to show that man makes mistakes; only God is perfect.

Treble end of Hubbard double, showing 8′ and 4′ bridges, nuts, rose, pinblock, and metal braces from pinblock to belly rail.

Because of Frank Hubbard's good nature he is not able to deal firmly with the many amateurs who descend on his shop. For a while he had any number of harpsichord enthusiasts working in his shop on their own projects, using his tools, supplies, and know-how. It was partly for this reason that Hubbard decided to bring out a kit, enabling him to get at least some return for the time spent with the amateurs. The kit, which he now sells at the rate of one a week, has slowly become the bread and butter product, keeping the shop going during lean periods. Since orders never slack off (Hubbard is 4 years behind), a lean period does not occur due to a business slump but as a result of poor organization, waste motion, supply failures, employee turnover, etc. Few harpsichord shops work efficiently—the work force is of necessity off-beat, coming in at irregular hours (Hubbard surprised them recently by installing a time clock), and quitting without notice. In Hubbard's shop visitors and amateurs take up a great amount of time, clogging the wheels of progress. Recently he has become stricter and more efficient, and his present staff seems the best he has had.

We will go into the whole question of harpsichord kits in great detail when we come to the end of the alphabet. Hubbard, as a serious maker with an international reputation, has drawn some fire from fellow makers for giving away the hard-won fruits of his knowledge for the price of a kit. Aside from taking orders away from other makers, it is argued, the kits bring the harpsichord from its high perch down to the common level of the tinkerer. To this one might reply that the Hubbard kit is not easy to assemble—only a skilled and intelligent worker should undertake it; but when successfully assembled, this kit turns out to be a better instrument than the majority of professionally built harpsichords, a point which was made recently by a German amateur writing in *Das Musikinstrument*.* Far from lowering the level of harpsichord making, the Hubbard kit has raised that level and has spawned a whole new breed of amateur builders, some of whom turn into serious professional makers. This is not to say that the Hubbard kit is fool-proof. From the point of view of kit design it leaves much to be desired. But

* Dr. Wolfgang Schroeder in *Das Musikinstrument*, Heft 7, Juli 1968, Frankfurt am Main.

133

The case of a Hubbard kit harpsichord (double manual), showing framing, pinblock, and nuts.

Detail of framing in Hubbard kit harpsichord.

Underside of soundboard of Hubbard kit double, showing curved 4′ hitchpin rail and cutoff bar and ribs. This is the classical method of reinforcing the soundboard. Note absence of ribs under the bridges.

Hubbard is constantly improving the kit, closing up the gaps in the instructions and eliminating the snags reported by his customers.

Frank Hubbard has had a profound influence on the modern harpsichord: first, through his association with Dowd in the first modern production of historical copies; second through his book *Three Centuries of Harpsichord Making* which unravels the long-buried mysteries of the craft; and third with the arrival of the Hubbard kit, spreading the word to distant places. Hubbard's work is well known in Germany and is one of the factors which promise an eventual change in the design of the German production harpsichord.

Frank Hubbard is that example of integrity and devotion to the craft that one expects in a harpsichord maker, but which one encounters so rarely in real life.

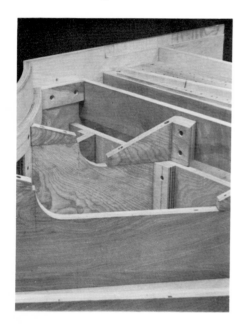

INSTRUMENTS BY FRANK HUBBARD

1. Virginal (copy of an Italian 17th Century virginal): 4½ octaves C–f3; 1 × 8′; 64 × 27 in.
2. Single manual harpsichord (based on 17th Century Italian): C–d3; 2 × 8′, hand stops; 73 × 31 in.
3. Single manual harpsichord (based on a Hans Moermans, Antwerp 1584): C–d3; 2 × 8′, buff; 78 × 31 in. Hand stops.
4. Single manual harpsichord (based on a 17th Century Flemish harpsichord enlarged in France during the 18th Century): FF–g3; 2 × 8′, 1 × 4′, buff; 85 × 38 in. Hand stops.
5. Double manual harpsichord (based on same as above): FF–g3; upper manual 1 × 8′; lower manual: 1 × 8′, 1 × 4′, buff; 90 × 38 in. Hand stops, manual coupler.
6. Double manual harpsichord (copy of a French harpsichord by Henry Hemsch, 1756): FF–e3; upper manual 1 × 8′; lower manual 1 × 8′, 1 × 4′; 95 × 35 in. Hand stops, manual coupler. Also available with buff stop, pedals, and compass FF–g3.

HUNNEL AND WITCHER

Renaissance and Baroque Musical Instrument Co., Randsburg, California 93554

According to a newspaper article (Los Angeles *Times*, June 24, 1969), these two makers work in an abandoned garage in a Mojave Desert town of about 300 residents. Henry Hunnel, 50, and his partner, 34-year-old Jay Witcher are the only manufacturers in this ghost town, where the absence of traffic allows them to work on their instruments out in the main street.

The two men, who are undersea engineers, started making harpsichords and clavichords a few years ago. They are still working at it part-time, and are not yet realizing a profit. They hope to put the enterprise on a self-sustaining basis, envisioning a half dozen employees at some future date, and production of other baroque instruments like krumhorns, citterns and lutes. They have made

Single-manual harpsichord by Hunnel and Witcher.

1 double, 6 singles, 9 spinets, and 4 clavichords, using wooden jacks, nylon plectra, and closed bottoms. As the newsstory remarks, Hunnel and Witcher may well be the biggest thing to happen to Randsburg since the gold strike of 1895.

KURT HUTZELMANN
652 Eisenberg/Thüringen, Ludwig-Jahnstr. 33, East Germany

Kurt Hutzelmann, born in Eisenberg in 1889, has been in business since 1919, and is still at it, *Werkzeug in der Hand* (tool in hand) at 80, as one of the many newspaper clippings about him puts it. Hutzelmann is basically a piano maker and has a number of patented inventions to his credit.

Harpsichords have been made at his Eisenberg location since 1927, and he has evidently spent a good deal of time on modernizing the harpsichord. ("I am always searching for new paths.") The new paths have led to a metal frame; a jack which forces the tongue out of the string's way upon the jack's descent; and an overhead damper and sustaining pedal allowing all dampers to rise as in a piano.

That Hutzelmann is somewhat out of touch with the rest of the world is revealed by his answer to the question of whether he had any instruments in America. "No," he wrote in his reply, "but in 1939 two gentlemen from Cincinnati visited me." Hutzelmann's brochure is almost totally devoid of technical information, even to omitting the number of strings or stops. An instrument referred to as "The Harpsichord of the 20th Century" (Model C54) seems to have $1 \times 8'$ and $4^{1}/_{2}$ octaves. Another one, Model C66, appears to have $5^{1}/_{2}$ octaves (GG-c⁴) and contains either one or two sets of strings. The one detail given, a weight of 320 lbs, speaks for itself. Except for the treatment of the slanted cheek fronts and the depth of the case, the instrument is almost identical to a small grand piano in appearance.

WILLIAM HYMAN
1018 Washington Street, Hoboken, New Jersey

William Hyman has been active since 1963, but he was relatively unknown until he finished a double in early 1969 which overnight made him the latest darling among the harpsichord players. Harpsichord players are fickle in their enthusiasms for the different makers; the moment they find a maker whose product they like better than their current instrument, off they go to the new find to place an order; and often that order is cancelled before the instrument is ready, and placed with yet a later discovery. This system helps to keep both players and makers busy, but it does make for less than the best relations between makers and players, some of whom are not on speaking terms.

The harpsichord which caused this rush to Hoboken was a two manual instrument based loosely on a Blanchet or a French type of rebuilt Ruckers. It was indeed impressive, both in appearance and tone, which is no mean accomplishment. No less impressive is Bill Hyman himself, an ex-commercial artist who is something of a renaissance man. Hyman does everything himself in a large loft equipped mostly with hand tools, where he and his wife also live. His cabinet work is precise, his soundboard painting spectacular, his outside case decoration a beautifully mellow dark green offset by panels of lighter

William Hyman playing his instrument.

The double manual in the Flemish–French style that caused the rush to Hoboken: harpsichord by William Hyman.

green. In addition, he plays the instrument very well, something which is certainly uncommon among harpsichord makers.

Hyman, who was born in Brooklyn in 1933, freely admits to having gone through a period of *Jugendsünden*, instruments of which he is not very proud. Unless a maker is apprenticed to another good maker, he is apt to inflict a few lemons on the world which will allow him to learn from his mistakes.

Hyman now works very much in the traditional way, using pearwood jacks with holly tongues (not adjustable except for a small bottom screw), and boar's bristle for a spring, although the plectrum is modern delrin. His slides and guides are made of beech and are leather-covered in the French fashion (an oversized slot in the wood and precise fit in the covering leather). The keyboard is made from linden (somewhat firmer than the basswood commonly used for keys) and the case, including lid and bottom, is also made from solid linden. Hyman does not believe in plywood, even for the bottom of the instrument, and judging by the tone he achieves he may have a point. The cases taper in thickness from front to back, like those of his prototypes, from about $5/8$ in. to $1/2$ in.

The soundboards are made from $1/8$-in. sitka spruce, thinned toward the edges and barred the classical way. The bridge gets thicker toward the bass, where it develops a concave section on the outside. It is also undercut for an inch or so at the bass end, which avoids having the soundboard encumbered by the bridge there. The bridge is double-pinned, with the second pin on the side of the bridge facing out. We have already seen that this is done to take pressure off the bridge and give it a slight "roll" (the double pin on the side tends to lift and force the bridge to twist slightly, creating an arch in the soundboard between bridge and hitch pins and a slight depression between bridge and spine).

Treble end of pin block and soundboard of harpsichord by William Hyman.

He achieves an extraordinary tone which virtually assaults the listener with its fullness. The harpsichord, when I heard it, was standing in a relatively small and enclosed room, and the lush and extraordinarily live sound would swirl all around you. I was not able to investigate what would happen in a large room or hall. Acoustics of a given room have unfortunately a lot to do with the tone of a given instrument, and one's judgment must therefore bear this fact in mind.

I have since heard the odd objection to Hyman's tone that it is "too" good. The tone imposes itself on the listener, forcing the shape of the music; the tone is so aggressive that, like not seeing the forest for the trees, you can't hear the music for the tone. There may be some truth to this objection, but I was able to hear different melodies played against each other with perfect clarity. I personally like a harpsichord that speaks to you boldly and with, perhaps, a romantic fullness of tone; such a sound takes some curse off the dry and somewhat precious nature of much of the harpsichord literature.

Hyman's action is a marvel. It is light, responsive, yet crisp. From the extremely light touch I assumed that the plectra were perhaps just barely stroking the strings, but upon investigation I found them projecting between $1/_{32}$ in. and $1/_{16}$ in. beyond the string. This would suggest a very careful voicing job, and it will be interesting to see how long the plectra, which are obviously quite thin, will last.

Hyman has made about twenty instruments, and now averages two to three yearly, alternating between the double and a small Flemish single.

WILHELMUS JISKOOT
Roosbergseweg 4, Bavel, Holland

Wilhelmus Jiskoot has been active for three years, largely putting together Hubbard kits. He has made a total of ten instruments, all doubles, and estimates his current yearly production at five or six. He is now preparing his own drawings and plans to branch out into singles, spinets and clavichords of his own design.

JONES-CLAYTON HARPSICHORDS, LTD.

2442 Hyperion Avenue, Los Angeles 27, California

This firm has been building harpsichords since 1952, making it the oldest firm of harpsichord makers in the West and one of the oldest in America. In this time they have made 372 instruments with the current yearly average often to twelve doubles, and twelve to fourteen singles.

They are now using a delrin jack with a flat brass spring and a long adjusting screw sticking up high above the top of the jack, which lends some credence to Richard Jones's amusing description of jacks he has used in the past which are "so exotic as to defy description, not to speak of regulation."

Jones uses aluminum slides, factory keyboards and a three-ply sitka spruce soundboard. (Spruce plywood is not readily available and is, in fact, rather difficult to come by, since few harpsichord makers can afford to buy the quantities demanded by special fabrication.)

Jones-Clayton's prices seem to me to be lower than those of most other American shops, a small single going for $650 and a double for under $2000. I have never seen one of their instruments nor known any one who has, and it is possible that the bulk of their output has been confined to the West coast.

INSTRUMENTS BY JONES-CLAYTON

1. Harpsichord, Model VI: C–d3; 1 × 8′, buff and half stops; 48 × 32 in.
2. Harpsichord, Model V: C–d3; 1 × 8, 1 × 4, buff on 8′; 54 × 33 in. Handstops or pedals.
3. Double manual harpsichord, Model III: FF–f3; upper manual 1 × 8′; lower manual: 1 × 8′, 1 × 4′, buff on 8′; 72 × 40 in. Handstops or pedals.
4. Double manual harpsichord, Model II: 5 octaves FF–f3; upper manual 1 × 8′; lower manual: 1 × 8′, 1 × 4′, buff on 8′; 96 × 40 in. Coupler, handstops or pedals.
5. Double manual harpsichord, Model I: 5 octaves FF–f3; upper manual 1 × 8′; lower manual: 1 × 8′, 1 × 4′, 1 × 16′, buff on 8′ and 16′; 100 × 43 in. Coupler, handstops, and pedals.

G. C. KLOP

Paleisweg 6, Garderen, Holland

Klop has for eight years been making harpsichords with a basically historical orientation. The fact that he has been influenced by Frank Hubbard, Martin Skowroneck and Gustav Leonhardt is born out by his closed bottoms, thin soundboards and self-made jacks and keyboards.

Klop, who was born in Landsmeer, Holland, in 1935, has two co-workers, and together they are currently averaging the brisk total of 21 instruments yearly, of which 3 are doubles, 5 singles, and the rest spinets, virginals and clavichords. He has produced a total of 60 instruments, most of which have been historical copies, sometimes with minor changes.

KNUD KAUFMANN

Rue Botanique 81, Brussels, Belgium

The Kaufmanns occupy a small building in a curving, cobblestoned Brussels street, with a store on the ground floor in which they sell pianos, Neupert harpsichords, and their own makes. This is another family operation with Kaufmann senior, of Danish descent, his wife, son, and daughter-in-law all working on the instruments at home and in a nearby country workshop.

Kaufmann has built a harpsichord from a drawing and suggested jack mechanism contained in the mid-fifteenth-century manuscript of Arnault de

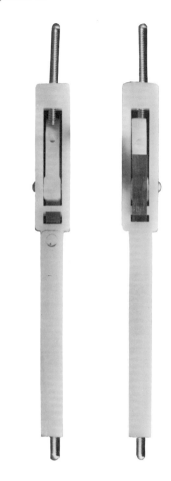

Jack by Richard Jones of Jones-Clayton. All delrin, including demountable plectrum; flat brass spring, machine screw for top and bottom adjustments.

Single manual harpsichord by G. C. Klop.

Zwolle, one of the earliest references to harpsichords on record. This has perhaps been the first attempt to construct an actual instrument from the Zwolle drawings, which are famous among historians. This instrument, which I heard, is of necessity fairly crude, having very short strings (it is roughly the size and shape of Challis' petite model, too short for 8′ strings and too long for 4′ and plucking with brass. Perhaps the pitch was meant to be higher than current usage).

Kaufmann has made some Ruckers virginal copies which are very handsome and have an extremely good tone; they are somewhat marred upon closer inspection by what seems to be embossed plastic covering, in place of the customary Ruckers block printed papers. Knud Kaufmann, as the only active maker in Brussels and environs, is kept busy with tunings, repairs, and restorations, and his own production is somewhat sporadic.

KÖCHEL HARPSICHORDS
67 Mint Road, Liss, Hants, England

This shop is run by Dennis Woolley, who has been active in the business for 15 years. Working with a staff of two, Woolley seems to specialize in smaller instruments. His literature shows two varieties of spinets, a virginal and two types of 8′ and 4′s. Some of the instruments show fancy cabinet work with crossbanding, inlays and extravagant veneering.

Woolley estimates his total production at 150 and is currently at work on a double, 10 singles, 8 spinets and virginals and 2 clavichords. The 45-year-old maker uses his own designs but has made copies of Kirckman and Taskin doubles.

ANTON LIGNELL AND RICHARD ALEXANDER
1281 Hearst Avenue, Berkeley, California

Anton Lignell was one of Eric Herz' apprentices and started his own shop in Boston a few years ago. He has recently moved to California and set up shop with a partner, Richard Alexander. All attempts to obtain precise information about their work have been fruitless.

O. LINDHOLM
72 Borna/Bezirk Leipzig, East Germany

This is another East German firm. Until recently they only manufactured reed organs. Since 1964 they have been making harpsichords, concentrating on spinets, clavichords, and singles. They are now making their first two-manual instrument. Their output is illustrated by the marvellous picture reprinted here. (What are those nine people doing out in the *Spielstrasse* (play street)? They are perhaps playing the harpsichord and organ concertos of Padre Antonio Soler. But why without music, and without looking at the keyboard?)

A Lindholm I saw in a piano store in Brussels had a jack very similar to the Ranftl jack. There was an enormous top adjustment screw ($1/4 \times 3/8$) sticking up, which always means that the adjustment screw hits the jack rail when the key is down, a function better performed by the top of the jack itself, since adjustment screws will be at different heights, thus causing different key dips.

Lindholm production models of spinets, harp-sichords, and reed organs set out in a Play-street on a foggy morning.

Like the Ranftl and Burton jacks, these had the plectrum moulded into the tongue. Aside from having to throw away the tongue (and often the entire jack) when a plectrum breaks, this has the disadavantage of possessing a moulded rather than a fabricated plectrum like the common delrin. There is evidence that a moulded plectrum behaves differently from a fabricated or extruded plastic, getting "tired" more easily and being subject to breakage. Delrin itself seems to have a "grain" and also breaks easily in one direction, but is extremely tough when cut in the right direction.

The Lindholm 8′ and 4′ I saw had a divided soundboard; where the cut-off bar should have been was a permanent frame member extending all the way down (there was no bottom). The triangle formed by spine, belly rail and cut-off was a non-functioning soundboard. The functioning soundboard had nine ribs $1/2 \times 5/8$ in. running straight across the bridge underside, suggesting the typically German production style. The lowest FF was $46^1/2$ in. long and used a heavy overspun bass string. In a very live instrument it should have been possible to use a solid brass string at that length.

These overspun strings are usually a nuisance, since they often just go dead after a few years' use. They are difficult to make and a slight error in their manufacture will result in a dead string immediately or at a later time. The steel core wire must be of a square cross section or at least filed flat so that the copper spinning can take firm hold; if there is any play or movement in the overspinning, the string will be worthless, resulting in false beats and irregular vibrations.

The tone of this instrument was, predictably, not better than that of the average German factory instrument. Lindholm employs 50 workers and has made some 500 instruments since they started harpsichord production 5 years ago. It is to be hoped that they, too, will benefit from the current trend towards classically oriented instruments with a clearer, fuller, more singing tone. (For those who wonder how much of such information passes across the iron curtain, I have freely corresponded with the East Germans, have talked to touring Russian players who have rented harpsichords in New York, and have recently supplied a kit to the government of Czechoslovakia.)

INSTRUMENTS BY LINDHOLM

1. Clavichord: 4½ octaves C–g3, single strung; 59 × 19 in.
2. Spinet: 4½ octaves C–f3; 1 × 8′, divided buff; 59 × 37½ in.
3. Harpsichord: 5 octaves FF–f3; 1 × 8′, 1 × 4′, buff on 8′; 59 × 37 in., 130 lbs. Knee lever on 4′.

THE LOCKWOOD HARPSICHORD
New York, New York

This was a venture of Richard Schulze, later of the Telemann Society. Schulze spent a day at Hubbard & Dowd's shop and then wrote a book entitled *How to Build a Baroque Concert Harpsichord* ("Use good-sized fish-sinkers and dig holes to put them in.") which had a 6-octave harpsichord as its jacket illustration, although the instrument described in the book as "typically" baroque was a small Italian single with 2 × 8′.

Schulze built one of his Baroque concert harpsichords, using shoe polish to blacken the keys (actually not such a bad idea!) and then convinced a businessman to go into partnership with him. That was a number of years ago; they made about five instruments and then gave up the ghost. The Telemann Society fared somewhat better than the Lockwood harpsichord, but eventually followed that venture into oblivion.

MAENDLER-SCHRAMM
Rumfordstr. 2–4, München, West Germany

Karl Maendler, 1872–1958, was one of the first of the modern builders, starting 1905/06 at about the same time as Neupert. He was associated with the piano house of M. J. Schramm, as the son-in-law of Max Josef Schramm, and his instruments bore the name of Maendler-Schramm.

According to the current owner of Maendler-Schramm, Ernst Zucker, Maendler built harpsichords after historical models and improved on them in the course of the years. It is probably more likely that he copied the old pianos he found at Schramm's, and his "improvements" led to a modern instrument (like one plaguing the Mannes School of Music for years) which was almost totally unplayable. The name Maendler alone was enough to strike terror into the heart of a harpsichord technician.

People who listened to harpsichord music in the 1930's will remember a performer named Yella Pessl who was then as well known as Landowska. Miss Pessl owned two large Maendler "Bach" models on which I had the misfortune to work. Maendler used piano-sized tuning pins, forcing the technician to drag a large piano-sized tuning hammer to Maendler jobs. It was never clear why he used these bulky pins, notably decreasing the space available on the pinblock. The instruments themselves incorporated all the deadly features of the German production model and were heavy and graceless, possessing thick soundboards, and what Zucker calls a *Panzerplatte*, literally armor-plate, an apt description of the metal frame.

The worst feature of the Maendler was the long spring which projected up and outwards from the bottom of the jack, intended to keep the jack to one side in its specially wide slot. The spring invariably got bent by getting caught under strings during jack removal and had to be clipped off, thereby making the action totally unreliable; the problem was compounded by the hard, brittle leather Maendler used for plectra, which could only work in one precise position, and was useless in a jack wobbling from side to side.

After working for hours on Yella Pessl's instrument, I finally was able to get some sound out of it and proudly played a few chords demonstrating this fact. Miss Pessl, perhaps startled out of her wits to hear the instrument playing, ran in from another room and exclaimed: "Mr. Zuckermann, you are breaking my instrument." I had trouble collecting the $5 fee which was all I thought she would willingly surrender.

Several years ago, when Ernst Zucker lost his only son and the firm's successor in an automobile accident, he gave up manufacturing Maendler-Schramms, but is still intending to resume this activity as soon as the question of a successor is resolved.

A Maendler-Schramm being played by Ernst Victor Wolff.

Case and soundboard of copy of an Italian harpsichord by Joe T. Marshall, Jr.

Detail of Marshall's Ridolfi copy.

Replica of a Ruckers 1648 by Marshall.

WALTER MAENE
Ooigemstraat 13, Desselgem, Belgium

Walter Maene has been in business for five years, evidently handling pianos as well as harpsichords. He has produced a total of 38 instruments, of which 8 have been doubles, 14 singles, and the rest spinets and virginals. The 32-year-old maker has been working from his own designs, but he is now preparing his first historical copy, a J. Couchet double of 1646.

JOE T. MARSHALL
36 Soi Chaiyos, Sukhumvit, Bangkok, Thailand

Joe Marshall, who was born in Paris in 1918, has been active in the field for 21 years. He works slowly, making precise copies of the 1665 Ridolfi at the Smithsonian, and a 1648 Ruckers, as well as a large Flemish single. His total production is six instruments.

Marshall uses solid spruce soundboards in Flemish instruments and Monterey cypress in Italians; his jacks are of pearwood with holly tongues and raven quills. His exact copies must often be made from pictures or illustrations because of the non-existence of historical models in Thailand. Dr. Marshall makes occasional trips to the U.S. to study the instruments he is copying.

MARS McMILLAN   Harpsichord Makers of Melbourne
269 Wattletree Road, Malvern, Victoria, Australia

This 25-year-old Australian girl has been making harpsichords for five years. It took her two years to finish her first double, and she has made a total of two concert doubles, two small singles, and an Italian harpsichord. Under construction (May 1969) are two further small singles, an Italian and a Flemish harpsichord, two clavichords, and a virginal.

Miss McMillan works with another enthusiast, Alastair McAllister, who has built some instruments on his own and hopes to become a full time maker himself. They work in the tradition of Ruckers, Taskin and the early Italians,

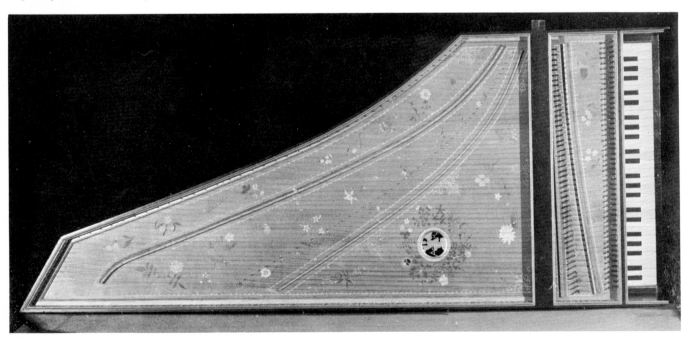

Double by Mars McMillan: upper manual 1 × 8′, 1 × 4′, peau de buffle, buff; lower manual, 1 × 8′, 1 × 4′, lute course, buff on 8′.

Mars McMillan at the keyboard of one of her instruments, with the wide Australian sky in the background.

using light case construction, light soundboards, light stringing, and "no gimmicks."

There is talk of the ex-Australian English maker Meridith Moon joining Miss McMillan in a short time to put Harpsichord Makers of Melbourne on a truly professional basis with larger quarters and more streamlined production methods. Unfortunately they will resist the temptation of calling the firm "Mars and Moon."

RICHARD MERZ
2473 Jackson Street, San Francisco, California 94115

Richard Merz has been making instruments for only two years, and in that time has made two doubles and one single. He works by himself, and makes about one a year.

Merz, who was born in Rochester, New York in 1937, makes his own jacks and keyboards. He is one of a growing group of West Coast makers in an area of great harpsichord activity.

WALTER MERZDORF
7501 Grötzingen/Baden, Löwenstr. 11, West Germany

Located in a tiny unspoilt German village, Merzdorf's workshop is housed in a former stable which only recently has had its outhouses modernized. Here Walter Merzdorf and his son Eckehart toil as in olden times, thinking of themselves as master and son, carrying on the sacred, God-given tradition. That priceless knowledge, handed from father to son leads, unfortunately, to our old friend, the German production harpsichord.

This is the sort of shop to satisfy the tourist who enjoys watching the master-craftsman and his eager apprentices at work. In fact, I have myself often thought of hiring an unemployed actor in a cobbler's apron to whittle away at a bench.

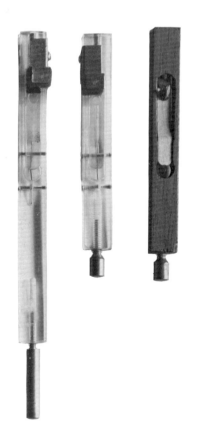

Walter Merzdorf working on a clavichord.

Merzdorf, now 74, has been making instruments for 49 years and has made a total of 1600. He currently produces 40 to 50 instruments yearly with the help of six co-workers. The instruments are a mixture of everything from suitcase clavichords to the inevitable "Bach" model.

Merzdorf harpsichords which have gone through my workshop I have found to be somewhat superior to the run of the mill German production harpsichord and some attempt has been made to copy historical models; the bottoms are closed (though this in itself may mean little) and the cases are somewhat more graceful than that of the typical *Serien* instrument. However, there is the same large box containing pedals, which looks so much like a clubfoot; and Merzdorf's keyboard supplier is not as good as Neupert's or Sperrhake's. The Merzdorf sharps are of solid, rounded, white plastic. (In "reverse color" keyboards, the sharps were usually made of fruitwood stained black, with ivory topping.)

I found the Merzdorf tone suffering from heaviness and lack of freedom; it was strongly suggestive of thick soundboards, cross-bridge ribbing, heavy cases and the rest. The leather plectra were usually beyond repair, and I have occasionally tried delrin on a Merzdorf and brightened the tone somewhat; however, in a harpsichord with little tone delrin tends to emphasize the percussive character of the sound, since the pluck itself is not drowned out by the musical tone.

The Merzdorfs have recently added to their production a Mozart piano, of which I have not seen an example. One would wish that they brought themselves up to date by going back a couple of centuries. Failing that, they could do with a thorough reading of Frank Hubbard's book.

INSTRUMENTS BY WALTER MERZDORF

1. Travel Clavichord, Size I: C–d₃; single strung; 39½ × 15 in.
2. Clavichord, Size II: C–f₃; single or double strung; 48 × 17½ in.
3. Concert Clavichord, Size III: FF–f₃; double strung; 59 × 22 in.
4. Klein-Cembalo, Size I: BB–f₃; 2 × 8′, or 1 × 8′, 1 × 4′, half and buff; 56 × 35½ in.
5. Cembalo, Size II and III: AA–f₃; 2 × 8′ or 1 × 8, 1 × 4′, half and buff; 79 × 36½ in. Handstops or pedals.
6. Cembalo, Size III: AA–f₃; 2 × 8′, 1 × 4′, buff on 8′; 79 × 36½ in. Knee lever on 4′.
7. Cembalo, Size IIIa: AA–f₃; 1 × 16′, 1 × 8′, 1 × 4′′, buff on 8′ & 16′; 79 × 36½ in. Handstops (knee-lever on 4′) or pedals.
8. Double manual harpsichord, Size IV: AA–f₃; upper manual 1 × 8′ with buff and half stops; lower manual 1 × 8′, 1 × 4′, or 1 × 4′, 1 × 16′; 86½ × 37½. Pedals.
9. Two manual harpsichord, Size V: AA–f₃; upper manual 1 × 8′, 1 × 4′, buff on 8′; lower manual 1 × 8′, 1 × 16′, buff on 16′; 90½ × 37½ in.
10. Concert Harpsichord, Size VI: FF–f₃; upper manual 1 × 8′, 1 × 4′, buff and half on 8′; lower manual 1 × 8′, 1 × 16′, buff on 8′ and 16′; 94½ × 42 in. Pedals.
11. Concert Harpsichord, size VII, 102′′ × 42′′ Same as 10; 5 pedals.

SHOJI MOMOSE

4–35–4 Den-en-chofu, Otaku, Tokyo, Japan

It is somewhat surprising that a country in which baroque music is immensely popular has produced only one harpsichord maker (so far). Although Vivaldi is common fare in Tokyo coffee houses, the harpsichord has not been seized on by the Japanese with their usual energy.

Shoji Momose was a piano tuner and technician who became interested in harpsichords in the 1950's, when he was called upon to service the few harpsichords in Tokyo. As could be expected, those few harpsichords were

Momose jacks in plexiglas and mahogany. Steel wire springs and top adjustment screws. Round holes for plectra.

German production instruments, and Momose's second instrument (after an initial spinet in 1956) was the inevitable "Bach" model. (Whoever converted the anonymous harpsichord No. 316 at Schloss Charlottenburg from $2 \times 8'$, $1 \times 4'$ on the lower manual and $1 \times 8'$ on the upper, to $1 \times 16'$, $1 \times 8'$ on the lower and $1 \times 8'$, $1 \times 4'$ on the upper probably had no idea that this odd and one-of-a-kind registration would make its way around the world under cover of Bach's name.)

Momose's soundboards are made of pine, 6 mm. (almost $1/4$ in.) thick, and this fact alone would bear out the opinion of a Japanese harpsichordist who reports that Momose instruments are just adequate and cannot in any way compare with the better American instruments. Momose speaks scarcely any English, and this combined with his piano background makes it unlikely that he will delve into a study of historical models. He has made a total of 21 instruments.

In view of the odd cultural gap between the English-speaking countries and the rest of the world in regard to the body of knowledge concerning historical keyboard instruments, large-scale Japanese harpsichord production at this point would be a disaster. Although a company like Yamaha, which makes 200,000 pianos yearly, and which has considered harpsichord production, is perfectly capable of making a good piano (in fact, a very excellent one), it would be much more likely to copy the German instruments (and thus swamp the world market with yet another bad harpsichord) than design an instrument based, say, on a Dowd. When the Japanese do get around to large scale production it is to be hoped that they will pick their models carefully.

The Momose harpsichord, patterned after German prototypes, and a Momose spinet.

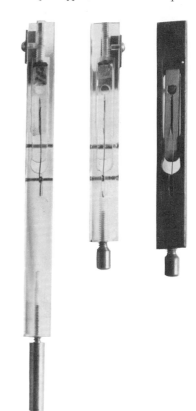

147

MERIDITH MOON
53 Wykeham Crescent, Oxford, England

By the time this appears in print, Meridith Moon may have returned to his native Australia, where he was born in 1928, to join Harpsichord Makers of Melbourne (see Mars McMillan).

In England, Moon has been active for seven years, six of them on a part-time basis. He has produced 19 instruments and is now turning out 3 or 4 yearly, working alone and along historical lines.

ROBERT MORLEY & CO., LTD.
4 Belmont Hill, Lewisham, London S.E. 13, England

This company is now the largest English firm making harpsichords and clavichords, turning out perhaps the English equivalent of the German *Serien* instrument, though the Morleys are generally superior and more classically oriented.

The Morleys were in the piano and harp business (to a certain extent they still are) when John Morley, the present head of the firm, got interested in historical keyboard instruments in 1955. John Morley, born near London in 1932, studied piano construction in Germany and England and made and repaired pianos prior to his entry into the harpsichord field.

The Morley factory is located in a London industrial suburb, some distance from the offices and showrooms at Lewisham. The factory is a spacious, airy, well-organized and well-equipped workshop with a staff of 25. The size of the shop accounts for the total of 1800 instruments Morley has made, and his current yearly production of some 240 instruments. Of this, an astonishing

John Morley, present designer and head of the firm.

Keyboards and pedals of a large Morley double. Note the pedals in the English style. The left pedal is split in two. Pedals so placed eliminate need for complicated under action. Knobs on key blocks are for shove coupler.

150 are clavichords; the rest are about 12 doubles, and about 25 each of singles, spinets, and virginals.

Whether by accident or design, none of the large harpsichord factories make copies of historical models. One could glibly conclude from this that historical models do not lend themselves to mass production, but they lend themselves to production no better and no worse than harpsichords in general, which is not terribly well. However, given a production set-up, it is as easy to design or copy something good as something bad, and both are affected in almost equal measure by the harpsichord's resistance to production methods.

There is a rather ambiguous sentence in Morley's brochure in which he states that as a designer he is "intrigued to observe how completely and exactly, without any alteration of shape or dimension, the traditional instruments fulfill the requirements of the modern home. Our task," he goes on, "is to continue in the footsteps of the great eighteenth-century makers . . .". Is Morley satisfied just with this intriguing observation or does he actually copy historical instruments himself?

Perhaps this statement only applies to the physical appearance; in any case it does not apply to the internal construction. Morley's soundboards are made of birch plywood (a hardwood!) topped with pine veneer for looks. There are no conventional ribs at all aside from one or two braces in place of the cut-off bar. The bottoms are open, and the whole instrument's underside, including the soundboard, is sprayed with a white, waterproof paint. This is presumably done to keep out moisture, but unless all open spots were equally protected, it would be a wasted effort since moisture can seep through any exposed area. The idea of a solid coat of paint on a soundboard is not appealing

A Morley dogleg jack: plastic body and tongue, brass wire spring, leather plectrum. The double end pins allow this jack to be played from either keyboard.

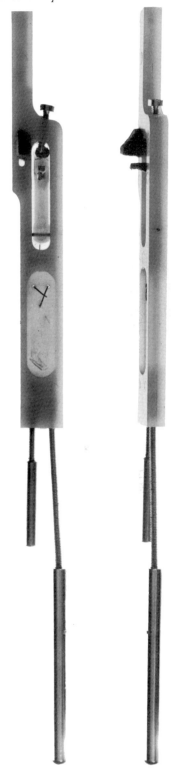

A Morley pedal clavichord.

The underside of a Morley harpsichord showing framing and underside of birch plywood soundboard. Bottom is left open and sprayed with white waterproof paint. Note lower end of L-shaped pedal lever at left.

—though one cannot say for sure that it would inhibit the tone. Morley himself has perhaps unintentionally described his tone aptly in his brochure as "subdued." (Perhaps he had the piano in mind as a standard). The tone is not unpleasant, and the instruments are well made. They, like many other English

The Morley pedal clavichord combined with two manual clavichords.

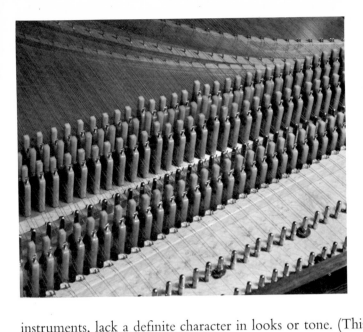

instruments, lack a definite character in looks or tone. (This, in any case, is preferable to a definite character, if that character is bad.)

Aside from the soundboard whitewash, Morley differs in other ways from common practice. His lids are made from "chip-wood" (pressed chips of wood) which he claims is more stable than plywood. The jackrails are held by a magnetic catch (an idea thought up by a workman) which is an ingenious way of solving the problem of holding the jackrail firm and yet make it easily removable.

His pedals are located near the side of the instrument (Kirckman style) which allows him to use a $^1/_2$ in. square steel rod in an L shape, pivoted in the crook of the angle. In place of the usual complex system of under pedal actions, this angle piece is pushed by the pedal rod, transmitting the upward thrust to a sideways motion at the jack slide. The pedals themselves are wood, and the split pedal allows use of either or both with one foot.

Morley's, like other English instruments, do not have a very good record of trouble-free performance in America. Part of the reason is to be found in the universal English custom of using leather plectra, which have been abandoned almost as universally in America in favor of delrin. Leather plectra, as we have seen, require extreme precision to work well, because the precise point on the leather plucking the string cannot be allowed any variation. Thus close tolerances are necessary, allowing little play for expansion, with predictable results in climates of extreme variations. Added to this should be the difficulty of finding properly trained leather voicers in a production shop.

Years ago, a harpist owning a large Morley harpsichord called me for a tuning, and upon examination I found the instrument a full tone below pitch. (This in itself is not at all unusual.) In trying to pull it up to pitch I started breaking almost every single string on the instrument. Perhaps the wire, which was tin-plated, had been weakened by the plating process, but whatever the reason, the instrument had to be totally restrung.

I don't want to leave the reader with the impression that Morleys are bad. They are reasonable production instruments, and well thought of by his many customers, including such American institutions as Goshen College, Mercyhurst College, and Moody Bible Institute.

Morley action showing three rows of jacks. The adjustment screws are handy for regulation.

A Morley traveling clavichord, 3½ octaves, single strung in phosphor bronze.

The gap of a Morley harpsichord showing metal braces between laminated pinblock and belly rail.

INSTRUMENTS BY MORLEY

1. Travelling Clavichord, Model C3: c–g3; single strung (phosphor bronze); 29 × 11 in.
2. Clavichord, "Bach" Model C4: C–d3; double strung (phosphor bronze); 43¾ × 15¼ in., 49½ lbs.
3. Clavichord "Phillipp Emanuel" Model C5: GG–g3; double strung (phosphor bronze); 52 × 19 in., 88 lbs.
4. Pedal Clavichord: CC–g (16′ pitch); 68 × 17 in., pedal board dimensions 53 × 36 in.
5. Virginal, Model V4: C–d3; 1 × 8′, buff; 57 × 22½ in., 71 lbs.
6. Spinet, Model S5: GG–g3; 1 × 8′, buff; 73½ × 29 in., 94½ lbs.
7. Continuo harpsichord, Model C12: GG–g3; 1 × 8′, 1 × 4′, buff; 75 × 37 in. Handstop to buff, two pedals.
8. Harpsichord, Concert, Model C23: GG–g3; upper manual 1 × 8′; Lower manual: 1 × 8′, 1 × 4′, buff on 8′; 81 × 37½ in., 185 lbs. Coupler, pedals, and hand stop.
9. Same as above, but with a second 8′ (lute) on the upper manual.
10. "Mozart" fortepiano: FF–f3; 2 strings to a note; 76 × 37 in. Una corda and sustaining pedal.
11. Mozart Piano: GG–g3; 2 strings to a note; 75 × 37 in.

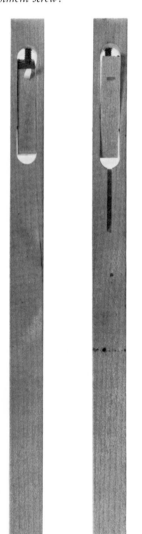

Wooden jack by John Nargesian. Nylon spring is attached to tongue; delrin plectrum; top adjustment screw.

JOHN NARGESIAN
63 Otis Street, Newtonville, Massachusetts 02160

Another maker of the Boston School, Nargesian spent two and a half years at Frank Hubbard's workshop. He is a church organist (as are a number of other makers), and studied at the New England Conservatory.

Nargesian works by himself in two rooms of a suburban house, turning out 3 singles or 2 doubles a year. He has made 9 or 10 instruments in the four years he has been active, all based on the Flemish-French style, and all very much in the "Boston" tradition. His work, which is excellent, proves again that the modern tradition of harpsichord making, based on the best historical models, can be transmitted from master to apprentice. It also leads to the observation that genius or special artistic ability is much less important to learning the craft than choice of a good workshop to learn in, and a good prototype to copy from.

J. C. NEUPERT
Am Knoecklein 9–13, Bamberg, West Germany

This is perhaps the most widely known of all firms making harpsichords.

The firm was founded by Johann Christoph Neupert (pronounced Noypert), born in 1842 in Munich, who learned piano building in the old tradition by apprenticing himself to various masters. One of his masters was Streicher of Vienna, successor to the Andreas Stein who developed the Mozart piano. J. C. Neupert set up his own piano shop in 1868, and six years later moved to Bamberg where the firm's headquarters are still located. In 1895 Neupert started a collection of historical keyboard instruments. The Neuperts started making harpsichords in 1906, which are said in an official biography of the firm to be based on the historical instruments of their collection.

The pre-war Neuperts I have seen, although better than their current products, do not bear this out. They certainly owed more to the pianos, which were once Neupert's main product, than to historical instruments in their collection. (This collection, which has had an erratic post-war history, being constantly shunted from one location to another, has not been seen by many people. Frank Hubbard was refused permission to examine the instruments for his book.)

Dr. Hanns Neupert, of the third generation of Neuperts, is the present

A Neupert double with a "Ruckers" disposition, and a case style in Queen Anne Modern, or perhaps Early Daddy Longlegs.

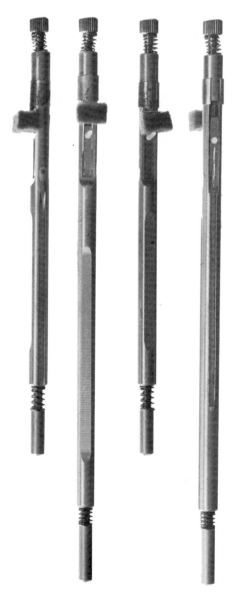

Neupert "OK" jacks entirely of metal. Top screws control plectrum projection, bottom screws, height. The vertical groove in jack body matches a projection in the box jackslide. Dampers are glued to a projection of a metal sleeve. These jacks have the conical plastic "silvertone" quill, but the "OK" jack is also available with leather plectrum.

head of the firm. He has given the total number of Neupert instruments produced as 24,000, but this figure includes the piano production as well. Probably half of this total are harpsichords and clavichords. Their current production is 400 yearly, making them one of the "big three." Sperrhake and Wittmayer, the other members of the trio, are more tight-lipped than Neupert and do not give out any production figures at all, but their yearly outputs are estimated at 600 and 400 respectively.

Neupert harpsichords, which one encounters everywhere, are perhaps slightly superior to those of their two big competitors, because it is at least possible to make them work. The fleet of Neupert rental harpsichords which I serviced for many years has been kept playable (despite rough treatment) by constant "babying." We have already mentioned the weaknesses of the German production harpsichord in discussing Ammer. The typical faults are open bottoms, comparatively heavy frame members, thick cases, thick soundboards, ribbing under the bridges, short bass lengths, thick strings, heavy 16′ strings resting on the 8′ bridge which spoils the 8′ tone as well as making the 16′ too short, complex or unreliable jack mechanisms, and the "Bach" registration. The instrument resulting from these building practices suffers

A Neupert "Silbermann" spinet.

Neupert ottavino in traveling case. Although in 4´ pitch, musicians find such an instrument useful for practice while traveling.

from laryngitis, possessing a coarse, whispering tone; and its appearance is graceless and without elegance.

Because of Hanns Neupert's published writings (*Das Cembalo* and *Das Klavichord*, Bärenreiter) he lays himself open to attack more easily than do his competitors. His critics also feel that Neupert bears the major responsibility for the faults of the modern factory harpsichord, since his building practices have been copied by the other major German manufacturers and have been found as far afield as Canada, Australia and Japan.

At the "Europianocongress" of 1965 in Berlin, Hanns Neupert said in a speech that the yearly turnover of five million D Marks by the four largest factories (presumably the big three mentioned above with the addition of Sassmann) are an indication that "one is perhaps not on the wrong path" with the building method known in Germany as *Rasten-konstruktion* or rigid case construction. He further said that the old instruments were of so many shapes and so lacking in any common practices that we have the right to achieve the goal of faithful sound reproduction with modern means. The obvious reply to this is that the old instruments were by no means lacking in building practices common to them all—there are few exceptions to closed bottoms, thin soundboards, light box constructions and the rest.

Skowroneck, in a paper which we will discuss in more detail later (*Hi-Fi Stereo Phonie*, Karlsruhe, issues 9, 10, 11, 1968) attacks Neupert frequently by name. He finds the heavy hand of the German makers reaching even into the past and cites numerous examples besides the *Bachfluegel* of alterations and falsifications.

Skowroneck likens the Neupert harpsichord to a guitar with the following alterations: leave out the bottom, put a thick frame in place of the thin box sides and increase the top board to at least double thickness. He takes Neupert to task for calling the Bach disposition *naheliegend* (natural), and for asserting that Handel had a Shudi harpsichord with a 16´. (The bass in Shudis sometimes went down to CC but there was no separate 16´.) Skowroneck quotes Neupert

Neupert action with jacks removed. The four box slides receive the round "OK" jacks; the bottom jack guide is eliminated. The heavy metal bar crossing the jackslides braces the pin-block against the belly rail.

A large Neupert harpsichord with "OK" jacks in position. Note the 16′ bridge superimposed on the 8′ bridge.

as saying about rigid case construction "surely it is heavier than the historical construction, but that is its only disadvantage; it has no tonal effect, since the frame belongs to the dead, or non-sounding part of the instrument." Neupert switches the emphasis by stating that on old instruments the "bottom board took the place of today's wood beam framing" when the bottom boards came first and the beams took *their* place.

Neupert calls the assertion that a closed soundbox alters the tone color not true. On the contrary, he says, the tone wins carrying power, since the soundboard underside of an open bottom will assist the soundwaves to travel outwards. Neupert, oddly enough, quotes Adlung, the German theoretician writing in the eighteenth century, who says that the soundwaves bring into motion both the soundboard and the bottom (provided it is of good wood), thus demolishing Neupert's own argument.

Neupert further urges the reader to go to the oft-cited Adlung for proof of his theories. Well, let us do just that, adds Skowroneck. Says Adlung: "They [the woods for the soundboard] may not be thicker than the 16th part of a Zoll, so that the board can let itself be moved easily and can be brought to tremble." Since the Zoll corresponds almost exactly to the modern inch, this would make for an extremely thin soundboard.

Neupert criticizes the "early instruments in their original form" (not altered by him?) for "suffering on account of being unable to stay in tune long, or being unable to maintain concert pitch, or from cracked soundboards, improper voicing in the jacks, uneven action of the keys, difficult or improper operation of the register stops and considerable noise caused by the action." But every one of these faults (with the possible exception of action noise) is associated with the German factory harpsichord, which, in addition, outdoes the early instrument by also being unattractive and dull sounding.

The keyboards (not made by Neupert) are undoubtedly the best part of the instrument. They are of the narrower "French" span ($6^3/_{16}$ in. C–B) and rarely cause any trouble. The soundboards are either solid or laminated, depending on the customer's request or the instrument's destination. They are often so highly varnished that the finish develops a fine network of small cracks (similar to old oil paintings) after a few years. The soundboard ribs run straight across under the bridge, usually at right angles to the bentside.

Two details showing Neupert hand-operated push-pull stop mechanism. Coarse screw threads translate push-pull motion into side-to-side motion against jackslides. Opposite end of jackslide is spring-loaded.

The cases vary in thickness from $1\frac{1}{2}$ to $2\frac{1}{2}$ in. near the bottom, and there are usually massive beams holding them together. Presumably the heavy framing is thought necessary because of the long treble scale often reaching to $16\frac{1}{2}$ in. for pitch c^2. The bass scale tends to be much too short, and this unevenness in scale may be one reason for the tuning instability. Neuperts usually require tunings every few days. (Someone is sure to counter this statement with the observation that his instrument came all the way from Germany and was still in tune! This is a common experience; the instruments are shipped wrapped tightly in oil paper and carefully crated and are thus better protected than they ever will be again; moving hardly ever affects a harpsichord's tuning in any case, but weather variations within a few days usually do.)

Neupert jacks now come in two versions—the rectangular plastic conventional jack or the modern O.K. jack with silvertone quill (German patent no. 836272/880537). The plastic jack is usually quilled with leather and is an outgrowth of the old wooden Neupert jack. Leather plectra develop the usual voicing problems which we have already discussed at length, and which are aggravated by the half-stop (usually a hand pull) forcing the plectra to pluck in one precise position without any tolerance.

The "O.K." jack, by far the more common on Neuperts nowadays, works on the whole quite well. Its "silvertone" quill is a plastic (nylon?) plectrum which fits into a tiny round hole in the tongue. Spare quills come on a "comb" or strip containing a number of the cone-shaped plectra. They have a tendency to curve downwards and get "tired" after much playing. They also occasionally break, but can easily be replaced by pushing out the old remnant and inserting the new quill. The Neuperts urge their customers to consult them in case of trouble, and if quills break, spares must be obtained from them since no other commonly used plectra will fit into the tiny hole of the tongue.

The O.K. jacks are made of metal and are set into a box slide, where a plastic ring at top and bottom holds them to close tolerances. They rarely stick, and then only if dust gets into the jacks, clogging up the small amount of play allotted the jacks. Neuperts supply a brush which will usually correct this problem. The jacks are guided like keys in the "rack system": the slotted jack moves past a stationary pin. Some Neupert owners complain of too much play between pin and slot, allowing a slight sideways twist, but this twist is usually not great enough to affect the amount of quill projection. More serious are the problems associated with the adjustment and end screws. Both are of metal going into metal, which means the tolerance between screw and thread cannot be very large. The screws must not be too tight for turning or too loose to stay put. To achieve the right tightness, Neupert puts coil springs between both of the screws and the jack itself. This does not always do the trick; I know of one customer who has put saran-wrap into all of her harpsichord's top and bottom jack screws, requiring some 400 operations, in an effort to tighten them. The same customer had broken pedal blocks, rather common in Neupert pedals, which end in a small soft wood pivot block not equal to the strain of constant foot pressure.

The "technician gap" being what it is, customers usually learn to cope with their problems, and one must grant the Neuperts that with a certain amount of common sense the actions can be kept playable, unlike those of some other instruments which are beyond home remedies. A harpsichord maker considering work on other than his own instruments is faced with an amusing paradox: if he uses all his skills and slaves over the instrument to make it work, the original maker will receive the credit, (those Neuperts are really great instruments!); if, because of time pressures he tries to do just the minimum to make it playable and it develops further trouble later on, he himself will be blamed for the failure (that Zuckermann doesn't know his jack's rear end from a hole in the slide!).

Neupert is perhaps the first harpsichord shop to sell exclusively through a franchise system, so that customers who wish to order an instrument direct from the factory are firmly referred to their local agent, if there is one. The agents work on a 50 percent mark-up, so that the originally low prices of Neuperts are not passed on to the final consumer. One of Neupert's American agents reports that Neupert, who is aware of the fresh winds blowing from Boston, is not planning to change his production style at this time. More's the pity, because the Neuperts have the set-up and capability to make a really good production instrument.

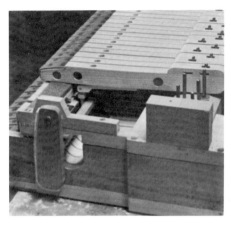

Neupert coupler in "off" and "on" positions. Dogs pivoted on lower key levers are held in slotted bar. When slotted bar turns dogs into vertical position, they engage underside of upper key levers and upper keyboard is coupled with lower. Slotted coupler bar can be operated either by handstop or pedal.

INSTRUMENTS BY NEUPERT

1. "Spinettino," ottavino in travelling case: 4 octaves c–c4; 1 × 4′, buff.
2. Clavichord, model 32/1, Philipp Emanuel: 5 octaves FF–f3; single strung; 53 × 20 in.
3. Spinet Silbermann: 4½ octaves C–f3; 1 × 8′, buff; 50 × 27 in.
4. Harpsichord Telemann: 4½ octaves C–f3; 1 × 8′, 1 × 4′, half stop, divided buff; 56 × 33 in.
5. Harpsichord Rameau: 5 octaves FF–f3; 1 × 8′, 1 × 4′, half to 8′, divided buff; knee lever for 4′; 79 × 40 in.
6. Double manual harpsichord Couperin: 4½ octaves C–f3; upper manual 1 × 8′, buff; lower manual 1 × 8′, 1 × 4′; 72 × 38 in.: Coupler, hand stops or pedals.
7. Double manual harpsichord Cristofori: 4½ octaves C–f3; upper manual 1 × 8′, 1 × 4′, buff to 8′; lower manual: 1 × 8′, 1 × 16′, buff to 8′; 72 × 38 in. Coupler, five pedals.
8. Double manual harpsichord Vivaldi: 4¾ octaves AA–f3; upper manual 1 × 8′, 1 × 4′, buff to 8′; lower manual 1 × 8′, 1 × 16′, buff to 8′; 80 × 40 in. Coupler, five pedals.
9. Double manual harpsichord Handel: 5 octaves FF–f3; upper manual 1 × 8′, 1 × 4′, buff to 8′; lower manual 1 × 8′, 1 × 16′, buff to 8′; 93 × 41 in. Coupler, five pedals.
10. Double manual harpsichord Bach: 5 octaves FF–f3; upper manual 1 × 8′, 1 × 4′, buff to 8′; lower manual 1 × 8′, 1 × 16′, buff to 8′; 103 × 41 in. Coupler; five pedals.

KAY NORDSTROM
Denmark

Nordstrom, who died in 1966, was one of two Danish harpsichord makers. (Bengaard was the other one.) So far as we can discover, there are now no active makers in Denmark.

JOSEPH NORRIS
9 North Preston Street, Philadelphia, Pennsylvania 19104

Norris has put together no fewer than 13 Zuckermann kits, but has now started to make instruments of his own design, having produced six of these to date.

Norris, who is 36 years old, was a student of John Challis, and has experimented extensively with different soundboard materials, including aluminum. Among other things he has discovered that a plywood soundboard responds to tapering at the edges. Testing the boards electronically, he found a definite increase in low frequency intensity where plywood boards were thinned at the tail. Norris, who works with a staff of two, gives his current yearly production as two doubles and four singles.

THE JOHN PAUL COMPANY
Parkway, Waldron, Heathfield, Sussex, England

From the name, the address and a picture and explanatory catalogue totaling 30 pages, I expected a busy parkway, with a grassy center strip, and a long, low factory building with one tall chimney pouring forth smoke. The smoke would come from the forge busily turning out metal frames for harpsichords and clavichords, and the large factory rooms would contain rows upon rows of tables at which English country girls would be assembling jacks, while John Paul himself, if there was such a person, would be sitting at an enormous desk writing brochures.

Parkway turned out to be the name of a house on a Sussex country lane just wide enough for one car. There were two milk bottles in front of the door and no one seemed to be home. Turning to leave I spied a small garage, and peering in saw a man in a clutter of wood and machinery. Although it was a cold and nasty day, there was no visible source of heat in the garage.

Mr. Paul, for it was he, turned out to be working on a harpsichord embodying a new theory of his. The "cavities" formed by the bracing in the case (see photo) had holes in the bottom which were placed so as to "tune" them, like organ pipes, according to Mr. Paul. These chambers are expected to resonate favorably in some fashion with the instrument. The wide board running diagonally across the top of the case is the base of the 4′ hitchpin rail. The soundboard will be glued solidly to this board. In view of the near fatal rigidity

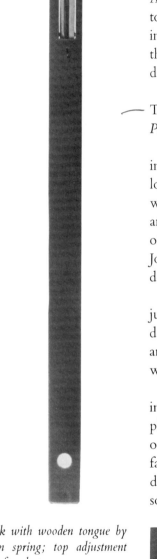

Tufnel plastic jack with wooden tongue by John Paul; nylon spring; top adjustment screw; square hole for plectrum.

The pensive John Paul in his workshop.

which will be imparted to the soundboard by such a wide board, one wishes Mr. Paul luck with his mysterious resonating cavities.

John Paul was born in Kent, England in 1920. He has been active in the harpsichord business for 23 years, getting interested in old instruments when he bought a spinet at auction. He then began buying old Broadwood and Stodart pianos (which were then still not very expensive) and converting them into harpsichords. (I personally think a conversion like that is more trouble than starting an instrument from scratch: the case, soundboard, bridges and layout are wrong, and even if they are put right one ends up with something quite different from the right design. But conversions are popular and almost everyone tackles them at one time or another; I've done so myself. It is just too tempting to have a silent antique instrument of some sort

Case and bracing system of a John Paul harpsichord, showing "resonating cavities," "tuned" by holes drilled in bottom. Soundboard will be glued to wide diagonal board supporting 4´ hitchpin rail.

sitting around, and one thinks of somehow fitting a harpsichord or clavichord action into it and turning it into something useful. The most interesting conversion I have heard of was made by the English-American builder Hugh Gough. He converted an early English square piano into a shirt cabinet. He advises that there is one type of English square which is wide enough to exactly accommodate an American shirt cardboard lengthwise.)

Some of Paul's conversions ended up in America, and I've seen several of them. Mr. Paul sells almost all of his instruments in America, and the idea of getting an ocean between oneself and the finished harpsichord is indeed an appealing one. Mr. Paul has made a total of forty instruments, of which three have been large doubles, and the rest singles and clavichords.

Paul builds almost no two instruments alike; he vacilates between metal frames and heavy wooden constructions, between running ribs all the way under the soundboard and using the classical system of cut-off bars, but sinking the cut-off bar into the case. His metal frames are superimposed from above, which seems to me not to be rigid enough because the frames lack depth (compare this with the Challis system). In any case, Paul has abandoned metal frames for now because of their high cost.

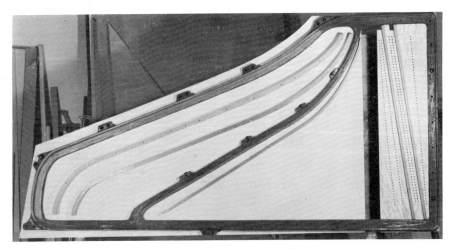

A John Paul harpsichord case showing metal frame superimposed from above.

160

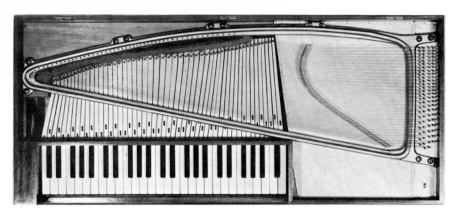

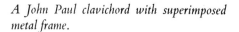
A John Paul clavichord with superimposed metal frame.

His jacks are made of an English product called tufnel, linen impregnated with phenol, which is also used by other English makers. His keyboards, like those of many other English makers, come from the London firm of Pynes, who are the subject of universal complaints for their poor workmanship. He uses a plectrum material consisting of leather topped by a thin sheet of Nylon, but admits that these materials don't bond easily and have a tendency to separate. The nylon top is supposed to protect the leather, but this practice seems to me akin to permanently keeping a slipcover on a beautiful couch. The beauty of the leather pluck comes from the leather's contact with the string, otherwise why bother with leather?

His most interesting and novel design is that of the upright harpsichord pictured here. It has an aluminum frame and soundboard and was sold for only $500. (In an upright harpsichord, called clavicythyrium in the old days, the jacks are returned by means of springs instead of gravity). He made three of these constructions, but had to abandon them when his metal frame maker demanded more money and greater quantities.

INSTRUMENTS BY JOHN PAUL

1. Clavichord Model II: 4 octaves and 2 notes C–d3; double strung; 48 × 20 in.
2. Clavichord Model III and IIIA: 4½ octaves CC–f3, and 4¾ octaves AA–f3; double strung; 56 × 23 in.
3. Triangular Harpsichord: 5 octaves FF–f3; 1 × 8′, 1 × 4′, buff; 78 × 41 in. Available with pedals or handstops.
4. Double manual concert Harpsichord: 5 octaves FF–f3; upper manual 1 × 8′, buff, lute (or second 4′); lower manual 1 × 8′, 1 × 4′, 1 × 16′, buff to 16′; 102 × 44 in. Six pedals.

CARL A. PFEIFFER
Stuttgart, West Germany

This piano firm, which has been in existence for 107 years, made a few individual harpsichords and clavichords prior to 1914, earning them a mention in Groves Dictionary. They have made no harpsichords since the first World War.

SOCIÉTÉ PLEYEL, S.A.
11, Ave Delcassé, Paris 8, France

This venerable old firm has lately been merged with two other famous French piano firms (also like Pleyel once renowned for harpsichords), Erard and Gaveau. The three firms now import a German upright piano called Schimmel, and market a television set named (in the best American tradition)

Pleyel two-manual harpsichord, "Grand Modèle dit de seize pieds," with 5 sets of jacks, 4 sets of strings, 2 × 8´, 1 × 4´, 1 × 16´. The seven-pedal control, from left to right: 16´, 8´, 4´, buff on 8´, coupler, nasal 8´, top 8´. The keyboards are only 1⁵/₁₆ inches apart, allowing both to be played by the same hand.

The tongue of a Pleyel jack (the leather has not been voiced).

Pleyelrama. The man responsible for most of the harpsichord activity, M. Lebal, is now over 80.

Pleyel was founded in 1807 by the composer Ignaz Josef Pleyel (1757–1831) in the days when composers and virtuosi went into the piano business to make money. Pleyel later took the famous German pianist Kalkbrenner into the firm. (Muzio Clementi is said to have started his own piano business in London to impress his future wife with his prospects; he was a rare combination of good composer and good businessman). Pleyel never amounted to much as a composer; he was friendly with Haydn and turned out enormous quantities of chamber music and symphonies, shamelessly imitating Haydn's style but not possessing even a fraction of his friend's genius. (When I was ten years old, my family string quartet played a lot of Pleyel since it was the only thing easy enough to keep all of us going. My cello part consisted of unending stretches of quarter notes played on open strings.)

Toward the end of the 1880's both Pleyel and Erard started making modern harpsichords, but it was not until the arrival of Landowska that Pleyel's harpsichords became famous. Landowska's relationship with the firm was probably quite accidental in the beginning.

The first harpsichord Wanda Landowska saw was a 3-manual Hass with a lid painting showing Catherine of Russia. (This harpsichord dropped out of

162

The Pleyel harpsichord, which might be considered the finest example of the piano-maker's art as applied to harpsichords, must excite our admiration for the thorough method by which was attacked every problem of "modernizing" the harpsichord. Shown here are the five highest treble jacks of a Pleyel harpsichord, lying across the ingenious damping system for the 16′ course. The rods of the overhead dampers act like a jack rail for the four rear courses of jacks; the 16′ jacks are long enough to raise the rods and thus the 16′ dampers. All this requires more energy than the crisp touch of a harpsichord should.

sight for many years but has recently reappeared and now belongs to Rafael Puyana, one of Landowska's students.) When Landowska, who was fascinated by the harpsichord, started to look around for a modern instrument, she quite naturally turned to her Parisian neighbors Pleyel. She took Pleyel's chief engineer to museums to look at harpsichords and made suggestions for improvements. The final product they concocted had, like the first Neuperts, much more in common with Pleyel's main product, pianos, than with the museum pieces they studied.

Since stories about Landowska's parsimony abound, many people assume that she chose Pleyel instruments because she got them free in exchange for publicizing them. According to Denise Restout, her long-time companion, this was not the case. Interestingly enough, Landowska never owned a harpsichord until she was 64 years old, and then she paid for it. What happened in the early days was that the firm would provide a harpsichord for Landowska to play "in" ("test-drive") and take it back only to provide her with a new one. (It is possible that Pleyel found it easier to sell a "Landowska's Harpsichord.")

The first Pleyel that Landowska actually owned in 1941 had a curious history. Landowska was then living in the South of France, hiding from the Germans who had ransacked her Paris quarters, and practicing on an old

Inside a Pleyel harpsichord. Note the complexity of the tuning system. The system takes up so much space that a two-story nut is necessary. The inscription on the jack rail reads: Le jeu grave dit par les Anciens "de 16 pieds" fut introduit dans le Clavecin Pleyel à partir de l'Année 1912 sur la demande et les suggestions de WANDA LANDOWSKA.

Underside of a Pleyel, showing the heavy framing and heavy ribs on the soundboard.

upright piano. A student of hers, observing this state of affairs, sold her life insurance and purchased the last Pleyel available in war-time France. When the instrument was shipped south, a German officer demanded a permit. He was told it was Landowska's instrument and he is supposed to have said: "Ah, Landowska, I admire her so greatly!" and let it pass. In any case, the harpsichord eventually made its way to Lakeville, Connecticut, Landowska's final home, and the student was reimbursed for the purchase price.

In trying to evaluate both Mme Landowska and the Pleyel harpsichord, we must remember that Landowska had that characteristic so lacking in present day harpsichordists which may be described as "star quality." She was a star, a virtuoso, and as such she caught the imagination of a public which was then still heavily involved with the nineteenth-century idea of genius and primadonna performers. Our dry, precise, scholarly modern approach was not then in vogue, and some of Landowska's extravagant performing practices were accepted as gospel. Her halo extended to her instrument which was accepted without question as "the" harpsichord.

Looking soberly at a Pleyel stripped of Landowska's glamour, we discover a "plucking piano" as someone has aptly called it. Pleyels use a soundboard made of spruce (epicea) in three plies 2 mm each for a total of $1/4$ in., or piano thickness. The Pleyel is built almost exactly like a piano, with a heavy cast iron frame, some eleven $1/2$-in.-wide soundboard ribs at right angles to the bentside, cases two to three inches thick, wooden beams $2^1/_4 \times 3^1/_2$ in. for framing, and overhead dampers. The tonal result of this enormous fortification is predictably poor—a thin harpsichord string cannot be expected to set this incredibly heavy and rigid structure in motion.

Aside from a tone which totally lacks any live quality, Pleyels are blessed with a fine-tuning system which is feared by professional tuners. This com-

The Pleyel Trianon model, available either with disposition of $2 \times 8'$, $1 \times 4'$, or $1 \times 8'$, $1 \times 4'$ and $1 \times 16'$.

plicated system works something like a fine-tuning peg on a cello, where many turns produce only a small change in pitch. Neither the metal frame nor the tuning system does much to keep Pleyels in tune, but changing a string becomes a chore, and I find that tuning Pleyels takes at least twice as long as ordinary harpsichords.

Pleyel pedals, unlike any others, used to be "on" when they were up and this has only recently been changed at the request of Rafael Puyana. Now the pedals are on when they are down, and pressing them even further will result in overplucking with increased volume. The jacks are made of wood, $7/16$ in. wide $\times$ $3/16$ in. thick with stiff leather pletra. The 16' is damped twice, once with the jack's own damper and once with the overhead damper.

Getting production figures out of a large company like Sperrhake, Baldwin or Pleyel is like getting blood out of a stone. When asked what their yearly production was, Pleyel replied: *Renseignement qui ne peut être communiqué* (information which cannot be communicated). Their total figure is given as 210,000 pianos and harpsichords, thus neatly camouflaging their harpsichord production. However, Walter Thoene in an essay on harpsichord playing estimates that Pleyel has made 70 harpsichords from 1920 to 1948, and cites another authority, N. Dufourcq, who states that Pleyel made two instruments a year. They have evidently given up everything but one or two double manual models.

Pleyels are still ordered by Landowska students and *their* students but their day has passed. The times, as Bob Dylan sings, they are a-changin'. We are moving forward, full steam, from the nineteenth to the seventeenth and eighteenth centuries.

CURT A. POULTON
1637 Dieter Street, St. Paul, Minnesota 55106

Curt Poulton spent most of 1967 working for Rainer Schütze in Heidelberg as *Praktikant in Cembalobau*. Schütze is one of the few German makers who uses light box constructions and generally follows classical models. While at Schütze, who was then busy tooling up for jacks and a keyboard suspension system, Poulton made seven clavichords to Schütze's specifications.

Since being on his own, Poulton, who was born in 1931 in St. Louis, Missouri, has made only two further clavichords and one Italian virginal, but he is now preparing to make harpsichords based on Dulcken and Taskin. He plans to develop a new plastic jack encompassing the best features of most modern jacks including removable tongues and integral tongue springs.

If he is planning to produce a jack similar to Burton's (which has these features) he might be able to get around Burton's patent by an alteration which would vastly improve the Burton jack—a slit for insertion of separate plectra instead of the Burton plectra which are of one piece with the tongue. And don't apply for a patent, Curt. It's not in the best tradition of harpsichord making and it is, in any case, useless. Most of the cumbersome "improvements" patented by the production makers no one has wanted to copy; if any one comes up with a really good idea (and most good ideas for harpsichords were thought up a long time ago) everyone will copy it anyway, patent or not.

GERHARD RANFTL
8671 Kirchenlamitz/Bayern, West Germany

This is a small shop which has been producing harpsichords for a few years. (All efforts to elicit precise information from Ranftl have been fruitless.) Ranftl has shown his instruments at the Frankfurt trade fair in 1967 and 1968. The instruments embody all the bad features of the German production harpsichord, plus a few thought up by Ranftl on his own.

The case hides a steel frame consisting of angle sections bolted together. Needless to say, a bolted frame does not have nearly the strength of a cast frame. To defeat tuning stability only the slightest "give" in the case is re-

The Ranftl jack; body and tongue are of plastic, with the round plectrum moulded in; aluminum end pins, flat brass spring. Damper is not adjustable.

quired, and a bolted frame can easily have such give at the joints. The sound-board has no ribs except for an immensely heavy 4′ hitchpin rail, and this fact together with the swirly grain, suggests a plywood board.

A straight bentside connects the cheek and tail pieces. This is not uncommon on small instruments (for example, the Zuckermann kit) but is rarely found on large harpsichords. Ranftl's bridges are straight as well, suggesting a some-what tortured scale. The hitchpin rail is placed at an angle between sound-board and outer case wall.

The jack is disastrous from almost every point of view. It has heavy top adjustment screws sticking up above the jack and making for uneven heights, and consequently uneven contacts with the jack rail. Both top and bottom screws increase the weight of the jack considerably; the jack dampers are not adjustable. But the worst feature of all is a green plastic tongue with stubby plectra moulded in. The one Ranftl I saw was unplayable because some plectra had broken off and others were weak or had bent down. There was, of course, no way to replace the plectra. The spongy feeling caused by the plectra was increased by the heavily bushed keys which felt as if they had a life of their own.

In appearance the instrument looked short and fat, with the usual vertical graining to emphasize its squatness, further accentuated by the straight bent-side.

In fairness to Ranftl it should be added that although the one instrument I saw did not work very well because of an unfortunate jack design, the tone (what there was of it) might be thought to have its own charm. The Germans like to use the word *rauschend* to describe their tone; it literally means the sound the wind or a rushing river makes, and it is certainly more appropriate to a description of organ sound than harpsichord tone. Both from the sound of the old harpsichords and from the character of harpsichord music, one would assume that harpsichords should sound crisp and sonorous, and neither grat-ing nor lush. It seems to me that those makers who construct such a rigid case that the tone issuing from it is that of the plucked strings only, do it not be-cause they particularly want to copy organ tone; they first are stuck with their tone, and then look around for an instrument to liken the tone to.

Jacks, bridges and hitch pin rails of a Ranftl harpsichord. Note adjustment screws on top of jacks, straight bridges, and 16′ bridge super-imposed on 8′ bridge.

The pin block of a Ranftl harpsichord through-bolted to heavy metal frame underneath.

Underside of a Ranftl harpsichord, showing heavy 4′ hitch pin rail which makes one of the principal framing members.

167

JOHN M. REED
30 Saddle Club Road, Lexington, Massachusetts 02173

This maker has been active on a part-time basis for six years, having turned out a copy of a Taskin double and Shudi single. He reports devoting about one thousand hours to the making of an instrument.

WILLIAM POST ROSS
791 Tremont Street, Boston, Massachusetts 02118

William Ross, who runs a bustling shop with some eight employees, has been on his own for four years. Ross, who was born in 1938, was at M.I.T. for seven years, studying architecture, engineering and math. He then worked for an organmaker and from there went to Frank Hubbard for several years.

Ross has made a total of twenty instruments, but hopes to make at least twenty more this current year, of which four will be doubles. I had the feeling that his large staff was a recent phenomenon, and there seemed to be a slightly higher rate of confusion in his two cluttered work rooms than is customary even in harpsichord shops. Perhaps his staff, which seemed to include a young girl with a baby in a beautiful hand-made cradle (it was hard to tell who was working and who was visiting), is fairly new at the game. The instruments in the shop, though bearing all the earmarks of the "Boston School," were perhaps not quite as meticulously done as those of the other Boston makers.

The virginal by William Post Ross, of which the soundboard view is shown in Chapter I.

Harpsichord by William Post Ross, after an Andreas Ruckers of 1646. Disposition: 2 × 8', buff. Finish outside is marbled paper with black plastic tape.

From past observation I would venture the guess that a new maker does better by growing slowly with his orders, learning from his mistakes as he goes along, than trying to cope with a large staff. From my own experience I know that just telling people what to do and supervising their work takes up all of your time, especially if the staff is green. It leaves little time for playing with ideas, designs, and tooling to improve your work. Once you get caught in the cycle of trying to provide enough work for your employees, this becomes a voracious monster, constantly demanding to be fed.

I found also that Ross' prices were somewhat high. Perhaps the master is entitled to charge more than the apprentice, but Ross seems to have reversed that natural order of things. (His prices exceed those of both Hubbard and Dowd.)

I cannot accurately gauge the amount of work and materials involved in the making of a small Flemish 4 octave single with 2 × 8', but $2400 would seem higher than necessary if the instrument is made in production. I can more accurately judge the virginal kit which Ross now produces, which is $525 including case parts cut to size. This would be more than double the price of the Zuckermann spinet kit, which is somewhat comparable in size and materials. This brings up the much more complex question of how the various makers arrive at their prices, which we dare not even get into. Do they make harpsichords because they like to and just charge the minimum to cover their expenses? Do they consider themselves artists and masters, whose work commands a price not related to the cost? Are they in it for money, for glory, for love of the craft, for meaning in difficult times? And how do they rate their work in terms of dollars and cents?

Ross lists a great number of different instruments in his catalogue including clavicytheria, pedal harpsichords, and claviorganums which I trust he has not made. What he seems to specialize in is the 4-octave Flemish single and the Italian virginal illustrated here. He uses Frank Hubbard's jacks, but makes his own keyboards. (Virginal keyboards *must* be produced in the makers own shop because the individually differing length keys and balance hole locations cannot be made in a factory set up for piano or organ keyboard production.) His soundboards are solid spruce, except for the virginal kits which now get poplar plywood, a material Ross is rightly dissatisfied with.

With so many inferior harpsichords being made in production, a shop like Ross's, being of the Boston school, has a special responsibility to work in the style of that school and with the same dedication. For the sake of the modern harpsichord's future, it is to be hoped that Ross, who has the potential, will take his place among our best makers.

RUTKOWSKI & ROBINETTE
153 Center Street, New York, New York 10013

Rutkowski and Robinette do not welcome publicity, shop visitors or curiosity seekers; they want to be left alone to do their work, and have consequently requested minimum exposure in this book. They have been making high quality, large double harpsichords since 1957. The makers personally construct these instruments one at a time and to order; production is therefore limited to three a year. The instruments are commissioned long in advance, chiefly by schools and professional musicians.

Rutkowski, who received his training from Challis (his most talented apprentice, according to Challis) retains some features of the Challis harpsichord, the most important of which is the aluminum frame. Unlike Challis instruments, which have no bottom, Rutkowskis have a screw-on bottom which is however not an integral part of the harpsichord. A Rutkowski & Robinette single with 2 × 8′ made in 1962 (No. 16) for the New York Pro Musica has jacks, wrest plank, and a stand almost identical to many Challis harpsichords.

This instrument, which I recently saw in the same room with an Italian 2 × 8′ copy by Martin Seidel, confirmed one of the notions about metal

Decorated soundboard and rose of a Rutkowski & Robinette harpsichord. Note 4′ metal hitchpin rail which sits on posts passing through oversize holes in the laminated spruce soundboard.

Action of an R & R harpsichord. Note bushings for tuning pins set into aluminum pinblock.

Igor Kipnis at the keyboards of the Rutkowski & Robinette harpsichord he has used in a number of recordings.

frames which we have discussed in these pages. Both instruments had not been tuned for about two months; the Italian copy, with case walls $^3/_{16}$ in. thick and a deep crack in the soundboard, was in reasonably good tune, while the Rutkowski, with a laminated soundboard, a cast aluminum frame, and tuning pins set into a metal plank was radically out of tune. This little confrontation does not, of course, disprove the efficacy of the metal frame, nor does it argue against Rutkowski and Robinette who are among our best makers. It does, however, lead to two conclusions: (1) a metal frame, alone and in itself, is no guarantee of tuning stability, since the stability can be lost before the frame ever has a chance to act; and (2) a maker has to exercise great care when dealing with modern (and possibly untried) materials.

The trouble with this instrument could be traced to the tuning pins, which were set into phenolic bushings, and were so loose that the mere act of placing the tuning wrench upon them made them unwind. A slight tapping of the pin was able to tighten it firmly, but since the pins were probably tapered like the ones Challis uses, they may well work themselves up after a time. A plastic bushing, as we have seen in the Baldwins, can be a dangerous thing unless it has a perfect fit both to the pin and to the hole in the plank and is of the right resiliency. Rutkowski and Robinette continue to use this system, but I have not encountered a similar instance of loose pins on any other of their instruments.

SABATHIL & SON
3911 W. 25th Avenue, Vancouver 8, B.C., Canada

The first Sabathil I ever saw was a virginal (or something resembling it) which came to my shop in totally unplayable condition many years ago. Under the veneer, which was peeling off, was a solid aluminum body. But the rigidity thus achieved had unfortunately no effect on the stability of the instrument, because the jackslide, which consisted of a piece of masonite completely unre-inforced, was hopelessly warped, holding all the jacks rigid in its twisted grip. This was a version of the three-legged (though rectangular)

"Virginal Amoroso" whose "graceful, singing timbre" I never had a chance to discover.

Sabathil and Son was founded in Munich, Germany (since Sabathil answered none of my communications, precise information is not available), and settled in Canada some time after the war. When we read in his brochure that Sabathil is "founded on a tradition and experience of 50 years in the building of fine keyboard instruments" we can be fairly certain that the tradition is not his own but that of our old friend, the German production harpsichord. Sabathil seems to have been chosen to bring this tradition to its highest pinnacle of non-achievement.

The Sabathil family of instruments, consisting of the Clavichord Dolce, Virginal Amoroso, Harpsichords Cantabile, Maestoso II and III, Concerto I and II, and Bach I, II, and III, are headed by the Bach models, which are "in every way the greatest works of modern harpsichord building," allowing the maker "to show his art at his best." The greatest of them all is the Bach III, a full 10′ long, which I had the privilege of seeing not long ago.

This enormous creature, crouching against an entire living room wall, has perhaps something endearing about it ("The appearance of the instrument itself could create a stir in the world of interior decoration."—*Canadian Music Journal*). It has been compared to a stegosaurus, the giant extinct animal with plated back. However, whatever charm it may have had was not sufficient to prevent its owner from ordering a new harpsichord from a Boston maker with the intention of selling his present one.

As might have been expected, the Bach III has the "Bach" registration. The soundboard ribs cross the underside of the bridge (about nine of them), and the scale is long ($15^1/_2$ in.). But there are also some astounding features not found on any other Germanic instrument. First there is the keyboard; the lower key levers are $1^1/_2$ in. thick (even modern piano keys are only $^7/_8$ in.) and they are stopped in front by a soft, bushy material causing a spongy touch. The upper keys have no lead weights, but are returned by a strip of foam rubber in back, against which they rise. (I did not see this arrangement myself, since the owner had to change it completely; the touch and action were thoroughly unsatisfactory when the instrument first arrived.)

The jacks are plastic, and the quills are similar to Neupert's "silvertone" quill; they seem to be less stable and resilient than delrin. The dampers were of a thick, hard, green felt which produced a second tone as it came down on the string. (The owner was able to remedy this defect by slicing a layer of felt from all the dampers and replacing it with soft felt. This operation was made extremely difficult by the non-adjustable dampers, since they allowed for no error in the thickness of the new felt.)

The buff stop pads were made of styrofoam, and one could rightly question this crumbly material for use against thin steel wires. However, the pads were still operating after about one year of use. Similarly, styrofoam was used as lining for the jack rail, receiving the constant pounding of the jack tops, which in this case consisted of adjustment screws sticking up above the jacks. Again, one year had not wrought any havoc here.

The soundboard was firmly glued to a frame member at approximately the position of the cut-off bar in classical instruments. Although there was a

---

THE GREAT WANDA LANDOWSKA had many good reasons to choose a metal frame harpsichord as her lifetime instrument. Such instruments—long the privilege of the Few Great—are now available at reasonable prices. Sabathil harpsichords unite authentic, beautiful sound with modern reliability. 3911 W. 25th., Vancouver, Canada.

We must not assume, although perhaps we are meant to assume, that the great Wanda Landowska ever played a Sabathil harpsichord, nor that the Pleyel metal frame had anything to do with the way a Sabathil is framed.

The Sabathil "Bach III" model. Both 8' and 4' bridges curve in prematurely. Slits in both the 8' and 16' bridges pass strings of 4' and 8' to outside hitchpin rail.

separate bridge for the 16', the bridge itself was some 2 in. high and could not reasonably be expected to transmit string impulses to the soundboard through its mass.

Inexplicably, Sabathil failed to take advantage of the enormous length of his harpsichord, making instead all three of his bridges curve in sharply at the bass end. Now a bridge usually curves toward the spine at the bass and, because the harpsichord ends there, it will not permit the bridge enough space to stretch out to its mathematically ideal length. Thus it is understandable that the 16' bridge curves in. But why do the 8' and 4' bridges curve in as well, leaving vast stretches of unused soundboard? The lowest bass string is $96^1/_2$ in. long, the 8' is $62^1/_2$ in. and the 4' is 40 in. Since the scale is $15^1/_2$ in. for pitch c^2, the correct mathematical length for the low C on the 8' is 124 in. (This instrument goes down to FF, with a consequently even longer theoretical length.) It would have been easy to make the bottom string say, 90 in. instead of 62 in., since the space is there and lying idle; similarly the 4' could have used the extra space to bring it closer to its theoretical ideal.

On an 8' and 4' Sabathil the 4' was not hitched to the soundboard (despite the board's extreme rigidity) but to the 8' hitchpin rail. The 4' strings must therefore travel through the 8' bridge, in this case going through slits coming up from the bottom. (A similar arrangement can be found on the 8' and 16' bridges in larger Sabathils.) I've occasionally seen 4' strings go through holes in the 8' bridge; these holes were drilled after the bridge was on, and usually were positioned so as to allow the strings free passage through the 8' bridge. On the Sabathil the slits in the bridge were obviously cut before the bridge was glued to the soundboard, so it would have been nearly impossible to locate the narrow slits with respect to the 4' strings, which come off their bridge at an angle. The result was that almost all the 4' strings "jammed" in the slits of the 8' bridge, thereby encumbering that bridge and in addition causing a tuning problem on the 4'. The 4' strings were not pulling through evenly because of friction against the 8' bridge slits, resulting in tuning irregularities.

That same instrument had 8' and 4' bridges of the same width, a nut consisting of individual metal pegs, dampers so thick that they rested on the second set of strings (the 8' and 4' strings were at the same level) and a braided

Sabathil action. Note size and double pinning of bridges.

Underside of Sabathil Bach III model, showing welded I-beam frame, and soundboard ribs.

cord around the edges of the soundboard. The latter is as much a hallmark of the production harpsichord as the steel wire running along the crown of bridges and nuts. The cord usually hides gaps between the soundboard and case sides. (A thick cord I once removed exposed sloppy soundboard fits all around the case.)

All Sabathils have a metal frame of welded aluminum channel, but the frame, as pointed out, usually doesn't get much chance to be effective because of the many other factors spoiling stability before the frame can ever do its work. The Sabathil brochure states that "on the American continent practically all professional harpsichordists own and play instruments with frames, a fact which speaks for itself." As of now, only a small minority play metal frame instruments; those that do, play instruments like a Challis or Rutkowski where the frame actually makes a difference.

The tone issuing from the giant Bach III comes out predictably not with a bang but a whimper; but again there are many people who like the quiet rustling quality of a subdued organ tone. Sabathils are reasonably inexpensive and are among the most quickly delivered of all makes (the owner of Bach III only waited seven weeks for his). Thus all isn't lost. Get to work, Sabathil and Son; all you have to do is change the design of your soundboard, jack, bridge, case and keyboard; and while you are at it, your firm's symbol as well. That tuning fork, entwined in a big S, looks suspiciously like the sign of a major world currency.

INSTRUMENTS BY SABATHIL

1. Clavichord Dolce: 4½ octaves; 45 × 18 in.
2. Virginal Amoroso: 4½ octaves; 1 × 8′; 45 × 18 in.
3. Harpsichord Cantabile: 4½ octaves; 2 × 8′, buff on both 8′; 54 × 36 in.
4. Harpsichord Maestoso II and III: 4¾ octaves; 1 (or 2) × 8′, 1 × 4′, buff on 8′; 61 × 38 in.
5. Harpsichord Concerto I: 5 octaves; two manuals 2 × 8′, 1 × 4′, or 1 × 16′, 1 × 8′, 1 × 4′; 72 × 41 in. Knee levers and coupler.
6. Harpsichord Concerto II: 5 octaves; two manuals, 2 × 8′, 1 × 4′, 1 × 16′; 72 × 41 in. Five pedals, coupler.
7. Harpsichord Bach I, II, III
   Bach I—5 octaves; two keyboards, 1 × 16′, 2 × 8′, 1 × 4′; 96 in. Five pedals.
   Bach II—5 octaves; two keyboards, 1 × 16′, 2 × 8′, 1 × 4′; 120 in. Six pedals.
   Bach III—5 octaves; two keyboards, 1 × 16′, 2 × 8′, 2 × 4′; 120 in. Eight pedals.

MARTIN SASSMANN
5609 Hückeswagen-Wiehagen, West Germany

Martin Sassmann runs one of the German production shops which are now beginning to turn out copies of classical instruments. According to Sassmann,

Martin Sassman

all of his instruments except models "Bach" and "Schütz" are now made in what is called *Kastenbauweise* (box construction), which suggests closed bottoms and thin sides. This is a comparatively new development, and most of the Sassmanns to be seen all over Europe, and especially France, were executed in the former *Serien-Instrument* style with the usual rigid case construction.

Martin Sassmann was born in 1924 and spent the war years as a German pilot. In 1948 he began to work for Neupert, passing his *Meisterprüfung* in 1953. After a stint as restorer in the Neupert collection, he began making instruments himself, plunging in right at the top by making a two-manual clavichord with 8′, 4′, and coupler, and a pedal clavichord with 4′, 8′, and 16′.

In 1955, Sassmann started his own shop, and since 1966 he has been at his present location, employing about 20 workmen. His shop has produced a total of 1500 instruments, and the current yearly production averages 45 doubles, 50 singles, 20 spinets, and 4 clavichords. The Sassmann jack is one of the simplest and most efficient of the Germanic jacks; there is little that could be expected to go wrong with it.

I have met with few Sassmanns in the U.S., and have not had one through my workshop. That could mean either that there aren't many in this country, or that they don't need much servicing. The one Sassmann I did see in Berlin was built in box-construction style, but it was by no means a close copy of a classical instrument. The essentials, however, were there, and the sound and action were basically good. Sassmann continues to produce "Bach" and "Schütz" models with Bach dispositions and production harpsichord characteristics. The Shudi copy of Sassmann's is somewhat grotesque looking because it can't make up its mind what it wants to be; there is the enormous Germanic pedal box, heavily braced, containing seven pedals, there are three clumsy legs ending in fat brass cups and casters, and there is a 16′ with a "theorbo" (buff) stop, all of it very un-Shudi-like. A footnote does state that the 16′ was absent in the original and has been added at customer's request.

The Sassmann models have the usual names after composers and historical builders, and the little 8′ and 4′ is called Modell "Kleinod" (Kleinod is a precious object). Sassmann, who spent some time as a restorer, undoubtedly has seen many old harpsichords. He would certainly have access to the modern books about historical harpsichords, including the careful study by Friedrich Ernst (*Der Fluegel J. S. Bach's*, C. F. Peters, Frankfurt, 1955) which demolishes the case for the "Bach" disposition.

Leafing through Sassmann's catalogue, one can almost feel the indecision on where to go from here; one page contains a typical *Serien* instrument, and the facing page has an illustration of a square-cheeked historical copy or near copy. In time, when more and more people demand instruments of decent sound and appearance, Sassmann may give up his models Kleinod, Schütz, Bach, etc., and have the first production shop of instruments based on true historical principles.

INSTRUMENTS BY MARTIN SASSMANN

1. Kleinspinett: BB–f3; 1 × 8′; 45¼ × 24¾ in.
2. Spinet Silbermann: BB–f3; 1 × 8′, buff on 8′; 63¾ × 24¾ in.
3. Harpsichord Kleinod: BB–f3; 1 × 8′, 1 × 4′, divided buff and half on 8′; 57 × 84 in.
4. Harpsichord Scarlatti: AA–f3; 1 × 8′, 1 × 4′, divided buff and half stop on 8′; 73 × 35 in.

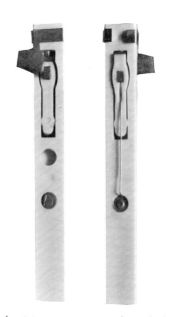

Jack by Martin Sassman. Plastic body and tongue, leather plectrum, brass wire spring, adjustable damper on metal clip, adjustment screw in top, and end pin (not shown).

5. Harpsichord Pertici: AA–f3; 2 × 8', 1 × 4' or 1 × 16', 1 × 8', 1 × 4' buff on 8' and 16'; 73 × 35 in.
6. Double manual harpsichord Baffo: AA–f3; upper manual 1 × 8, buff; lower manual: 1 × 8', 1 × 4'; 78¾ × 35 in. Knee coupler.
7. Double manual harpsichord Schütz: AA–f3, GG–f3, or GG–g3; upper manual 1 × 8', 1 × 4', or 1 × 8', or 2 × 8'; lower manual 1 × 8', 1 × 16', or 1 × 8', 1 × 4', 1 × 16', or 1 × 8', 1 × 4'; 82½ × 40½ in. Coupler.
8. Double manual harpsichord Bach: FF–f3; upper manual 1 × 8', 1 × 4', buff on 8'; lower; manual 1 × 8', 1 × 16', buff on 16'; 102½ × 40 in. Coupler, four pedals.

R. A. E. SCHÄFER
6075 Offenthal, Feldstrasse 15, West Germany

This is a small workshop, making instruments which radically depart from traditional harpsichord design. Eckhard Schäfer sent only meager details on his instruments in fear that a thorough description would encourage copyists. He makes a spinet with electronic amplification, which does not seem to have a conventional jack action. Another spinet (Model 61) looks like a small upright, set on three inverted umbrella handles. He also makes a *Tafel-Pianino* and a "harp" piano, formerly called the Chopin I, but now, in what seems to be a concession to modern tastes, renamed the "Haydn."

MARTIN SCHOLZ, HUG & CO.
Freie Strasse 70a, Basel, Switzerland

Martin Scholz works with Hug & Co., the largest music dealer in Switzerland. Scholz at one time worked as restorer in the collection of Dr. Rück in Nürnberg, but has been making harpsichords since 1936. He has produced a total of some two hundred instruments and his current yearly average is 4 doubles, 2 spinets, and 4 clavichords, with an occasional fortepiano.

A two-manual harpsichord by Martin Scholz, Hug & Co., with 2 × 8', 1 × 4', 1 × 16' disposition.

According to a Swiss piano tuner who is familiar with the Scholz production, the harpsichords are basically classically oriented. However Scholz himself adds the following cryptic note to a description of his instruments: "if desired, we build instruments after old measurements. Harpsichords with 16′ are based on dimensions of Ruckers and Kirckman." Now Scholz, who has worked as a restorer and is still doing a lot of repair work for collections and museums, must know that neither Ruckers nor Kirckman ever made a 16′, and that these two makers also differed considerably from each other.

Igor Kipnis, who has played Scholz instruments in Europe, reports that they are Neuperts in disguise. Be that as it may, Martin Scholz, who was born 1911 in Thuringia, is turning out instruments at a steady rate, employing three co-workers. He uses ready-made keyboards, but makes his own wooden jacks. Until recently Scholz was the only maker working in Switzerland, but an organ maker named Fleig is now making harpsichords on a small scale.

RUDOLF SCHÜLER
8031 Hechendorf am Pilsensee (near Munich), West Germany

Schüler is an oddity among the German shops—he works in neither the typical production style, nor in the style of historical copies. His is neither a large factory nor a one man workshop. Schüler's average yearly production of 3 doubles and about 30 singles suggests the type of small operation which is not common in Germany.

Rudolf Schüler was born in Saxony in 1911. He has been making harpsichords for 20 years, and the total produced by him runs to some four or five hundred instruments. Of his four models, the two larger ones are built with a separate inner and outer case in the Italian style. The inner instrument is described as being built "somewhat lighter" because it is protected by the outer case. In view of the lighter inner case, obviously based on Italian harpsichords, the enormously long scale which Schüler gives as 430 mm (17 in.) for pitch c^2 seems incomprehensible.

His jack embodies some details which have the look of potential trouble about them. One is the plastic quill, very similar to the Neupert "silvertone" quill which has not proved very durable. A second detail is the odd spring arrangement which holds the damper. A very soft white felt is glued to a thin wire loop, providing a minimal glue surface to materials which have little affinity for sticking together. The wire loop holding the damper is part of a spring wire clip going over the top of the jack and presumably hitting the jack rail each time the key is depressed. The delicate up and down adjustment of the damper would thus be easily disturbed in playing.

The worst feature of the jack is the long end pin assembly, consisting of a thin brass wire some 2 in. long, bent at an angle, and threaded at the end. Two little nuts $3/8$ in. from the end suggest that this arrangement fits into a hole in the key itself. Although I haven't seen a Schüler harpsichord, the endpin arrangement is identical with that of Wittmayer jacks which have no lower guide but go into the key itself. This means, of course, that the keyboard cannot be removed without taking out all of the jacks. We shall hear more about this inconvenient arrangement when we come to Wittmayer.

From catalogue pictures the Schüler instruments look lighter, more grace-

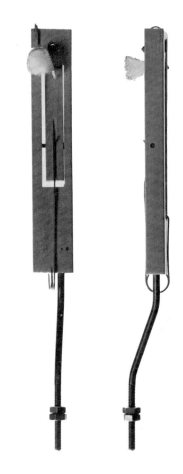

Wooden jack by Rudolf Schüler: spring clip damper carrier, steel coil tongue spring; brass end pin goes into key itself; round plastic quill.

Rudolf Schüler

ful and more classical than the typical German instrument. They have square cheeks and five thin legs instead of the three heavy ones. Schüler's prices seem low—the small 8′, 4′ is about $750, and the double is under $2000.

INSTRUMENTS BY SCHÜLER

1. Small Harpsichord: C–d3; 1 × 8′, 1 × 4′, buff on 8′; 58¼ × 28¾ in., 66 lbs.
2. Harpsichord Model 180: C–e3; 2 × 8′, 1 × 4′, buff on 8′; 71 × 30½ in. 83½ lbs.
3. Harpsichord Model 195: AA–f3; 2 × 8′, 1 × 4′, buff on 8′; 76¾ × 33½ in. 132 lbs.
4. Double manual harpsichord: AA–f3; upper manual 1 × 8′, 1 × 4′, buff on 8′; lower manual 2 × 8′, 1 × 4′; 83½ × 35½ in., 176 lbs. Knee coupler, five hand stops.

RAINER SCHÜTZE

Mühltalstrasse 128, Heidelberg, West Germany

Rainer Schütze, whose name is invariably preceded by Dipl.-Ing. (degree in engineering) was born in Heidelberg in 1927. When he was 17 years old he found himself a German prisoner-of-war in Russia and spent the next five years as the prison wood-carver and carpenter. After his release he went to Karlsruhe to study architecture and in 1950 joined Walter Merzdorf for three years, where he learned the rudiments of harpsichord making. In 1954 he became an independent industrial designer, making harpsichords on the side, but it wasn't until 1959 that he devoted himself full time to harpsichord making.

Schütze, who is a good friend of Martin Skowroneck, works generally in the style of historical instruments. He has a relatively small shop with about five workmen and spends a good deal of time travelling, writing and lecturing about the differences between historical and modern harpsichords, a subject on which he has elaborate theories. His own instruments use box constructions, closed (and solid-wood) bottoms, and classical scales and ribbing, and as a result have a good, lively tone. There are still many evidences of his industrial design days which surface in such details as slanted braces on stands, modernistic music racks, thin slanted metal braces to hold up clavichord lids, and round tapered legs with casters.

In spite of Schütze's Dipl.-Ing. and his numerous gold and silver medals from trade and world's fairs, the jacks of an 8′ & 4′ he made in 1963 were very poorly designed. The delrin plectra could not be inserted from the back since the hole in the jack did not go all the way through the tongue. There was a square niche, into which the plectrum had to be squeezed from the front, held by a filler. In order to make the plectrum insertion work properly, it was necessary to cut slots through the tongue so that the tapered delrin could be pushed in from the back, seating itself firmly in the slot.

A second incomprehensible feature was a rail sticking up in back of the keys, which prevented the removal of the keyboard unless all the jacks were taken out first (the rail would catch against the bottoms of the jacks as the keyboard was being pulled out). Since individual keys could not be removed for servicing due to a very narrow removable name batten, it became necessary to remove the entire keyboard, and with it all the jacks, to fix a single sticking key. In view of these features, one looks forward with a certain amount of apprehension to the new Schütze "axle-less" jack (DB and US patent), whose mould is now in preparation, and the keyboard suspension system which Schütze is reportedly working on.

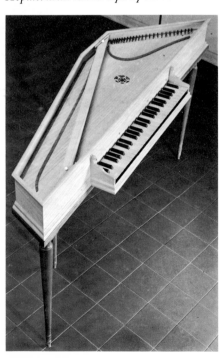

A spinet in the Italian style by Rainer Schütze.

Harpsichord by Rainer Schütze after Dulcken. Upper manual 1 × 8′, nazard; lower manual 1 × 8′, 1 × 4′, compass FF–g³.

In an article appearing in the German publication *Das Musikinstrument* (Issue 9, 1963) Schütze summarizes the findings of various authorities regarding the sound of the old versus the new harpsichords. He quotes Kirkpatrick (1942) complaining about the difficulty of achieving a "rich simplicity," as in two historical 8′ stops, on the many but monotonous stops of the modern harpsichord. Professor J. Mertin of Vienna is cited next, with his publication in 1957 of the results of his investigation into acoustical differences; Mertin finds that the modern harpsichord (meaning always the German production model) sounds "tired" and "boring," and lays this to wrong scales and piano-type soundboards and construction. Mertin adds that the quantitative addition of registers is no substitute for the qualitative loss in sound.

Gustav Leonhardt is cited as observing the fullness and depth of tone of the classical harpsichord, connecting it with the transmission of sound vibrations to the bridge and case. Nikolaus Hornoncourt in Vienna (1960) is mentioned as having found that "the modern harpsichords are much softer and one hears

The Schütze keyboard, with projecting rack in back which makes it necessary to remove all jacks before keyboard can come out.

Schütze's solution to hand stops.

only a metallic rustling, while an old harpsichord was capable of becoming the centerpoint of an ensemble."

Schütze further cites J. Stadelmann with the opinion that the modern harpsichord lacks a certain "timbre," it is too dull or too shrill, while the historical 8′ register was truly fundamental, eliminating the need for a 16′. Annemarie Bohne is quoted as observing that the 16′ lowers the tone quality of the entire instrument (we have already seen that 16′ strings passing over an 8′ bridge encumber and therefore inhibit that bridge).

In another paper ("Die Unterschiede in der akustischen und musikalischen Qualität bei alten und modernen Cembali"—*Musikinstrument* 5, 1966) Schütze develops his elaborate theory involving tone rays of a zero order. One of his points is that an open bottom leads to an acoustical "short-circuit," since soundwaves emanating from above and below the soundboard interfere with each other and cancel each other out. He attacks Neupert for his statement that modern man has a different threshhold of hearing than his baroque predecessor; what Neupert does, in effect, is to lower the volume of the modern harpsichord only to suggest electronic amplification to correct the lowered volume.

Schütze is one of the lively forces now at work in Germany undermining the "establishment" of the modern harpsichord. It is possible, even likely, that we shall soon see the whole edifice of the production harpsichord, for which Neupert and Pleyel must accept a special responsibility, come tumbling down to make way for a more accurate conception of the harpsichord. If that happens, we will owe thanks to the forces which brought about that downfall and which will have included such figures as Kirkpatrick and Leonhardt, Hubbard and Dowd, Skowroneck—and Dipl.-Ing. Rainer Schütze.

INSTRUMENTS BY SCHÜTZE

1. Clavichord: C–f3; double strung; 51 in. long.
2. Clavichord: FF–f3; double strung; 59 in. long.
3. Spinet: C–f3; 1 × 8′, buff; 55 in. long.
4. Flemish style harpsichord: C–f3 or AA–d3; 2 × 8′ or 1 × 8′, 1 × 4′, buff on 8′; 79 in. long.
5. Double manual Flemish style harpsichord: upper manual 1 × 8′; buff; lower manual 1 × 8′, 1 × 4′; 86½ in. long. Coupler and hand stops.
6. Double manual French style harpsichord: upper manual 1 × 8′, buff; lower manual 1 × 8′, 1 × 4′; 98½ in. long. Coupler and hand stops.
7. Double manual harpsichord after Dulcken: FF–f3; upper manual 1 × 8′, lute, buff; lower manual 1 × 8′, 1 × 4′; 98½ in. long. Coupler, hand stops.

Copy of an Italian harpsichord by Martin Seidel. Note two "split sharps" in the bass.

MARTIN SEIDEL
Corina 117, Coyoacan, Mexico 21, D.F.

It would be romantic to envision Mexico's only harpsichord maker with a wide-brimmed hat, taking a siesta outside his adobe shack. Martin Seidel, however, is not a native Mexican and does not work in the Spanish tradition.

His first instrument, made in 1963, is a copy of an Italian harpsichord, which was eventually acquired by the New York Pro Musica. It is, on the whole, a faithful copy, except for a number of details. One of these is a one-inch-wide cap moulding which serves no purpose other than catching on objects; most of the overhung moulding had, in fact, ripped off. (The Italians, who were practical, usually ended their cap mouldings flush with the case mouldings.)

An interesting feature of the instrument is the split sharps in the bass, often found on the old harpsichords, but rarely copied by modern makers. Each half of the sharp works a different key, allowing extension (by way of the short octave) to GG. The scale of the harpsichord is $c^2 = 10^3/_4$ in., with a speaking length of 63 in. for the lowest bass string.

Crack in soundboard of the Seidel harpsichord shown above. This crack seemed to have no effect on tuning stability or the tone of the instrument.

KLAUS SENFTLEBEN
2150 Buxtehude, Jahnstrasse 28, West Germany

Senftleben hybrid spinet-harpsichord.

Like Schüler, Klaus Senftleben runs the small to medium sized workshop which is comparatively rare in Germany. Senftleben learned instrument-making in East Germany, where he started at the age of fourteen. His apprenticeship was spent at Ammer, and from there he went to Blüthner in Leipzig and Bechstein in Berlin, learning piano building with these two famous makers. He possesses "Meistertitel" in harpsichord, piano, and harmonium (reed-organ) work.

Since 1955 Senftleben, who was born in Breslau 38 years ago, has had his own shop in the appropriately named town of Buxtehude near Hamburg. Senftleben has produced about 300 instruments, of which one-third have been doubles.

Senftleben instruments have open bottoms, heavy cases, and slanted cheek fronts, giving them a fairly Germanic look. An oddity is a hybrid, combining a triangular spinet and a small Italianesque harpsichord. (See illustration.) Senftleben works with a painter named Peter Knauer from the island of Föhr, who often decorates his harpsichords.

INSTRUMENTS BY SENFTLEBEN

1. Travel Clavichord Model S IV A: C–f3; single strung; 41½ × 15 in.
2. Clavichord Model S IV: FF–f3; single or double strung; 50½ × 19 in.
3. Spinet Model S V: FF–f3; 1 × 8′, buff; 73½ × 47¼ in.
4. Klein-Cembalo, Model S I: C–f3; 1 × 8′, divided buff; 39⅜ × 21¾ in. This instrument is also available in kit form.
5. Harpsichord Model S II B: FF–f3; 1 × 8′, 1 × 4′, divided buff; 59 × 36¼ in.
6. Harpsichord Model S II: same as above, but 69 × 37½ in.
7. Double manual harpsichord Model S II A: FF–f3; 1 × 16′, 1 × 8′, 1 × 4′ or 2 × 8′, 1 × 4′, divided buff on both 8′; 76¾ × 41¾ in.
8. Double manual harpsichord S III: FF–f3; 1 × 16′, 2 × 8′, 1 × 4′, divided buff on both 8′. Pedals.
9. Double manual concert harpsichord Buxtehude: FF–f3; 1 × 16′, 3 × 8′, 1 × 4′, buff and half stops on 8′s; 96½ × 41¾ in.

Senftleben S II double-manual harpsichord.

JOHN SHORTRIDGE
P.O. Box 95, Aldie, Virginia 22001

John Shortridge is well known as the author of U.S. National Museum bulletin 225 *Italian Harpsichord Building in the 16th and 17th Centuries* (now out of print) which he wrote while he was curator of musical instruments at the Smithsonian Institution. In this pamphlet Shortridge advances the theory that Italian harpsichords with ranges up to f 3 have considerably longer scale averages than those which ascend only to c3. From this he infers that the long-range instruments were tuned a fourth lower than the others, equating c3 and f3 and resembling the transposing doubles made in Antwerp.

Frank Hubbard points out that Shortridge lumps Italian harpsichords and virginals together for the sake of his theory, and that nearly all the virginals have long scales and extended ranges, while few of the harpsichords do. While Shortridge finds an average scale of 12¾ in. for pitch c2 on the extended ranges, Hubbard, by giving many more examples, brings that average down to just a little over 11 in. Comparing this to just under 10½ in. for the shorter range, it will be seen that the small difference is not nearly enough to account for a fourth difference in pitch.

Shortridge has been active for eight years and built some instruments while still at the Smithsonian. He has since moved to an old stone house some 50 miles from Washington, where he works slowly and meticulously, turning out precise copies. The bearded, 39-year-old maker, together with his partner Linda van Sweden, is now working on three replicas of the 1665 Ridolfi harpsichord at the Smithsonian.

Shortridge, who (somewhat in jest) puts his yearly production at "1.375 and rising" is currently working on instruments for the New York Pro Musica Society and Yale University School of Music (staff). He has made a total of 11 instruments, but is forced to teach at a nearby school to supplement his income. His partner used to be an urban planner for the National Capitol Planning Commission but is happy to be out of politics and to be making an estimated 75 cents an hour doing really meaningful work.

ANTHONY SIDEY
55 Rue Sedaine, Paris 11, France

Anthony Sidey is an Englishman, born 1942 in Hertfordshire, who has been making harpsichords in Paris for five years. He has produced twenty instruments, of which 5 have been doubles, 7 singles, 3 spinets and virginals, and 5 clavichords. He makes his instruments to his own designs, unless asked to make a copy.

Sidey, who works alone, uses open bottoms, and on his big concert double a light alloy frame which he says improves tuning stability considerably. His jacks are made from diakon, a plastic used by other English makers. On his instruments with 16′ stops, Sidey places the 16′ bridge on pillars over the 8′ bridge.

A listing of Sidey's instruments shows nine models, ranging from a four-octave clavichord to six different types of two-manual instruments, culminating in the nine-foot concert double shown here.

The nine-foot concert double by Anthony Sidey: upper manual 1 × 8′ delrin, 1 × 8′ leather; lower manual 1 × 8′, 1 × 4′, 1 × 16′, buff to 16′; coupler, 6 pedals, 2 hand stops.

MARTIN SKOWRONECK
28 Bremen-Oberneuland, Am Heiddamm 47, West Germany

Martin Skowroneck, whom the reader has already encountered many times in these pages, was born in Berlin in 1926, and went to the Musikschule

A Ruckers model by Martin Skowroneck. (Courtesy Dr. C. Truesdell)

The Skowroneck jack of beechwood with holly tongue. No top or end adjustments; boar's bristle spring, delrin plectrum.

in Bremen from which he graduated in 1950 as a flute and recorder teacher. He built his first clavichord and harpsichord three years later, copying the modern production style which was to be seen everywhere. Skowroneck soon abandoned the style of these early instruments, which he considers his *Jugendsünden*, and immersed himself in the study of historical harpsichords.

In spite of Skowroneck's comparatively young age and his small output, he is considered by many a legendary figure among harpsichord makers. Few people have seen the man or his instruments; Skowroneck refuses to compete with his fellow German makers. He does not show his instruments, give them to dealers, or promise commissions to music teachers or professors as other makers do; as it is, he has a 12-year backlog of orders. His importance stems from the quality of his instruments and the effect he is slowly having upon his fellow German makers.

Martin Skowroneck is a large man with a high forehead, bushy receding hair and rimless glasses, looking very much like the kindly, absent-minded college professor. He lives with his wife in a two-family house at the end of a quiet, unpaved suburban lane, a 30-minute bus ride from downtown Bremen. In his house there is one enormous studio room containing some completed instruments. In the center of that room, seated formally with Skowroneck at a table, I spent some three hours sitting nearly rigid in the austere and almost unheated room. The studio did not have the look of a workshop about it, and this, together with what seemed to me Skowroneck's unusually heavy hands made me wonder where his instruments really came from.

Next to the studio there was a tiny workshop with some very simple tools. The antiquated little circular saw I noticed there would certainly be considered sub-standard in the shop of any American maker. The conclusion to be drawn from the shop and the man is that, above all else, he has the will—and the knowledge—to make really fine instruments. All the equipment of a shop like Neupert's or Sperrhake's, all their experienced shop foremen, all their modern materials and technical know-how cannot produce the quality which Skowroneck manages to wrest from his meager equipment.

Skowroneck works entirely by himself, without any help whatever, even

to the point of decorating his soundboards. Between working, teaching, playing, and writing, it is surprising that he has managed to produce the total of fifty-five instruments which have come out of his workshop. Skowroneck's classical copies are played by the historically oriented Dutch harpsichordist Gustav Leonhardt, and recordings made on these instruments have given a large public an idea of the sound of historical harpsichords.

We have made reference to a paper by Skowroneck ("Probleme des Cembalobaus aus historischer Sicht" *Hi Fi Stereo Phonie*, issues 9, 10, 11, 1968, Verlag R. Braun, Karlsruhe) which discusses the problems involved in making historical copies. Since Skowroneck was largely unacquainted with the recent awareness of historical instruments in America (harpsichord makers, aside from the mass producers who encounter each other at trade fairs, are notoriously provincial and self-contained) his paper presented the case for classical instruments against a background of rigid lack of comprehension on the part of most of the other makers.

As we have already seen, Skowroneck laments the fact that few if any harpsichordists play on the original instruments, something which is commonplace with violinists. The modern harpsichord makers have been able to evolve a new instrument (quite suitable, incidentally, for modern music), which has little in common with the classical instruments in tone, appearance and mechanics; and this has been possible, according to Skowroneck, because few players had the chance to compare the modern and historical products (especially side by side) and could thus be easily mistaken in their conception of tone. He discusses the departures of the modern harpsichord from the old practices under the headings of construction, scale, mechanics, disposition, tone, and materials, and makes many of the points with which the reader of this book must by now be thoroughly familiar. (Skowroneck's paper is unfortunately not yet available in an English translation.)

Skowroneck's obsession with the historical instruments leads to some opinions which are probably unjustified. Thus, he is strictly opposed to any kind of production, even that of using only a few workmen and good machine tools; he insists on boar's bristle for jack tongue springs, maintaining that

Action of Skowroneck Ruckers model.

Soundboard of the Skowroneck Ruckers. Even the Ruckers rose has been duplicated. Soundboard painting was done by Skowroneck as well.

Another view of the Skowroneck soundboard.

historical builders could have used the cheaper music wire had they wanted to dispense with the bristle (Skowroneck forgets that music wire in those days had no "spring" to it as it does today); he opposes the use of plywood anywhere in the instrument; he warns against leather plectra and deplores the use of plastic jack tongues as being too slippery to hold a quill. Skowroneck goes so far as to maintain that the lidstick must be of the same wood as the lid, to transmit the sound vibrations from lid to case without any loss, an idea that amuses the good American makers. He correctly rails against the "Bach" disposition and takes Neupert to task for citing Adlung in its support. What Neupert probably had in mind, however, was a remark of Adlung's quoted in Friedrich Ernst's study of the Bachfluegel to the effect that "one could exchange one of the 4′ in a disposition of 2 × 8′, 2 × 4′, for a 16′ in order to enrich the tone possibilities."

What Skowroneck does would appear to be very simple. He carefully studies and measures historical models and then picks a particular one and copies it closely, both in regard to measurements and materials. The outcome of this simple procedure (it really is often easier to copy then to make one's own design) is an astonishingly beautiful instrument, proving once again the validity of the old harpsichords.

Skowroneck's instruments have flute-like (not silvery) trebles, reedy (not rustling) tenors, and sonorous (not booming) basses. On a first hearing a Skowroneck is almost a disappointment; it does not overwhelm the listener (the way Hyman's instrument did, for instance) but keeps its distance. It does what the player, the listener and the music want it to do. It is the ideal *instrument* (in the sense of "tool"), because it neither resists nor encourages its user but mirrors precisely his own strengths and weaknesses. This allows the skilled performer to do almost anything he wants with it, a characteristic which was also found in the Ruckers instruments of old.

KURT SPERRHAKE
Passau/Bayern, Steinweg 14, West Germany

Sperrhake is the factory with the largest harpsichord production today. Although, as is customary with the large companies, precise figures could not be obtained from Sperrhake himself, his current yearly production is estimated at six hundred instruments, and the total since 1948 a staggering eight thousand. In 1956, long before the current German *Konkurrenzkampf* (competitor's squabble) among the major producers, I visited Sperrhake and was cordially received. I even spent a night on his living room couch and was given a grand tour of the factory (I was then completely unknown). When Eric Herz tried the same thing many years later, he was refused a tour of the factory point blank.

Kurt Sperrhake, who was born 1907 in Thuringia, was a piano-maker before the war and reportedly sold Ammer harpsichords along with his pianos. In 1948 he went into the harpsichord business himself, knowing little about the instrument. With German industry and efficiency he finally arrived at his present large plant and work force of some 60 employees. In the course of 21 years, Sperrhake has changed many features on his instruments to make them work better and more efficiently, but he has as yet not made any conces-

The Sperrhake jacks. Center of jack is wood, outer layers and tongue are bone. Felt damper is glued to adjustable metal clip. Plectrum is leather.

sion in the direction of classical instruments (his "Ruckers" model notwithstanding).

My visit in 1956 resulted in my ordering a "Silbermann" spinet from Sperrhake, intended for an instrument rental service in New York. With exactly
one year of harpsichord experience under my belt, I thought the Sperrhake
spinet a very nice instrument. (It is actually still among his best products.) The
rental service soon ordered a whole fleet of spinets and a two manual harpsichord. The double was rented to the Metropolitan Opera, and they found it
such an improvement over their upright piano with thumbtacks in its hammers, that they bought it on the spot.

Now one decided advantage of a Sperrhake spinet over a large harpsichord
is that it has only one set of 54 jacks which need servicing. The Metropolitan
instrument with its three sets of jacks soon fell apart, and at the end of two
seasons it was a wreck with a whimpering sound completely inadequate to the
size of that enormous hall. I next offered to trade them one of my own 8′ + 4′
singles for the Sperrhake double just to cut down my constant service calls,
and this trade accomplished, I took the Sperrhake to my shop for revoicing
and eventual sale. It was the first of a long string of Sperrhakes which came to
my shop, many of them almost completely unplayable.

In those days the principal problem lay in the jacks and plectra. Aside from
the fact that even under the best circumstances the instruments did not possess
a very live sound, most Sperrhakes were not playing at maximum efficiency.
The leather he used then was extremely hard and brittle and was subjected to
an artificial process of rolling and compressing in an effort to improve its
natural stiffness. There was not much more than half a year of playing life in
those plectra before they would break and pluck with the limp, half broken
end, causing a soft sound, and hanging on the string.

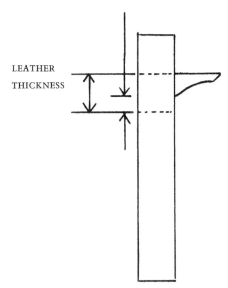

WASTED SPACE

LEATHER
THICKNESS

Diagram of relative thickness of Sperrhake leather.

Underside of Sperrhake harpsichord showing framing. Total weight of this instrument was 330 lbs.

The jack was then, as now, made of wood laminated with processed bone, but the tongues, which are now plastic, were then also of bone. This material was extremely brittle, and between the square hole and the tongue's edge was no more than $1/_{32}$ in. of material. (Sassmann's present jack design incorporates a useful feature which would have improved the Sperrhake jack immeasurably —the tongue bulges out at the leather hole to provide thicker tongue walls at that point.) Since the leather was completely hard, and solidly glued into the tongue, tongues would invariably break when an attempt was made to remove the leather. I learned later that the tongue had to be soaked in warm water to make removal of leather possible, but soaking would also loosen the tongue felt pad which was to silence the tongue's contact with the adjustment screw. Once the leather was out, the hole was found to be of such a size as to accept only an enormously thick leather, not easily available. Most of the leather's thickness was wasted, since the actual slant of the voicing cut only affected one third of the leather's thickness (see illustration). Even worse were the tongues with round holes, into which leather sharpened to a point like a pencil was supposed to fit.

With the double curse of leather constantly breaking and being almost impossible to replace, Sperrhakes became a major threat to the harpsichord player and technician. Many of his instruments changed hands, sometimes at ridiculous prices, and finally I took to using delrin instead of replacement leather, with somewhat better results. It is disconcerting to think of all the Sperrhakes in all parts of the world with broken leathers, whose replacement is beyond the capability of the average owner.

Sperrhake has made a number of improvements in his current product. He now uses plastic tongues with a somewhat more pliable leather, but the bone and wood laminated jack is still inclined to break at the axle pin. The spinet jack slides are now adjustable, allowing an overall adjustment of spinet jacks without having to adjust jacks individually. In a spinet this is very important, since any movement in the case will take all the strings in one direction. Because the strings are arranged in pairs and the jacks face each other, half of the jacks pull away from the strings (i.e. get softer) and half go toward the strings (get louder). One move of the slide can even this out. (I pointed this problem out to Sperrhake in 1956, but he did nothing about it for many years.)

The Sperrhake pedals mercifully use steel pivot blocks unlike the Neupert wooden blocks which frequently split. The soundboard is now laminated spruce, so it at least does not crack; but it is still varnished to such a high shine that the finish develops the network of hairline cracks which we already found in Neuperts. The frame of large Sperrhake doubles is still some 3 in. thick and braced with a criss-cross maze of 1 × 4 in. framing boards. All this wood does not seem to help the tuning stability; according to a number of observers light box-construction harpsichords actually stay in tune longer than the rigid case harpsichords. Sperrhake used to make his own keyboards but now uses the good German ready-made factory keys, which have the narrower French octave span.

He has abandoned the two extra top treble strings with no corresponding jacks which used to be a feature on his spinets. (No one has ever been able to

One of Sperrhake's more graceful instruments to be contrasted with the one shown in Chapter III.

explain what they were for, unless they were supposed to resonate with the plucked strings.) Still to be found is the braided cord running along the inside of the harpsichord and hiding the soundboard edges, and the wire running along the nut and bridge crowns underneath the strings. This wire is never found in good harpsichords, because it may well inhibit the sound transmission from string to bridge.

Sperrhake's American representative, Robert Taylor of Bethesda, Maryland, has written a maintenance manual for use with Sperrhake instruments which covers the subject in admirable detail. We will deal with some of the points Taylor makes in our maintenance section. Taylor is an exception among agents dealing in production harpsichords, since he is technically knowledgable and works with a modest commission; in addition he does not abandon his customers, as so many of the piano dealers selling harpsichords are forced to do since they know nothing about the product.

The appearance of the Sperrhake has changed little over the years, and the heavy lines are, as usual, emphasized with vertical graining. An exception is the model 168, illustrated here, which has square cheeks and horizontal graining, and is among the most successful of his products, tonally as well as in appearance. Sperrhake has changed his system of leg bolts and plates several

Detail of Sperrhake 16′ bridge showing extreme double pinning.

times, from the wooden and easily worn out threads to thin $1/4$ in. metal bolts. None of them are equal to the strain of frequent screwing and unscrewing of legs.

The Sperrhake "Ruckers" model, perhaps an attempt to keep up with the "now" generation among harpsichord enthusiasts, is as solidly built as the rest of his oeuvre, but has in addition a bottom. Just to be there "fustest with the mostest," Sperrhake provides the player with a keyboard coupler operated by a handstop, a shove coupler, and dogleg jacks. On the bottom of the Ruckers model can be seen round plugs, perhaps 2 in. in diameter, with a number of screwheads showing. On unscrewing one of these plugs, I discovered that it held a post which in turn supported the 4′ hitch rail by pushing up against it. The pull on that rail, however, would only be upwards, so no bottom support could do any good. It is another odd Sperrhake innovation.

The hope that Sperrhake, whose harpsichords one encounters everywhere, will lighten up his cases, improve his action, and change the appearance of his instruments is slim indeed. Sperrhake's instincts are basically those of a piano maker, and he feels that if a $1/2$ in. thick case (as on the classical instruments) is good, then a 1 in. case is better, and a 2 in. or 3 in. case is best; if three soundboard ribs are good, then six are better, and nine are best, etc. But Sperrhake is a businessman as well as a piano man; perhaps, if his customers demand light and pretty cases and lively sounds, he can be budged. In view of the volume coming from his shop, one can only hope for the best.

INSTRUMENTS BY SPERRHAKE

1. Clavichord Model 12: C–f3, single strung; $46\frac{1}{2} \times 15\frac{3}{4}$ in. 66 lbs.
2. Clavichord Model Hubert: FF–f3; single strung; $57 \times 19\frac{3}{4}$ in., 100 lbs.
3. Klein-Spinett: C–f3; 1 × 8′, buff; $37\frac{1}{2} \times 21\frac{1}{2}$ in., 66 lbs.
4. Spinet Model Silbermann: C–f3; 1 × 8′, divided buff; $60\frac{1}{4} \times 23\frac{1}{2}$ in. 88 lbs.
5. Harpsichord Model 145 Stingel: C–f3; 1 × 8′, 1 × 4′, divided buff on 8′, knee lever on 4′; 57×34 in., 155 lbs.
6. Harpsichord Model 168: C–f3; 1 × 8′, 1 × 4′, buff; 66 in. long.
7. Double manual harpsichord Model 161: C–f3; upper manual 1 × 8′, buff; lower manual 1 × 8′, 1 × 4′, buff on 8′; $63\frac{1}{2} \times 37\frac{3}{4}$ in., 198 lbs. Keyboard coupler; pedals or handstops.
8. Double manual harpsichord Model 205: AA–f3; upper manual 1 × 8′, buff; lower manual 1 × 8′, 1 × 4′, buff on 8′; $80\frac{3}{4}$ in. long. Coupler, pedals or handstops.
9. Double manual harpsichord Model 200 "Bach": FF–f3; upper manual 1 × 8′, 1 × 4′, buff on 8′; lower manual 1 × 8′, 1 × 16′, buff on 8′ and 16′; $78\frac{3}{4} \times 43\frac{1}{4}$ in., 330 lbs. Coupler, five pedals.

JOHANN GEORG STEINGRAEBER
Berlin, Germany

This former builder, who started making harpsichords in Germany at the same time as Neupert and Maendler, died in 1932. He never made very many instruments, but for some reason achieved the reputation of being a very fine maker whose rare instruments were of special value.

One of those rare instruments, which I saw in New Jersey, struck me as being very similar to pre-war Neuperts. It is possible that Steingraeber achieved his reputation because he died before he could incorporate in his work all of the worst features of the *Serien Instrumente*, although enough of them were already present.

From Skowroneck we learn that according to Friedrich Ernst, the former restorer of the Berlin Collection who worked for Steingraeber at one time, a

A Sperrhake two-manual instrument. Note 16′ bridge doubledecked on 8′ bridge.

third manual was added to a 1631 Baffo double-manual by Steingraeber himself, who covered the third manual naturals with ivory instead of the bone found on the other two keyboards.

ROBERT STRATTON
416 Hume Avenue, Alexandria, Virginia 22301

Stratton has been active since 1964, producing a total of eight instruments. He estimates his current yearly production at one double, and two or three singles. Judging by a picture of a double, Stratton, who was born in Paris France in 1904, seems to be working in a style reminiscent of his countryman Pleyel.

THIERBACH CEMBALOBAU
Thierbach near Dresden, East Germany

No attempt to reach this East German firm was successful, either at their own address or through the East German organization for foreign exports called DEMUSA, 108 Berlin, Postfach 1209.

However, judging from a Thierbach I saw in Brussels, this is not a great loss. This instrument, an 8′ and 4′, was nearly seven feet long, but the tone was extremely coarse. No attempt had been made to fine-voice the plectra, cut from an unidentified plastic, and I counted 35 "hangers" (jacks which would not return of their own accord because of rough plectra catching on the strings) on the 8′ alone. The instrument had Sperrhake-type hand stops (wide brass $1/8 \times 9/16$ in.), soundboard bars $7/8 \times 5/8$ in. going straight across, case walls 2 in. thick, and three framing beams 4×4 in.

In addition the 8′ bridge was double-pinned with pins over $1/16$ in. in diameter and the hitchpins were almost piano sized. (Generally thin piano center pins are used for harpsichord bridge pins, and piano bridge pins for harpsichord hitchpins.) The music rack assembly rests on four dowels going into tight holes, and the rack must be lifted straight up, and with a good deal of force, to remove it for tuning.

MICHAEL THOMAS
The Manor House, Hurley, Berkshire, England

Michael Thomas is less of a harpsichord maker than a phenomenon on the English scene. His instruments are scattered about in a Charles Addams type heatless mansion, but Thomas himself lives in a modern bungalow at the edge of the property. Hurley is another quaint picturesque English village, but Thomas is much too atypical to qualify as the village harpsichord maker.

When Hugh Gough still had his shop in London, Michael Thomas spent some time there, picking up whatever information came his way. Thomas is too nervous, impatient and disorganized to be a meticulous woodworker, and he now has parts of his instruments made all over the English countryside. He is something of a wheeler-dealer and is very good at locating sources for antique instruments. (Thomas and the famous English Haydn scholar H. Robbins Landon work as a team to acquire antique Italian harpsichords— "Robbie" spots them and Thomas gets them out of Italy and does the restoration.)

A number of antiques of all kinds, sizes, shapes, and conditions are strewn about the house. Italian harpsichords with dubious stands and newly and crudely made keyboards, antique chamber organs, a Stodart piano, and a Shudi with Venetian swell in excellent condition can be found in different corners. There is not much evidence of actual work, and it seems that most of the building is done by a Thomas associate, John Horniblow, who is publicity shy and just wants to be left alone to do his work.

The one Thomas harpsichord I was able to hear had a remarkably good tone, somewhat reminiscent of the instrument by Clayson and Garrett, who at one time worked with Thomas. Thomas himself is responsible only for the soundboards of his instruments; they are extremely thin and arched, and sometimes have ribs only $1/16$ in. wide running straight across. Evidently ribs as thin as this do not interfere with the tone or bridge in any way when run straight across the bridge underside; in fact, far from interfering, this soundboard structure produces an extraordinarily live tone, which in this instance was probably helped by fairly thin case walls as well.

Thomas gets his jacks partly from his own suppliers and partly from Sassmann in Germany. He estimates his production at about one instrument per month, but his method of operation has the appearance of being extremely sporadic. A story, which may be apocryphal, concerns a Thomas clavichord which arrived at Harrod's department store in London without a music rack. Thomas was called, and showed up with a raw piece of wood, a hammer and two nails. He then proceeded to nail the piece into the clavichord lid. Thomas is an unpredictable mixture of good and bad, capable of the crudest workmanship and the finest tone.

WILLIAM THOMAS AND J. J. K. RHODES
Easterhaughs, Burntisland, Fife, Scotland

These two makers have been on the English scene since pre-war days and have devoted much time to restorations, particularly at the Raymond Russell collection now in Edinburgh. They are said to be residing in a rambling baronial castle on the Firth of Forth, which they reconstructed with their own hands. They have made very few, though elaborate, instruments, but are apparently not building at the present time; they are said to have faded out into a position of god-like inaccessibility.

TURNER CORPORATION (Turner-Bainbridge)
401 East Main Street, P.O. Box 1461, Charlottesville, Virginia 22902

This company returned a questionnaire from me almost totally blank. The length of time they have been in business, the number of instruments made, their yearly production, their scale averages, the number of staff, etc., seem all to be guarded secrets.

According to their literature, they are making a spinet (Model K), four types of singles (Models A1, A2, A3 and A4) and four types of doubles (Models D1, D2, D3, and D4). The soundboard, at least in the spinet model, is made of a "highly sound sensitive and extremely temperature and moisture resistant high pressure melamine laminate." Their advertising copy, as high pressure as the melamine laminate, asks "whoever heard of a harpsichord that doesn't need a sales talk!" (And whoever heard of one that does?) The copy continues, calling the Turner-Bainbridge "the only precision crafted harpsichord in the world. Grace. Beauty. Flawlessness." (So much for Hubbard; so much for Dowd.)

Resting on the melamine laminate soundboard is a bridge "formed from heat and moisture resistant phenolic." An internal frame "cast from a specially developed aluminum alloy" and jacks made of "steel and tenite" complete the contribution of modern science to this instrument. If the reader is dying to find out what all this "modern precision crafting" has done to the tone, so am I. I haven't heard a Turner-Bainbridge and can't take much comfort from the ad which claims that "it speaks a language that's bigger, brighter—a sound that's all harpsichord."

There are many industrial products today which turn out to be considerably better than they appeared to be through their extravagant advertising copy, and Turner-Bainbridge may be one of them. They would be wise however, to realize that harpsichord people are, on the whole, a literate group, and that copy like the above is more likely to end up on people's bathroom walls as examples of camp than sell harpsichords.

— JOHAN VAN LEER
520 West Belden Avenue, Chicago, Illinois 60614

Johan van Leer comes from Java, Indonesia, where he was born in 1927. He has been active in the field since 1960, restricting himself to the making of clavichords only. Of these he has made thirty-four, currently producing one to three yearly.

His clavichords have a five-octave German keyboard, FF-f^3. He uses a 3-ply birch soundboard, .055″ (or less than $^1/_{16}$ in.) thick. Since this is by far the thinnest plywood soundboard of which I have heard, I am sorry to report that I have not had the chance to hear this instrument. Van Leer undoubtedly chose birch because a softwood as thin as this might have caved in and is, in any case, not commercially available. In a clavichord, the S-shaped bridge itself acts as a soundboard brace, allowing the safe use of thin soundboards.

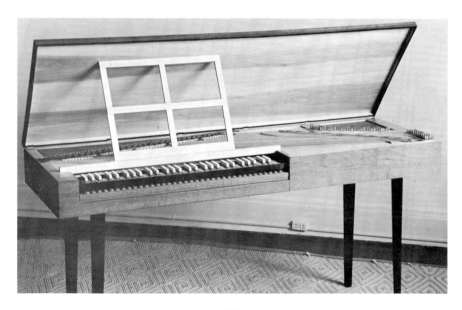

Five-octave clavichord by Johan van Leer.

JULIUS WAHL
Los Altos, California

Julius Wahl, who died a number of years ago, was described in an article in *Musical America* (February, 1950) along with John Challis as "the only generally known maker of harpsichords and clavichords in the U.S. today." Twenty years later, few people have heard of Wahl, who had made some forty instruments up to 1950 and produced about three per year, working alone in Los Altos.

Julius Wahl was a piano maker by trade and worked at Chickering from 1905–1911; he was thus at Chickering with Arnold Dolmetsch, perhaps providing the "missing link" in the American harpsichord tradition which started with Dolmetsch in Boston. It is more likely, however, that Wahl worked exclusively on pianos and was only mildly interested in harpsichords at the time. He later became the curator of the Belle Skinner collection (now part of the Yale collection) before setting up his own shop.

The one spinet of his which I have seen repeatedly for repairs is not impressive, possessing short stubby leather plectra and a thick case, but Frank Hubbard reports having been pleased by a Julius Wahl clavichord he saw.

THOMAS WESS
44 Bluecoat Chambers, School Lane, Liverpool 1, England

Thomas Wess has been making instruments commercially for only six months, but has made them for his own use at intervals during the past ten years. His total production has been seven instruments, all clavichords, but he is planning to make harpsichords as well, basing them on instruments of the Italian school.

The 33-year-old maker works by himself and estimates his future production at seven to ten yearly, which he concedes may be too optimistic. His clavichords embody the odd five-sided shape also associated with Michael Thomas (who claims to have originated it) and Clayson & Garrett.

Clavichord by Thomas Wess, double strung throughout with copper beryllium wire.

S. R. WILLIAMS
1229 Olancha Drive, Los Angeles, California 90065

S. R. Williams, who was born 1920 in San Francisco, has been active for six years and has produced a total of twelve instruments, but his current yearly production estimated at 7 to 9 instruments suggests a brisker pace than past activity. Williams' doubles are copies of a 1617 Hans Ruckers (after ravalement) and his standard single is based on the "Jesses Cassus" harpsichord cited in Frank Hubbard's book (p. 142). Although he copies classical harpsichords, Williams designs his own spinets and clavichords, using such unclassical materials as laminated luan mahogany for soundboards. His jacks are the same as those used by Jones-Clayton (see Richard Jones).

The major part of the Williams production is now devoted to kits, although an elaborate price list describes a Flemish double with five options, an Italian single with three options, a Flemish single with seven options, a triangular spinet, and a large, medium, and small clavichord, all made to order in finished form. Until recently only one of these, the triangular spinet, seemed to be out in kit form, but Williams has recently added a small Flemish single to his kit production.

E. O. WITT
Route 3, Three Rivers, Michigan 49093

Witt has been active since 1950, but has concentrated on making instruments in his own shop only since 1963. He has produced a total of 40 instruments, in addition to kits which he offers for some of his models.

The 45-year-old maker, who rightly objects to being reduced to a mere statistic in a survey of this kind, works alone except for an occasional helper. He makes his own keyboards and jacks and uses redwood for soundboards, claiming it to be superior even to Sitka spruce. He seems to be the only modern maker building fretted clavichords.

KURT WITTMAYER
8190 Wolfratshausen/Obb., Obermarkt 8, West Germany

With Wittmayer we come to the last of the big German production shops, and the one most reluctant to part with any information. A questionnaire was returned to me by Wittmayer showing only his recently instituted copies of classical instruments and omitting any of his standard production models, which comprise the bulk of his output. At the bottom of the questionnaire Wittmayer appended the following note: *Unsere Serien Modelle möchten wir in einem solchen Buch nicht angeführt haben, weil sie nicht dem Ideal Klangcharakter entsprechen.* (We do not wish our Serien models mentioned in such a book, because their sound characteristics do not correspond to the ideal.)

Perhaps Wittmayer's concern about being dissociated from his production models reflects a new tendency in Germany to take classical models more seriously. Wittmayer has now gotten a former restorer from the Berlin collection (perhaps even the very Friedrich Ernst whom we have encountered in these pages) to supervise the construction of his historical models. Unfortunately I have not seen any of these, although Wittmayer claims to have made four hundred of them.

The production models, of which Wittmayer makes an estimated four hundred yearly, have most of the features of the typical *Serien* instrument but add an unfortunate touch of his own. This is a complicated jack which is described in a catalogue of Wittmayer's California agent (The Baroque Instrument Company, 3101 Summit Road, San Bruno, California) as a "Wittmayer invention," giving his harpsichords "the most satisfactory performance of any harpsichord." This Wittmayer invention, which is a Maendler invention, consists of a spring rising upward from the bottom of the jack, to keep the jack from either sticking or having too much play in its slide slot. In practice the spring adds a complicating factor. If the spring bulges out too much, it may prevent the jack from returning, and if it is too flat it won't do its job of pushing the jack to one side. Springs also get caught under strings upon removal of the jacks and often get so hopelessly bent that they are clipped off, thus producing the wobbly jack that Wittmayer went to so much trouble to prevent. Wittmayer's springs are bent in at the top, making string entanglement less likely.

A second type of jack used on the smaller instruments has a little hook on the tongue which holds a looped spring which serves both as a tongue spring and to keep the jack to one side of its slot. In order to remove a jack, the loop has to be disengaged from its hook. This feature, coupled with the thin threaded end pin which fits directly into a hole in the key itself rather than a lower guide, can have some pretty unfortunate results. If a key sticks and there is no room to lift out the individual key, each single jack must be disengaged carefully from its loop and pulled out in order to allow removal of the keyboard. To fix one sticking key is thus a good hour's work, and if one finds, at the very end of the job, a second sticking key, the temptation is great never to confront a Wittmayer again.

The tone of the Wittmayer is no better and no worse than that of the typical *Serien* instrument. The big Bach model has the usual disappointing lack of volume and heavy tone, and cannot be heard above an ensemble in a large hall. This peculiarity of German production instruments led a Berlin Steinway representative to develop a magnetic amplification system for harpsichords and clavichords. (The Berlin Steinway branch handles Wittmayers.)

Rolf Drescher, the Steinway man, had been interested in harpsichords for years. He noted that the instruments were usually drowned out in concert and decided to do something to make the harpsichord more useful in the concert hall. Drescher proceeded to develop a complex system of magnetic pickups poised above the strings, demanding all-steel music wire throughout the instrument. The speaker was built right into the soundboard. The amplification resulted in a faithful reproduction of the sound of a plucked string, but, as Skowroneck points out, the sound of the string itself is only one aspect of a harpsichord tone—there is still the soundboard structure and case, producing the timbre. In that sense, a microphone placed under the instrument or above the soundboard would have a better chance to pick up the whole tone rather than the string tone only.

Drescher built his amplification into two Wittmayer Bach models, both of which were unveiled in an astonishing concert by the Berlin Philharmonic in Carnegie Hall, New York. Herbert von Karajan imported the two ampli-

Wittmayer jacks. Wood bodies and tongues, delrin plectra, adjustable damper on metal clip. Top adjustment is by eccentric screw. The end pins with nuts insert into key levers. Left jack has its own tongue spring and also a wire spring on the face of the jack to keep it aligned in slide. Right jack has hook on tongue for spring which also serves to pull jack to one side of the jack-slide slot.

fied Bach models, weighing a total of over 1500 lbs., to use them as continuo instruments in a Bach clavier concerto—in which the solo part was taken by a piano. Any small but lively single harpsichord would have comfortably replaced these two machines, but von Karajan conducted from one of them (in the baroque style) playing a few chords now and then when his arms were not engaged in beating time; the rest of the time a poor performer, playing second harpsichord to the conductor and completely obscured by the orchestra, picked up the threads dropped by von Karajan. All this time the solo piano contributed a foreign sound which mixed uneasily with the continuo. I am pleased to report that all the New York music critics derided this ludicrous performance. But one of the two amplified Bach models has subsequently been sold to the Indianapolis Symphony.

On the occasion of the New York debut of his amplified harpsichords, Wittmayer made a quick trip to New York, prodded by Rolf Drescher who was trying to convince him that a small revolution in the harpsichord field had taken place in America. I hope Wittmayer took more back with him to Germany than he left behind in America—a pair of pants and some shoes which I am storing in my shop. He has been in business for twenty years and is not at the stage in life in which changes are easily accomplished.

A small scandal was precipitated when a Munich harpsichordist named Dr. W. Schroeder wrote an article in *Das Musikinstrument* (issue No. 7, July 1968) in which he quoted a critic attending the 1967 Salzburg Easter festival calling an amplified harpsichord (presumably the Wittmayer) a *transistorisierte Scheusslichkeit* (transistorized monstrosity). Wittmayer is reported to have appeared at the editorial offices of the magazine and demanded a retraction, as well as threatening to cancel his advertising.

The point made by Dr. Schroeder, however, was well taken. While granting the factory harpsichord a "rustling" tone which surprises a nearby listener with its fullness, Schroeder points out that this tone quickly dies as it travels outward, unlike the tone of a good violin which actually increases in its travel. Instead of following the principles of the violin and lute soundbox construction, the modern harpsichord builders have gone in the opposite direction, trying to make up electronically what they cannot achieve intrinsically.

Schroeder relates having visited the U.S. with his instruments, proud of his German factory harpsichords, only to be rudely awakened from his *Dornröschenschlaf* (Sleeping Beauty oblivion) when an American instrument shared the stage with his own harpsichord. "Everyone, especially the producers and defenders of the rigid case construction, should have a chance to hear such a confrontation," Schroeder wrote. He went on to relate how he bought a Hubbard kit and was able, as a layman, to build an instrument which was superior to the professionally built factory harpsichords. "And yet," Schroeder pointed out, "this is so simple to explain: the Americans went back to the sources, while the Germans went to the piano for instruction."

Wittmayer's historical copies are considerably more expensive than the corresponding production models, yet there is (or should be) much less material in them. The price may be influenced by a separate process for making keyboards, jacks, cases, etc., using fairly rare and expensive woods like pear, cedar and cypress. Like Neupert and Sperrhake, Wittmayer is worried

Action of a Wittmayer "Bach" model with magnetic pickups and woofers and tweeters built into the soundboard.

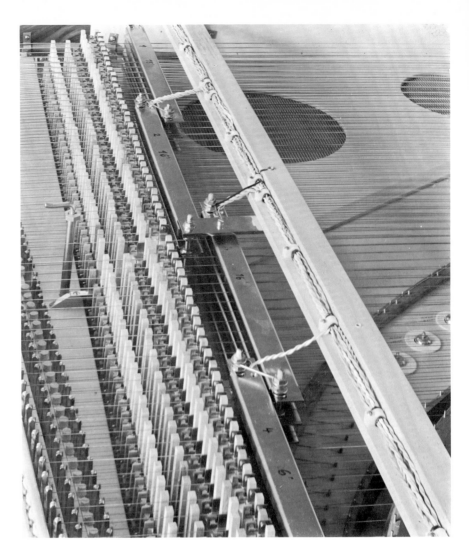

by the increasingly knowledgeable harpsichord public, but Wittmayer, at any rate, seems to be trying for a share of the more educated market.

PRODUCTION INSTRUMENTS BY WITTMAYER

1. Portable clavichord: C–d3; single strung; 41½ × 14 in., 39½ lbs.
2. Clavichord "Salzburg": C–f3; double strung; 49½ × 16½, 79 lbs.
3. Portable spinet: 1 × 8'; 45 in. long, 61 lbs.
4. Italian spinet: C–f3; 1 × 8', buff; 59½ in. long, 83 lbs.
5. Harpsichord "Klein-Cembalo": C–d3; 1 × 8', 1 × 4', buff; 51 × 32 in., 99 lbs. Knee lever on 4'.
6. Harpsichord "Christofori" /sic/: C–f3; 1 × 8', 1 × 4', buff; 78 × 36 in., 162 lbs. Knee lever on 4'.
7. Double manual harpsichord "Scarlatti": C–f3 2 × 8', 1 × 4', buff; 67 × 40½ in., 217 lbs.
8. Double manual harpsichord "Chambonnières": FF–f3; 2 × 8', 1 × 4', buff on both 8's; 92 × 45½ in., 343 lbs. Coupler, four pedals.
9. Double manual harpsichord "Frescobaldi": AA–f3; upper manual 1 × 8', 1 × 4'; lower manual 1 × 8', 1 × 16', buff on 8' and 16'; 83 × 42 in., 360 lbs.
10. Double manual harpsichord "Monteverdi": FF–f3; upper manual 1 × 8', 1 × 4'; lower manual 1 × 8', 1 × 16', buff on 8' and 16'; 90 × 45½ in., 389 lbs. Five pedals.
11. Double manual harpsichord "Bach": FF–f3; upper manual 1 × 8', 1 × 4'; lower manual 1 × 8', 1 × 16', buff on 8' and 16'; 107 × 45½ in., 409 lbs. Five pedals.

HISTORICAL COPIES BY WITTMAYER *(all jacks quilled with condor)*

1. Virginal, after Ruckers 1604: C–c3; short octave; length 56 in.
2. Polygonal spinet, after Pisaurensis 1540: C–f3; short octave; length 62 in.
3. Italian harpsichord: BB–f3; 2 × 8'; length 88½ in.
4. Double manual harpsichord in the Flemish style: FF–f3; 2 × 8', 1 × 4'; length 95 in.
5. Double manual harpsichord in the English style after Kirckman (with four rows of jacks): FF–f3; 2 × 8', 1 × 4', lute course; length 94½ in.

198

GEORG ZAHL
8033 Planegg/bei München, West Germany

Although Zahl has been working on harpsichords since he was 14 years old, he has had his own shop only since 1965. Prior to that, the 37-year-old maker worked for Sassmann.

I had heard in Germany that Zahl was one of the small number of new makers working in the historical tradition, but a glance at his brochure reveals such model names as Hubert, Silbermann, Kleinod, Schütz, and Bach, all of which can be found in the brochures of the production makers. In addition, the Schütz and Bach models have the "Bach" registration, with the 4′ in the upper manual.

On the other hand, we also find Ruckers, Taskin, and Kirckman models, which appear to be related to the makers with whose names they are associated. Zahl has made a total of ninety instruments and now has a staff of five coworkers producing an average of twenty to thirty instruments yearly. He is currently at work on 5 doubles, 8 singles, 7 spinets and 2 clavichords.

ZUCKERMANN HARPSICHORDS INC.
115 Christopher Street, New York, New York 10014

The reader is likely to be disappointed by this account of my own work. I have never made a two-manual instrument, having always been primarily interested in efficient and economical production of small instruments; and secondly, my instruments are not close copies of the traditional historical instrument so often lauded in these pages.

I became interested in harpsichords in 1954, largely through playing the cello in baroque chamber groups. Having worked as a piano technician, I built a harpsichord after looking at an old Italian and a modern Dolmetsch harpsichord. For my first harpsichord, I made my own keys and jacks, but for the sake of cabinet simplicity I straightened the bentside, eliminating the curve. When the instrument was done I decided to make another one, and I put a two-line classified ad in the New York *Times*, which brought an overwhelming

A group of Zahl instruments on display. At the left is the "Silbermann" spinet, in the center the "Ruckers" harpsichord and a pedal harpsichord, at the right the "Kleinod."

199

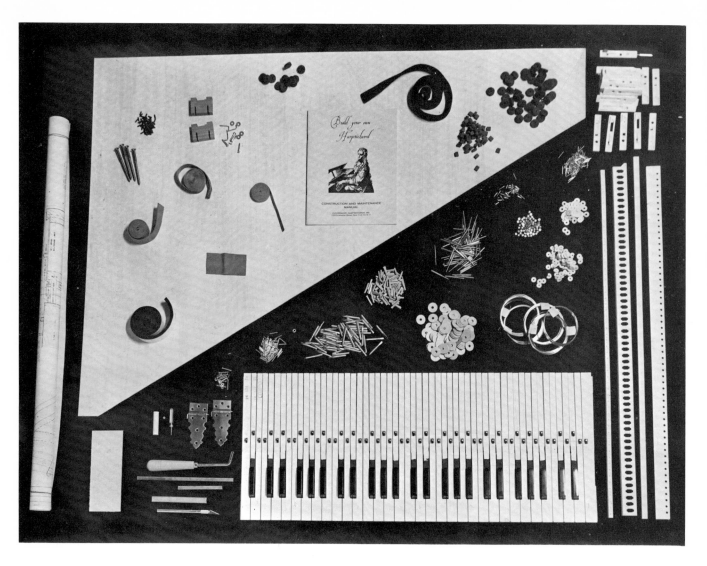

The Zuckermann harpsichord. Add eighty to one hundred hours of work and a few hand tools. Shown here are the basic kit, and the cabinet parts of carefully matched and mitered pre-cut walnut plywood which makes up the outer case. Overleaf are shown the bridge and pin block which can also be ordered.

response. In those days there weren't many people making harpsichords and I received five orders and a lot of visitors, including harpsichordist Sylvia Marlowe.

During the next few years I worked by myself, turning out about 12 instruments yearly. I had the keyboards made by a large American piano action shop, but continued to turn out wooden jacks myself. In 1958 my shop went up in flames, destroying all my equipment and five nearly completed harpsichords, of which one was destined for Columbia University and another for the captain of the U.S. Equestrian Team. The fire, although disastrous, made the New York *Times* which patiently explained to its readers what a harpsichord was and how it works. With the resulting publicity and further orders, I took a new workshop, hired an old-time cabinet maker who had been a neighbor, and started the painful process of assembling tools and jigs all over again.

By 1960 we were in full production and had made some 60 or 70 instruments. I began to calculate the number of service calls I would have to make if I had only 180 instruments out in the world and if their owners only called me twice a year for tuning and adjustment. That would come to a call every single day, or rather evening, since I was too busy to leave the shop during the day. With this gloomy prognosis I began to think of other possibilities.

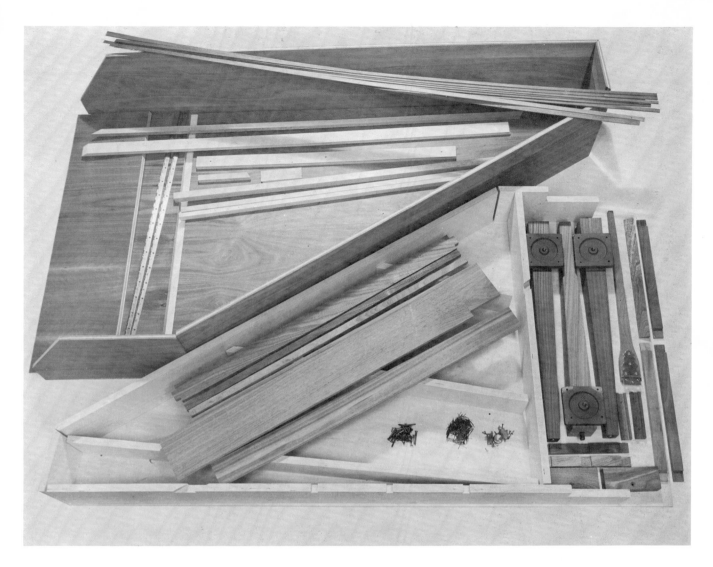

Realizing that most people approach a harpsichord with caution, the way they do a vicious dog, I decided that the only way they might lose their fear of harpsichord maintenance was to go through the process of building the instrument for themselves.

Several friends had already asked me for parts and instructions to make their own instruments; in most cases they wanted to save the price of a finished harpsichord; but some actually looked forward to the kind of meaningful experience associated with building an instrument. Out of this came the first "kit," the price of which I almost arbitrarily set at $150. This price (for the basic kit) has remained the same over the years; increasing mass production and simplification of design have offset the steadily rising costs of materials.

The most popular kit harpsichord is an instrument 62 × 35 in., with 57 keys, AA–f³; there is one set of strings in 8′ pitch, a buff and a half stop. The construction consists of a bottom, braces and inner case which makes a complete unit, to which the outer case shell is glued. The reason for the inner and outer case is mainly its ease of construction. Even if the inner case is botched up, one can still make a neat job by fitting the boards of the outer case carefully around the inner structure.

The components of this harpsichord are: (a) the inner and outer cabinets; (b) the soundboard, bridge and ribs; (c) the pinblock, nut and stops; (d) the

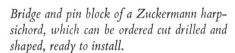

The Zuckermann harpsichord again, after all the pieces are put together.

Bridge and pin block of a Zuckermann harpsichord, which can be ordered cut drilled and shaped, ready to install.

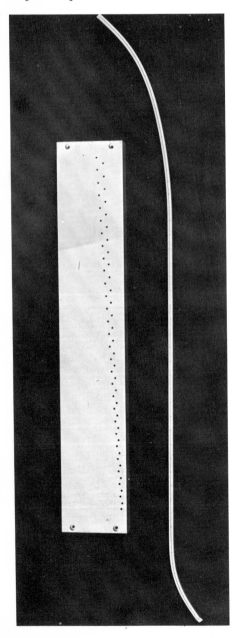

keyboard; (e) the strings, pins, felts, etc.; (f) the slide and guide; and (g) the jacks. Let us briefly consider the manufacture, supply and potential trouble spots of each of these components, so that we may get a glimpse into the problems facing the makers.

A. *The cabinets.* The inner case is made of $3/4$-in., 13-layered Finnish birch plywood; the outer case is cut from $1/2$-in. plywood with walnut veneers on both sides. There are between 30 and 40 pieces in the two cabinets, and the idea of cutting and mitering some 3,500 pieces (100 kits) monthly in a relatively small shop was out of the question. Through a friend in Philadelphia I was introduced to a giant woodworking plant, covering several city blocks, with automatic-feed circular saws, gang drills (14 drill presses coming down automatically at the same time) and gang combinations of automatic saws and drills which can cut a piece to size, miter it and drill it on several sides, all in one operation.

Now it is obvious that no harpsichord maker, even one with a large production, can afford machines of this kind, which must be kept constantly busy to earn their keep. The management of the Philadelphia plant, dubious at first about taking on the harpsichord project (they specialize in displays), found the work to their liking because it involved repeated runs at regular intervals which did not require new designs or jigs. (Continually changing designs are considerably more costly and wasteful than a constant production.)

The key to the quality of production work is the presence of one or two really experienced and careful shop foremen, whose task it is to set up the

The Zuckermann clavichord after the kit has been assembled.

machines. Many of the machines are almost fully automatic and require no great skill of operation, but the setting up of jigs, tools, saw fences, blades, etc., is absolutely critical. It is at this stage that careful miters, cleanly cut saw edges and correct drill spacing are determined. In Philadelphia, the shop foremen are old, European craftsmen. When they are gone, the questions of successors will loom large.

The plant can handle a run of 300 units in a couple of days, including wrapping and packaging all the wooden parts plus accompanying hardware in large flat corrugated boxes, and marking and storing them ready for immediate shipment. Provided the parts are properly designed and the machines are carefully set up, these production runs on the cabinets are capable of turning out a very high quality product.

B. *The soundboard, bridge and ribs.* With these parts we move to an area of the harpsichord more resistant to mass production. At the quantities we supply, and for purposes of home construction, we had to make a decision many years ago to provide a laminated board rather than a lumber soundboard. The lumber board would have had to be joined of 3 or 4 strips, entailing a complex process either on our or the kit builder's part. We would have also faced the problems of cracking, shrinking and warping boards. Looking around for a suitable commercial $1/8$ in. softwood plywood, the only choice seemed to be Italian poplar. This material, manufactured in Italy, turned out to be full of blemishes, skipped inner layers, and badly matched surfaces. In addition it was not very stable and would expand during humid weather to

The jig for bending Zuckermann bridges.

203

The inner case of a Zuckermann harpsichord, ready for the soundboard and pin block to be installed.

such an extent that the board would bulge up to touch the strings, causing a buzz. We first decided to cope with this by letting the grain run crosswise (spine to slanted side) thus providing much more strength, since two of the three layers did not have a long unsupported run from belly rail to tail.

Shortly after this (and after many complaints) we switched to 3-ply basswood $^1/_8$ in. thick, which is not commercially available but had to be made up specially in a New England plant. It meant that a minimum of 300 sheets (each making two boards) had to be ordered at one time, with a waiting period of four months and at a much greater cost. But the boards were clean, even and stable, and have given no further trouble.

The bridges were originally cut on a bandsaw from a flat piece of solid maple, but we soon abandoned this time-consuming process which often resulted in bridges broken during shipment because of weak cross grain in the curve of the bridges. We next made a bending form intended for three pieces of solid $^1/_8$-in. maple wide enough to cut out about six bridges. The three pieces of maple were covered with glue and clamped into the form, resulting in one piece $^3/_8$ in. thick, some 4 in. wide and in the right shape for bridges. This was then cut into six or seven $^1/_2$-in. strips, and these were drilled and "crowned." At first we found that bridges would change their outlines after they were cut apart, but we dealt with this by letting the bridges lie around until they had assumed their final shape before inserting them in the drill jig. There was then enough leeway to line them up in the jig so that the holes could come into the proper position in the bridge outline.

Many years ago we switched from ribbing straight across to the classical system of a cut-off bar and three smaller ribs parallel to the spine. On plywood boards this is especially safe, since the board does not need the support of crossing ribs. Lately we have experimented with lightening and thinning the soundboards at their edges and the results suggest that this practice improves the tone.

C. *The pinblock, nut and stops.* We have always used solid maple for pinblocks, but lately lumber has been expensive and of poor quality. Many blocks show hairline cracks after they are processed, forcing us to discard them. We are now experimenting with the laminated pinblocks used in the piano industry and by many harpsichord makers. They are cheaper than solid maple blocks, presumably free of cracks, and perhaps stronger.

The nut is a straight maple piece which causes no problem except for the fact that it must be drilled accurately, since the nut determines string spacing to a large extent. The price of brass for hand stops almost doubled in recent years.

D. *The keyboard.* Most harpsichord builders who make their own keyboards cut them out on a band saw. They mark the pattern of the keyboard, often by silkscreening, on a glued-up piece the size of the keyboard; then the pin holes are drilled and marked on the key frame before keys are cut apart. This process is time consuming and takes considerable skill. In the large piano action factories, the wood for the keyboard is pushed through two gang band saws, spaced to correspond with the backs and fronts of keys. A factory keyboard can thus be made to sell for about $25 even at today's inflated prices.

The American keyboard factories will not consider altering their manufacturing processes to make the two modifications most common in harpsichord keyboards; one is the narrower lateral spacing and the other is a covering of naturals with ebony, boxwood or some other hardwood, and sharps with ivory.

The difference in lateral spacing from $6^1/_4$ in. (C-B) for the French keyboard to just under $6^1/_2$ in. (C-B) for the modern piano keys (derived from the English harpsichords) is only about $^3/_{16}$ in. to the octave. An Italian keyboard which came through my shop had an octave span of a full $6^1/_2$ in., so the contention that the narrow spacing is "correct" for harpsichords doesn't hold water. However, more than half of the modern harpsichord makers use narrow keyboards, especially since German keyboard factories supply the narrow spacing. For the player switching from piano or organ to harpsichord, the wider modern spacing is perhaps more practical, but a player adapts quite easily to either spacing. We are neither set up to make our own keyboards in quantity, nor wish to depend on the uncertain supply of imported keyboards, which are also considerably more expensive by the time customs duty and shipping are considered.

As for the keyboard covering, we have already encountered the three traditions: English and Flemish, white (ivory or bone) naturals and ebony sharps; French, ebony naturals and ivory topped sharps; and Italian, boxwood naturals and ebony sharps. The German keyboard makers will accommodate the harpsichord makers by covering keys with material of the makers choice; the American factories glue the covering in sheet form on the keyboard before cutting, and will not consider wooden coverings which have to be laid on in pieces. We therefore supply uncovered keys and separate wooden

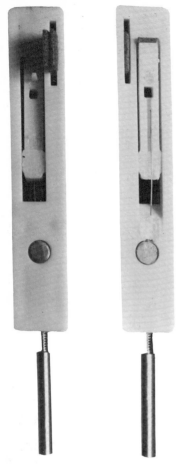

Zuckermann jacks: plastic with wire spring, lead weight, felt damper, and provision for either delrin (or quill) or leather plectrum.

key covers to those customers wishing to have a wood-covered keyboard. There is no "correct" harpsichord keyboard. It should be pointed out, of course, that all piano keys are thick (almost 1 in.) and heavily bushed and that the ideal harpsichord key is only half that thickness and unbushed, since it has to perform a much lighter duty than a piano key.

E. *The strings, felts, pins, etc.* These parts are, on the whole, available from piano supply houses, although we have located many cheaper sources of supply. Most harpsichord makers use zither pins for harpsichord tuning pins, piano center pins for bridge pins, and piano bridge pins for hitchpins. We buy key leads from a lead supply house, and felts from a felt supply house, both at lower prices than piano supply houses charge. We buy music wire from wire houses, though piano suppliers stock harpsichord sizes. (Skowroneck, Schütze, Rutkowski and others are now experimenting with spring-less music wire to approximate the wire which was used on the old harpsichords.) We are using tinplated wire to prevent rusting. This has to be approached with caution because the plating process may weaken the wire, but we have had no trouble, and the lack of corrosion helps to prevent jack hangers, caused when a plectrum sticks on a rusty string. In the bass we use solid brass wire, though many builders have gone to phosphor bronze. We do not use covered strings (copper winding on steel core) although our last three bass notes could undoubtedly benefit from their use. However, it is difficult to get good covered strings made. The core must be square or at least filed flat so that the winding will stay put. Any slippage of the winding will "kill" the tone completely— commercially produced strings are often useless for harpsichords.

F. *The slide and guide.* These pieces represent the heart of the instrument and must be spaced and dimensioned correctly with respect to the rest of the action. We started out by punching aluminum channel with a foot-operated punch press. The shape of the slide slot which admits the jack is generally rectangular to match the jack, with a cutout to allow for the tongue's backward swing.

The slots punched into the aluminum turned out to have abrasive edges which would roughen up the wooden jacks we were then using, causing a noisy action. We then changed to punching $1/16$-in. Finnish plywood strips, mounting them on a frame consisting of two wooden runners and end blocks. In order to provide a close fit from slot to jack, we made the slot slightly under-sized and allowed the kit builder to file the slot to fit. The system did not work out very well, since kit builders would vigorously ram a file into the slot and widen it so much that it allowed the jack too much play. With wooden jacks some play was necessary to allow for expansion in humid weather, but with the advent of plastic jacks the slot could be a close fit.

We next had a die made and had brass sections punched, each of which contained 12 jack slots. The advantage of these 5 adjustable sections mounted on the frame (see photo) is that an overall string spacing error can be corrected. One of the most frequent complaints among kit builders was the lack of correspondence between slide and string spacing, and the adjustable slide sections enabled the builder to correct overall spacing errors. We are still using this system and find it basically satisfactory.

The guide is also made from the $1/16$-in. Finnish plywood. We are now experimenting with punched out plastic guide rails, set directly into a rabbet in the belly rail.

G. *The jacks.* Our first jacks were made by the same American firm supplying our keyboards, but they were not particularly well made. We next got jacks in Germany, but uncertain supply, and duty and shipping costs, drove us to set up jack making in our own shop. We soon found that we had to stop everything else to get enough jacks together to supply the kits (we use almost 100,000 jacks yearly) and the next logical step was to go to plastic.

We decided on high impact styrene mixed with a rubberizer which took the brittleness out of the plastic and allowed screws to make their own threads easily. Next we had a single-cavity mould made which turned out one jack body and one tongue with each injection. For those who think of all machines working completely automatically, operated by an attendant with a pushbutton, it may come as a surprise that we struggled with this mould for three years. No lot of jacks looked exactly alike. The thin mould pins around which the material flowed, and which upon retraction would provide the holes for the tongue axle pin, would often bend under the pressure of material injected into the mould, thus leaving crooked holes. If the injection pressure was lessened the jacks would come out looking ragged and irregular and would vary in size.

In the end we had to discard our first mould altogether and go to the expense of a new mould which was designed much more efficiently (I was forced to learn about injection moulding to help with the design). The jacks from the new mould have been coming out to standard specifications. In the new mould we decided to provide the tongue with both a square hole for leather and a slit for delrin, giving the builder a choice between the materials.

The biggest flaw in the kits has been the inability of many builders to do a proper voicing job. Many people would make elaborate and beautiful cabinets, only to be defeated by the complexities of the jack and plectra. We are now supplying delrin already stamped out in the right plectrum shape and needing only some fine cutting at the tip. This has greatly reduced the number of builders who end up with balky or unplayable actions.

The reasons for the popularity of harpsichord kits are the same as those for the popularity of the harpsichord itself, with two additions: that kits are cheaper; and that kits provide a meaningful activity to many people whose own work lacks such meaning.

The variety of people who buy harpsichord kits is astonishing. Some buy kits because they are home craftsmen looking for a project; some live in dormitories or hotel rooms and want an instrument for practice. High school kids who are fascinated by baroque music, and retired pensioners who want to fill out their time with constructive work, buy kits. Nuns, organists, housewives, and convicts put harpsichords together. Doctors, rock musicians, executives, missionaries, foreign ambassadors, army captains, Wall Street lawyers, Broadway stars, riders and writers construct their own instruments. Families, college and high school classes, and orchestras make group projects out of the kit construction. The do-it-yourself kit builders range in age from 12 to 80, are men, women and children, and whites and blacks. There seems to be no limit to the variety of kit customers.

Treble end of a Zuckermann 2 × 8′ instrument, showing two nuts, buff stop on one set of strings, jack slide control and capstans. (On this instrument, rear jack slide is controlled from under the pin block.)

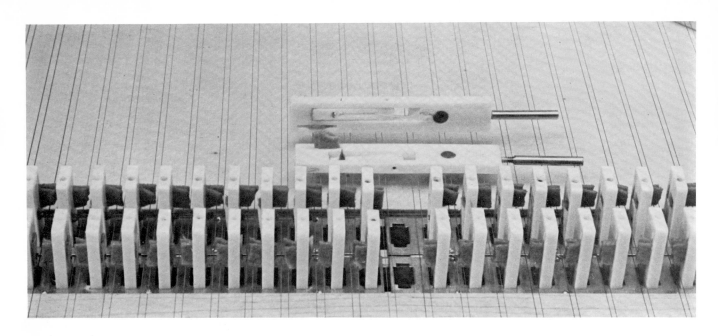

Jacks and jack slides in the gap of a Zuckermann harpsichord.

Once a 300-pound truck driver walked into the shop, sat down, rattled off a Bach invention, and pulled out the cash to buy a kit, all in dollar bills. A 13-year-old boy appeared with the contents of a piggy bank. An old lady bought a kit for her son in Israel; a soldier took a clavichord to Vietnam; a famous playwright bought an instrument for his summer home.

A prison warden once wrote us that a convict had made a harpsichord while serving time for murder. Another kit customer, building a clavichord, wrote us for help in the final stages. When we asked him to bring the instrument into the shop, he wrote that he was not allowed to leave the premises. I finally found time to call on him and found him in a state mental institution. I worked on the premises for two or three hours surrounded by the inmates who regarded me as a new arrival.

I have found doctors, lawyers and architects for my personal use among the kit builders. When I needed a surgeon for a recent operation I chose from

A missionary in the Philippines relaxes with
cigar and bottle and two monkeys at his
Zuckermann harpsichord.

The ingenuity of Zuckermann builders is infinite, and not even the straight bentside is left unchanged. Here are two more examples of instruments built from Zuckermann kits.

among a number of doctor-kit-builders by looking at their harpsichords. The man I picked on the basis of his neat work turned out to perform a flawless operation. The publisher of this book is a kit builder who has made a clavichord and a 2 × 8′ harpsichord.

Not less astounding than the variety of kit builders is the lengthy correspondence they engage in. One mid-western doctor wrote us: "I hope your brochure explains how dextrous and intelligent I have to be to finish the project (and how stupid I have to be to start it). I once built a catamaran from a kit in nine and a half months, just fourteen days beyond the period of gestation in the human. The brochure claimed that 28 hours, a hammer, a screwdriver, and average manual dexterity were all that was necessary to complete the project." The doctor wrote us enough rambling 10-page letters to make an entertaining book. Others write letters in Old English script and eighteenth-century sentence structure. Still another correspondent writes us in Pennsylvania Dutch only, calling the harpsichord a *Tinkelbochs*.

Not all the letters are friendly. One starts off: "First of all I have to say, that I wish, I would never have the idea, to get a H. kit from you." Another correspondent asked for a "two-manure" harpsichord. We recently received a letter in which the writer has "nothing but contempt for your company." He had a great deal of trouble with the transport of his kit, and blamed us for his shipping problems.

With a weekly shipping schedule of at least 25 kits both from New York and Philadelphia, we are beset by shipping woes. The nearly bankrupt Railway Express Company is the only carrier who will deliver across the U.S. to private homes, but it is constantly delaying shipments, delivering to wrong addresses or losing kits. It is true that the shipping instructions we get sometimes invite disaster. We wonder, for example, whether the shipper was able to deliver a kit with the message "Leave package with C. H. Taylor near center of town." The trucker who was instructed as follows: "Doorbell is broken, so ring any bell to get in, then go to third floor and *knock* (that bell's also out of

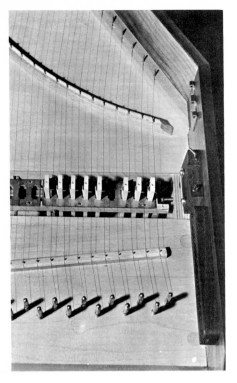

The brass-topped jackslide, one of the recent improvements in the Zuckermann kit harpsichords.

order)" may or may not have made his delivery. And one can certainly have doubts about the patience of the shipper whose instructions read "If no answer, or door is answered by elderly lady speaking no English, trucker should go to lawn on left side of house and yell *loudly* into the garden way at back. Someone will be there."

The U.S. Post Office is only slightly superior to Railway Express, but they employ a "fragile jumper" whose presence makes the transport of any long, thin article extremely risky. The jumper's task is to stomp on any fragile package, and a nut or bridge invariably arrives in two pieces unless reinforced with a hardwood or a steel bar. In view of all this, the miracle of the kit business is not that so many kits are sold, but that so many get to the customer, are put together by him and actually end up being played and greatly cherished.

We don't know how many kits never get finished since we rarely hear about them, but an unfinished kit is often sold, traded or given away, and we frequently get the new owner's request for replacement parts. A voice from the grave reached us recently when the brother of a deceased kit builder wrote to ask about squeaking jacks, one of the last concerns of his dying brother.

Tuning remains a problem for a certain percentage of builders, in spite of our (necessarily complex) tuning instructions and tuning aids like chromatic pitchpipes, chromatic sets of forks and the visually oriented Strobotuner. We are now considering issuing a tuning record with chromatic organ tones which may alleviate the problem somewhat.

A great deal of the success of a kit builder depends on his ability to read and understand what he is reading, and this is by no means a common phenomenon in our McLuhanesque and vertically oriented culture.

At present our staff consists of a secretary-demonstrator, a production manager, a cabinet maker and his helper, a kit supplies manager (my brother), three assemblers and a packer, a total of 10 including myself. With our present space, equipment and work routine, it would hardly be feasible to expand the work force. We have made a total of 210 finished instruments but have given them up long ago in favor of kits, of which we have now sold some 10,000.

The future of the kit business is, of course, tied to the future of harpsichords in general. Barring any unforseen developments (like mushroom clouds) harpsichords show every evidence of remaining with us for some time to come. We have fairly accurate figures about the effectiveness of various advertising media, and by extension, about the kind of people harpsichords appeal to. Television is worthless; the number of times I have been on national TV (once on the 7 p.m. NBC newscast) have brought nothing but crank letters, considerably less amusing than those of our own cranky customers. Radio, even FM, is only slightly better.

The general circulation magazines like *Life* and *Look* would elicit a response from one out of 100,000 readers, and only one order out of perhaps 100 responders. For that reason we would reject even a free full page in *Life*, since it would cost us considerably more in brochures and postage than the couple of orders it may bring would be worth. Harpsichord people are, in any case, not oriented toward full or half page advertising. They need not be convinced or exhorted—just given the facts, which can be done with a tiny notice.

With the literate magazines like the *New Yorker* and *Saturday Review* the response goes up to as high as one out of 10,000 readers, with one order from some 25 responders. In every college and university town there are twice, three and even four times as many kits as in non-college communities.

With the increasing use of the harpsichord in popular music it is possible that this instrument will broaden its popular base and make its appeal more directly to the masses. The emergence of harpsichord kits has certainly brought the instrument within the reach of a much broader segment of the population. But there is, and always has been, something precious, rare and exclusive about the instrument which no amount of kit or mass production can, or should, do away with.

INSTRUMENTS BY ZUCKERMANN HARPSICHORDS

1. Clavichord: C–f3; single strung; 48 × 16 in., 60 lbs.
2. Spinet: C–d3; 1 × 8′, buff; 49 in. wide, 68 lbs.
3. Harpsichord: AA–f3; 1 × 8, buff and half stops; 62 × 35 in., 130 lbs.
4. Harpsichord: as above, 2 × 8′, buff on both 8's.
5. Harpsichord: as above, 1 × 8′, 1 × 4′, buff on 8′.

In summarizing our discussion of the modern harpsichord and its makers, we may draw the following firm conclusions:

1. Instrument makers of the past rarely produced harpsichords which were not elegant and extremely handsome in appearance; they had a sure flair for the aesthetically proper shape. Modern makers trying for the physically beautiful appearance of which the harpsichord is so easily capable should study and copy historic models in this regard.

2. The old instruments have a tone infinitely superior to that of most modern makes. The reason for this does not lie in some lost secret of the craft, but in many quite obvious practices related to instrument construction. Harpsichord strings, unlike the strings of a piano which are made to vibrate with a forceful blow, require a light soundboard, bridge, and case construction to get a live response from the instrument. It is instructive to place a hammer or heavy object on a harpsichord bridge and note the spectacular deterioration of the tone; thick cases, ribbing under the bridge, heavy, rigid, and untapered soundboards, fat bridges, excessive string bearing on the bridge, and the addition of heavy 16′ strings to an 8′ bridge—all of them associated with many modern harpsichords—contribute to the "hammer-on-bridge" effect.

3. There is now no excuse on the part of harpsichord makers and players to pretend ignorance of old building practices and tonal characteristics; there are enough good old instruments in playing condition, in private hands and collections all over the world, to give the modern maker a clear idea of the tone to strive for. Further, we now have three excellent and thorough books, the works of Messrs. Russell, Boalch, and Hubbard, to teach the builder almost all he needs to know about old harpsichords.

4. The addition of heavy frame members, metal plates, thick cases, and elaborate action adjustment mechanisms does *not* make the modern instrument notably more stable or more reliable than its historic predecessor. The weakest links in the chain of factors bearing on harpsichord stability and reliability are the light strings, the thin soundboards (if any tone at all is to be achieved), the plucking action, and the return of the jack by gravity.

No matter how strong the other links in this chain are, it is going to break at its weakest points. Complex adjustments in the action set up a "cycle of complexity" in which each adjustment requires a further adjustment. A mechanical object almost always works best in its most simple form, and action reliability can be achieved not by making the jack more complex and adjustable, but by eliminating the need for most adjustments through careful choice of materials and workmanship in the action parts.

5. The most successful departure from old building practices concerns the use of plastic in harpsichord jacks and plectra. Plastic, which is both revered and despised by modern man, works extremely well if used intelligently and in the right places. Plastic has the right smoothness, durability, imperviousness to moisture, and most importantly, the capacity for being turned out cheaply in quantity, to make it eminently suitable for jacks.

6. The use of plywood in casework and soundboards has not been sufficiently tested to draw any firm conclusions.

7. The best looking, sounding, and working modern harpsichords are made (with one or two exceptions) in the United States.

8. The best harpsichords in America, again with a few notable exceptions, are associated with the "Boston School," the workshops of Frank Hubbard, William Dowd, and their apprentices.

9. Testimonials by harpsichordists, given in a moment of enthusiasm and frozen on paper forever, are not very useful in guiding the prospective buyer. The player may have changed his mind, his instrument, or his profession years ago; he may never have owned the subject of his testimonial but played on it only once (after careful preparation by a technician) because no other harpsichord was avilable.

10. Negative testimonials, on the other hand, are instructive. American harpsichordists travelling in Europe without their own reliable instruments report European harpsichords in the most shocking conditions. Igor Kipnis, who owns an excellent American instrument made by Rutkowski and Robinette describes a European trip during which he found it almost impossible to locate harpsichords in acceptable playing condition. He reports instruments by Neupert, Sperrhake, and Scholz, used by radio stations and therefore presumably serviced regularly, with only one or two of four sets of jacks working at all, and the sound was invariably dull and insufficient for recital use. English harpsichords fare no better with American performers; according to Kipnis, the best instrument in London is a Dowd. An American accompanist, who travelled in the U.S. with the flutist Jean Pierre Rampal, reports that 75 percent of the Sperrhakes, Wittmayers and Neuperts furnished by local colleges and communities are unplayable, not working properly or useless for recitals. This is not an example of chauvinism on the part of American players; we have tried to show why American instruments, which are basically patterned after the old ones, and make use of new materials with discrimination and intelligence, are generally superior to their European counterparts.

11. The harpsichord is curiously resistant to mass production. This is due partly to critical building processes such as soundboard construction, and voicing and regulating techniques which do not lend themselves easily to production, and partly to the mentality of the good makers who do not wish

to exchange the work bench for the front office. In addition, the harpsichord resists conventional advertising and distribution techniques, appealing as it does to a group of extremely literate consumers shunning hard-sells and sales talks.

12. The introduction of harpsichord kits has served to educate the musical public to the peculiarities of the instrument as well as to distribute harpsichords in much greater quantity than would have been possible without them. The average kit builder has been found to make up by his enthusiasm, care, and dedication for much of the lack of professional experience—with the result that kit-built instruments are often superior to production harpsichords made by workmen who have no such dedication. In addition the kits have spawned a whole new generation of serious harpsichord makers who otherwise would not have been motivated to choose this career.

13. There can now be seen emerging a general return to the principles of classical harpsichord construction, not just in brochure prose but in the actual instrument. It is hoped that our discussion of the modern harpsichord will contribute to this development.

14. A modern builder who copies the features of historical instruments for which they are justly famous, namely physical appearance, light box construction, thin soundboards, and scaling and geometry, and adds to this a carefully

A two-manual harpsichord in the French style by Rainer Schütze, which may serve as an example of the new wind blowing in German harpsichord production. In spite of some minor criticism that can be made of Schütze's instruments, they are based on historical principles, have good lively tone, and look like harpsichords.

fitted action, consisting of plastic jacks and plectra, as well as stable and neatly executed slides and guides, can produce a harpsichord as good as a classical model in tone, and one which is much superior in action dependability, thus lifting the age-old curse that "it never works" from the harpsichord once and for all.

Harpsichord makers reputed to be working now, who did not confirm their existence:

Atlas Piano Mfg. Co.; 2576 Kandacho, Hamamatsu, Japan. (Information supplied by another harpsichord maker).

Christian Aubin; Domain de Roquecave, 46 Cénevières, France. (Information supplied by another harpsichord maker).

Gianrico Cella; Successori Brocco, San Marco 510, Venezia, Italy. (Information supplied by a harpsichord maker and a Dutch editor).

Alec Dobson; Tour de Cesare, Aix-en-Provence, France. (Information supplied by a harpsichord maker and a staff member of the Conservatoire Nationale Supèrior de Musique, Paris, France).

Wilhelm Gertz; P.O. Box 104, Vrededorp, Transvaal, South Africa.

Kanzler; Reilschulgasse 10, Graz, Austria. (Information supplied by a harpsichord maker and a staff member of the Smithsonian Institution, Washington, D.C.).

Emmo Koch; Lauenbrueck, Barbarahof, West Germany. (Information supplied by two harpsichord makers.)

W. Kroensberger; Jeruzalem Straat 20, Utrecht, Holland. (Information supplied by a Dutch editor).

Wm. H. Newman; 17053 4th N.E., Seattle, Washington 98155. (Information supplied by the International Harpsichord Society, Denver, Colorado.)

Felix Wolff; Akeshof-Knivsta, Sweden. (Information supplied by a Dutch harpsichord maker).

Chapter V

The
Well-Regulated
Harpsichord—
A Manual of
Maintenance,
Tuning
and Repair.

Two COMMON ATTITUDES on the part of harpsichord owners towards their instruments are fear and exasperation. The fearful owner will blame his instrument's malfunctioning on the weather, the room, the movers, the heating system, or just the fates, but will struggle with a nearly unplayable action without daring to look under the jack rail. The exasperated owner will blame the maker or tuner and turn every screw in the instrument at once in an effort to get it going. Neither of these approaches will do much to make the instrument playable.

Keeping in mind that the most important rule in buying a harpsichord is *caveat emptor* (let the buyer beware), the key factor in coping with it, once the instrument has been acquired, is proper *diagnosis* of the problems. A harpsichord is one of the few modern industrial products whose mechanism can be thoroughly grasped without knowledge of electronics, higher mathematics, the internal combustion engine or quantum mechanics. A harpsichord action is entirely mechanical in the old Newtonian sense, having to do with forces acting on each other, pivot points, friction, and gravity. Close observation, a little bit of knowledge, and a great deal of common sense are all that are necessary to unravel the mysteries of malfunctioning harpsichords.

When confronted with any of the typical problems—sticking keys, balky actions, sticking jacks, buzzes, ringing strings, uneven volume, small tone, and any number of others—the first rule is always to *isolate* the problem. If, for example, a note "sticks" (the way this word is commonly used it covers a multitude of sins), it is necessary to find out what it is that "sticks." This means that one single note on one single stop which shows the problem must be isolated; since each single tone is produced by the two moving parts, the key and the jack, we must further isolate the components to determine the offender. Removing the jack and playing the key alone will show up any problems with the key itself; and if there are none, we can then turn our attention carefully to the jack, again studying each possible malfunction (jack sticking in slide, jack sticking in guide, tongue sticking in jack, plectra catching on string, etc.) until we have pinpointed the origin of the problem.

To enable the reader to make the proper diagnosis of his harpsichord's malfunctions, let us now proceed to discuss the potentially troublesome areas of the harpsichord in the order of their importance: I. The jacks; II. The keyboard; III. The jack slide and lower guide; IV. The hand stop and pedal systems; V. The strings and the soundboard; and VI. The rest of the harpsichord.

I. THE JACKS

The function of the jack is to carry the plectrum past the string, thus effecting the plucked sound, and return the plectrum to its original position under the strings, ready for the next pluck, without producing another sound. Jacks ride up through downwards pressure on the front of a pivoting key, and return by gravity to rest position. Jacks can be exposed by removing the jack

A jack raised by pressing on its key is adjusted for amount of tongue projection.

rail above them, which is always easily removable; they can then be just lifted out. The following are the components of the modern harpsichord jack, their function and possible failure:

A. *The tongue.* The tongue is the central part of the jack holding the plectrum. While the jack body remains rigidly vertical, the tongue must be allowed to swivel backwards to permit the plectrum's gliding downward and around the string on its return journey after the pluck. The tongue's swivel is generally accomplished by means of an axle pin running through jack and tongue. (The Burton jack has side prongs on the tongue which fit into matching depressions in the jack, thus eliminating the axle pin, and Schütze will soon come out with an "axle-less" jack altogether.) The axle-pin hole in the tongue should be large enough to allow the tongue to swivel *freely* but not so large as to make it wobble. The tongue is returned to rest position by a spring, mounted either on the tongue itself or on the jack body.

Malfunctions of the tongue. The tongue must swivel freely enough so that it falls backwards of its own accord when jack is held horizontally (face up) and the spring is pushed out of the way. If the tongue does not swivel freely it will either cause a "hanger" by preventing the plectrum from gliding out of the string's way or, having accomplished the plectrum's backward flip, will then prevent the spring from returning the tongue and plectrum forward to rest position. In wooden jacks a tongue binding on the axle pin is a frequent occurrence. To repair this the axle pin must be pushed out carefully and the pin hole in the tongue enlarged by drilling it out. In some jacks the axle pins are relatively loose and can be pushed out with a thin nail or awl. In others it has to be hammered out, preferably by laying the jack on a metal surface with axle pin poised over a hole in the surface. Again a thin nail or brad, smaller in diameter than the pin, will make an acceptable punch. The point of the nail must be filed flat, so that it can't slip off the axle pin and into the side of the jack. Special caution is necessary on Sperrhake jacks which are so brittle that a slight tap on a jack not properly supported on a solid surface can crack the jack. Axle pins must be put back flush with the sides of jack or they may interfere with jack movement through the slide.

A second potential problem is the tongue's alignment in the jack itself. If the tongue holes or the jack axle pin holes have been drilled at an angle, the tongue will lean toward one corner in its slot, possibly rubbing against the sides. The side of tongue rubbing against the tongue slot side must then be sanded or filed until it is free. In jacks with wire springs, the spring can be given a sideways twist to keep the tongue away from the critical side.

The tongue must come to rest against the jack adjustment screw. During playing, the jack spring will throw the tongue against the adjustment screw with some force, and this may cause a clicking noise. Many jack tongues are provided with a patch of leather or felt to deaden this impact, but other makers do not bother with this time consuming operation, claiming that these clicks cannot be heard above the tone itself.

B. *The jack adjustment screw.* Most modern makers (exceptions are Skowroneck, Ahrend) provide the jack with an adjustment screw (never found on old harpsichords) which regulates the amount of plectrum projection. For convenience most makers now put this screw through the top of the jack, whence it bears on the tongue's inclined top surface. By turning this screw to the right or downwards (clockwise) it will have the effect of pushing back the tongue and plectrum. Turning the screw to the left and upwards (counter-clockwise) will result in the tongue's forward motion, and thus increased plectrum projection. Some makers (Neupert, Ranftl, Thierbach, Sabathil, Jones) allow the screw to protrude above the top of the jack, but a much neater way is to use slotted or allenhead set screws, which disappear completely in their holes. Other makes (Dolmetsch, some Ammers, some Sperrhakes) still use the older system of adjustment screws in the center of the jack, bearing against the back of the tongue. This forces the adjuster to remove the jack, guess the amount of adjustment, drop the jack back in, try it, and repeat if necessary, a process not necessary with a top adjustment screw. The adjustment screw should only be used to even out individual differences in plectrum projection (and thus volume); to change the volume of an entire set of jacks it is much easier to move the slide itself.

Adjustment screw malfunction. In some cases the tongue will not come to rest against the adjustment screw because of burrs or splinters protruding from adjustment screw hole. Remove burrs with file, emery board or knife, provid-ing clean contact between slanted top of tongue and matching slant in jack. (It is common for people to turn the adjustment screw quite far up in an effort to get the tongue to come forward for increased plectrum projection. Turn-ing the screw may be in vain, however, because the tongue may be stopped by burrs or by rubbing against the sides of tongue slot.)

A second problem concerns adjustment screws too loose or too tight. These screws have a plus or minus tolerance of .003 in. which may be enough to make some of them very loose or very tight. In addition, the drilling of adjustment screw holes may have been sloppy and oversized, or, in plastic jacks, may have come out the wrong size because of varying injection pres-sures. Screws that are too loose should be taken out and reinserted with a piece of heavy (carpet) thread which will generally provide enough body to tighten screws. Screws that are too tight and stuck inside their holes must be worked out carefully, since strong screwdriver pressure can shear off the top of set screw, thus eliminating any possibility of retrieving the screw. Once the screw is out, the hole should be drilled out one or two sizes larger.

C. The end pin. The end pin is the bottom adjustment which determines the point in the downward travel of the key at which the pluck occurs. The plectrum should rest about $^1/_{16}$ in. below the string for comfortable playing. This means that the pluck occurs high enough to allow the key further travel downwards after plucking, and low enough so the key need not return to com-plete rest position to get repetition; an important point for trilling. Turning in the end pin (clockwise) lowers the jack, turning it out (counterclockwise) raises the jack and plectrum. When making end pin adjustments it is often necessary to change the damper adjustment as well, since the damper may prevent lowering of the jack. Some makers (Dowd, Challis, Sperrhake, Herz) provide holes in the end pin for easy turning with an awl; plain end pins should be turned either in the chuck of a hand drill or with a pliers whose jaws have been taped, since any marring of the end pin's finish may result in scratching contact between end pin and lower guide and resulting action noise.

This Momose jack of transparent plastic shows the anatomy of a jack quite clearly, from the adjustment screw at the top which fits against the slanted, felted end of the jack tongue, and the damper, to the bottom adjust-ment screw.

Jack by Rudolf Schüler with end pin that inserts into a hole in the key lever. Height of jack is regulated by the two lock nuts. This arrangement eliminates the need for the lower jack guide, but makes necessary the removal of all jacks before keyboard can be removed.

Some makers (Wittmayer, Schüler) have end pins going directly into the keys, with two locking nuts adjusting jack height. Hubbard jacks rest on a Phillips head screw in the key, which is raised or lowered for jack height adjustment.

Malfunction of end pin. End pins, like adjustment screws, can be too loose or too tight and should be fixed in a similar fashion. If end pin surface is marred, sand and steelwool until it is smooth. A tiny drop of machine oil spread over the pin's surface will often cure action noise emanating from the end pin passage through lower guide.

D. The damper. The damper is the piece of felt or cloth whose function it is to stop the string's vibration after plucking. When the damper is not doing its job, the string continues to ring after the jack is in its rest position. On many jacks (Skowroneck, Burton, Dowd, DeBlaise, Zuckermann) the damper is wedged into a slot and is adjustable by pulling up or down. On others (Neupert, Sperrhake, Wittmayer, Sassmann) the damper is glued to an adjustable metal clip or carrier. On still other jacks (Sabathil, Ranftl, Thierbach) the damper is not adjustable at all.

Damper adjustment is one of the few features present on all historical jacks, perhaps because it did not involve screws. It is an essential adjustment, since any change in end pin and height of the jack must usually be accompanied with a change in the damper adjustment. The jack in its rest position must hang (ever so slightly) from the damper to allow the damper firm string contact. If the end pin is shortened without an accompanying raise in the damper, there will be "lost motion" between the key and the end pin. The jack should rise with the first motion of the key, so there must not be a large gap between key and end pin. If the end pin is lengthened, it will naturally lift the damper off the string, unless it is pulled down to match the added jack height. The damper's bottom edge should be about $1/16$ in. above the plectrum's top surface, allowing the plectrum a gap of $1/16$ in. below the string when the damper rests firmly on it.

Malfunction of damper. "Flag" dampers, the pieces of red cloth wedged into a slot in the jack, sometimes are too loose and slide up, failing to extinguish a string's vibrations when the damper comes to rest. The resulting continuous ring of the string is often called a "sticking" key by the layman. This can, of course, be easily fixed by pulling the damper down until it can make firm string contact. However, if it has slid up causing a "leaking" damper, chances are that pulling the damper down will not be a permanent solution. A small shim cut from file card stock and inserted in the slot with the damper will usually tighten dampers enough to hold. On plastic jacks it is sometimes possible to roughen up insides of damper slot to provide more friction.

In adjusting dampers which are glued to metal carriers it will be found that the damper felt often sticks to the body of the jack as well as to its carrier, and that an adjustment involves cutting the damper loose from the jack body first. Some dampers are made of very hard felt, and while this perhaps lasts longer, it will often produce a second tone at a higher pitch when it comes down upon the string in the manner of a clavichord tangent. To cure this, it is either necessary to procure new and softer damper felts, or attempt to make a number of tiny incisions in the bottom edge of the damper in an effort to make it more pliable. A "hanger" can sometimes be caused by a damper which has been pulled below the plectrum, preventing its return under the string. A leaking damper, or one which is too high, will sometimes allow its open string to vibrate sympathetically with a note lower down and related to the open string by octaves or fifths. This will be heard as a high, unpleasant aftersound.

E. *The jack spring.* The spring serves to return the tongue to its rest position after the plectrum has journeyed down and around the string. It must be strong enough to perform this function quickly so that an instantly repeated note will find the plectrum in its proper starting place under the string; yet weak enough to permit the plectrum's slide backwards around the string. Next to the plectrum itself, this spring is probably the most crucial part of the action. Some actions are full of hangers (and consequently, of notes which work only sporadically) solely because a stiff and thick wire spring prevents the tongue's smooth return. Other actions have such poor repetition that trills or ornaments cannot be executed on them for the sole reason of having extremely weak springs.

In jacks with wire springs, .010 or .011 seems to be the best size; however, the tension of almost any thickness wire can be changed by manipulating the base of the wire with a pair of tweezers. The flat brass springs often found on Italian harpsichords and used by some modern makers (Ranftl, Jones, Williams) are hardest to manipulate. Plastic springs moulded into the jack or tongue (Dowd, Hubbard, Burton, Herz) work well if they are long and thin. They, too, can be manipulated by tweezers, either straightening them or making them more convex for added pressure.

To arrive at the right spring pressure takes some trial and error. I find that when a jack is held horizontally and face up, the tongue should tremble when the jack is shaken slightly. If it doesn't, the spring has too much tension. If the weight of the tongue is enough to displace the spring downwards more than just a small amount while the jack is shaken, the spring will be too weak. The final test of spring tension is, of course, the performance of the action. A hanger can often be cured by weakening the spring, but that should be a last resort since one will pay for a weak spring with poor repetition.

Malfunction of spring. Aside from the incorrect tension already discussed, springs sometimes break or get bent completely out of shape. A broken flat plastic spring has no other remedy than a new jack (or tongue, if that is where the spring is). Wire springs, boar's bristle and nylon bristle can be replaced either by following the same system of attaching the spring that was used before, or by drilling a small hole into the jack at the base of the tongue slot, doubling over the end of the spring and inserting the doubled over end into the hole with the proper glue (considering both spring and jack material).

Wire springs sometimes have sharp ends digging into the tongue's spring groove and thus preventing proper spring action. The upper and final end of the spring should have a gentle curve away from the tongue. The spring should also end well below the back of the plectrum, as plectra sticking out in back could provide an obstruction for a long spring.

F. *The plectrum.* The plectrum's function is to pluck the string. It does this by rising with the jack and catching the string from underneath with its tip, setting the string in motion. To do its job properly, the plectrum must be flexible enough to bend fairly easily, yet firm enough to pluck the string

Side view of a Zuckermann jack showing delrin plectrum and flag damper. In this picture, damper is probably too close to plectrum.

vigorously and yet spring back quickly to its original shape. We have already seen the no material performs this function ideally well, but no matter what the material, the shape of the voicing cut can do much to determine the final functioning of the plectrum.

Modern harpsichord makers are almost evenly divided between using leather and delrin as plectrum material, with the trend of the times going in the direction of delrin. Some makers use a round plastic quill (Neupert, Schüler) which looks like a bristle from a plastic hairbrush. Some of the historical copyists still use crow, raven or condor quill, but even the conservative Skowroneck has now switched to delrin.

Delrin. The first use in harpsichords of this material, which is a relatively new commercial product, should probably be credited to Hubbard and Dowd. These makers realized that the nearly universal modern use of leather was not based on historical fact. Hubbard himself cites few possible uses of leather (mostly on Italian harpsichords) and Skowroneck states flatly that leather was *never* used. Realising also that bird quill is uneven, unstable and difficult to come by, Hubbard and Dowd cast about for a good quill substitute and thus chanced upon delrin, a hard, slippery material which had been used for gears, automobile, and machine parts. Delrin's chief flaw is its hardness and inflexibility, but any softer plastics like teflon and polyethelyne were found to lose their shape after repeated plucking.

A second fault of delrin is a subtle change in the material after it is exposed to repeated plucking. The repeated shock of plucking affects the material's internal composition, perhaps rearranging its molecular structure, making it in effect harder and stiffer. Good voicing can do much to minimize both of these flaws. A third and more minor drawback is delrin's imperviousness to most commercial glues (we've discovered that a brand called Pliobond sticks better to delrin than most other glues). This characteristic of delrin demands a very close "press" fit between plectrum and tongue slit to keep the material from slipping out.

In this country delrin is not commercially available in thicknesses under .020, but this is just as well since anything thinner would probably not have enough body to keep the plectrum stiff at the tip of its $1/4$ in. unsupported length. The delrin plectrum should taper in width from .085 (under $3/32$ in.) to .035 ($1/32$ in.) at its tip. Of its $13/32$ in. (.408) length, about $1/8$ in. will be wedged into the tongue, with $1/4$ in. left to stick out for possible trimming. To remove old delrin it is generally sufficient to push delrin from the front with a pliers. It is either held just by wedging or a small amount of glue, but should slide back with the application of a little force. We will discuss the actual voicing procedure under a separate heading.

Leather. The most suitable leather for plectra is cut from hard cowhide sole leather, used by shoemakers. Unfortunately, there is little one can tell from feeling a leather skin about its hardness and subsequent behavior when cut down to the size of a plectrum. The leather in skin form is also thicker than it must be to fit into most square tongue holes. The average tongue has a hole $3/32$ in. square which gives leather about the right beginning shape for voicing. Some jack tongues have a rectangular hole (Dolmetsch, Morley, Paul, Sassmann), higher than it is wide, perhaps to allow the insertion of the original leather skin thickness. Once such thick leather is inserted in the jack, how-ever, it must be thinned right at the base, since a straight slant from base of leather to its tip would make the entire plectrum too stiff and heavy. To thin the leather at its base requires an operation much more difficult than cutting it before insertion into a square hole, where it will have the right thickness for a slanted cut to its tip.

Some makers (Sperrhake, Ammer) did at one time or still do supply jacks with a round tongue hole. I have never solved the mystery of fitting a square leather peg into a round hole. Most makers insert the leather from the back of the tongue, so that the wedge-shaped plectrum's point will stick out towards the front and the wider rear of plectrum will seat itself firmly in the tongue hole. Presumably the plucking pressure tends to pull the leather for-ward and thus wedge it more tightly. To remove old leather plectra, cut it flush in the front of the tongue and push backwards. (Zuckermann leather is wedged in from the front and must be pushed out frontwards.) The operation can probably be done best by holding tongue in a vise and tapping out plec-trum with a punch or small screwdriver. Many European makers glue in their plectra, and these will have to be drilled out, cleaning off the remnants with a square file. (Sperrhake leathers can be soaked out in warm water.)

G. *Voicing delrin.* Delrin must be lodged firmly in the tongue and be-cause delrin is slippery the tapering plectrum should be just wider in back than the tongue slit. In jacks with square holes a filler made of leather or a square wooden peg must be used. The flat delrin is wedged against the upper edge of square hole. When converting from leather to delrin, the leather can be cut flush in front and a slit made between upper edge of square hole and leather itself. A good tool for making this slit, and for voicing in general, is an X-acto knife (holder and exchangeable blade No. 11). (Frank Hubbard recom-mends a Beaver office knife with a No. 35 blade.) Two suggested voicing positions are illustrated here. Many modern jacks do not permit the swivelling out of the tongue for easier voicing access. With delrin this feature is not serious since voicing takes place at the tip and access to the base of the plectrum (the point at which it leaves the tongue) is not required. Some jacks (Sabathil,

Voicing a delrin plectrum. Jack spring has been slipped aside to let tongue fall back. Delrin, which tends to stiffen in time, may need successive thinning after intervals of several months. Entire length of tongue may need thinning to eliminate the characteristic explosive pluck. Considerable trial and error is required to find the voicing best suited to a given harpsichord.

Another method of voicing plectra, using a hand-held end-grain block of hard wood.

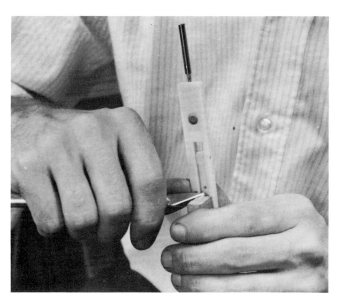

Diagrams of jack tongues and plectra in relation to the string; delrin and leather. The shape and stiffness of the plectra has a great deal to do with the sound of an instrument. The plectra diagrammed here are cut à la Zuckermann. Other voicers will thin the delrin plectrum all along its length and cut it off square at the end. The leather cut shown will give considerable difference of volume on the half stop, and a bright tone. A stubbier cut of the leather without undercutting (as Challis cuts) will give a louder and somewhat more "piano-like" tone, but needs very close tolerances between jack and jack slide and allows very little movement of the slide (if any at all) for the half stop. A shallower wedge going straight to a point gives a tone closer to a horn or trumpet tone. You cut your leathers and you take your choice.

Ranftl, Thierbach, Schütze) have dampers going across the entire width of the jack, making access to the plectrum difficult. In these cases, a thin ($^1/_{16}$ in.) hardwood block must be inserted between damper and plectrum to provide a solid surface against which the knife can cut.

With delrin, which must be obtained from the maker, it is best to leave the plectrum as long as possible. The length of the plectrum is, of course, determined by the amount of space available to the jack. In a spinet this will be precious little. In a multi-stop instrument, room must be allowed the jacks to recede to the "off" position in which they fail to pluck altogether, and yet be a safe distance from the set of strings in back of them. Before voicing an entire set of jacks, careful attention must be paid to the position of the jack slide. A good average distance between the body of the jack and its corresponding string is $^1/_8$ in. in the "on" position. Since jack tongues are usually recessed, and since the plectrum projects beyond the string, a plectrum length of $^3/_{16}$ in. is thus a good average.

The object in voicing delrin is to thin the tip of the plectrum; this operation should serve three purposes: achieving a clean, pleasant tone; getting a light, even action; and eliminating the chance for hangers. Many people report using files or emery boards on the delrin underside for even thinning; I prefer a sharp X-acto knife, but slicing the delrin underside in *thickness* sometimes leads to a mistaken cut shortening the length. The final $^1/_{16}$ in. cut should always be made with a knife to provide a smooth surface enabling the plectrum to glide downwards around the string.

Since the plectrum's function is to pluck the string, and since it will pluck the string whether it projects a great or a small amount beyond the string, it is best for ease of playing and operation to allow the plectrum the *minimum* projection. More harpsichord actions have become unplayable because of excess plectrum projection than perhaps from any other cause. Frank Hubbard stipulates a plectrum projection the amount of the string diameter, but $^1/_{32}$ in. would probably be safer in case the jack has some play which could cause an occasional miss. Projection beyond that small amount serves no purpose other than to make the action stiff and balky, and the plectra's return uncertain.

The actual voicing cut, made on the underside of the plectrum, is a $^1/_8$-in.-long wedge in *thickness* tapering to almost nothing at the very tip. If this cut doesn't result in a light action (a weight of $3^1/_2$ ounces placed on the key should result in a pluck) the delrin has to be thinned all the way along its length, or cut narrower in width. Massaging the plectrum will make it temporarily more pliable, but generally doesn't last.

Instruments equipped with a half stop are a special case. The jacks must be allowed a small movement (no more than $^1/_{32}$ in.) from loud to soft and from soft to off in a multi-stop instrument. The half stop works on the principle that the thin tip of a tapered plectrum will pluck the string more softly than the thicker, more central section. This works well with leather, but delrin, which is flat and consistently thin, does not usually achieve much contrast between loud and soft. In addition, the half stop forces added plectrum projection to allow an adequate "reserve" for the soft position.

The tone to strive for in delrin voicing should be crisp, clean and light. A stiff plectrum which overprojects will be forced to bend excessively as the key is depressed, and rebound after the pluck with the sound of a small explosion which adds an unpleasant mechanical sound to the musical tone. A light and minimally projecting plectrum, on the other hand, will lift the string only slightly during the pluck (incidentally minimizing the pitch rise of a stretched string) and achieve a non-explosive release.

Leather. Much of the above applies to leather as well. Voicing leather however, is considerably more difficult than voicing delrin. The voicing cut in leather usually starts at the base of the plectrum and goes all the way to the tip. It isn't a completely straight diagonal cut, however. The illustration shows my own way of cutting leather, but it is by no means the only way. Almost every maker using leather has his own way of cutting it. The best cut is the one that works best, i.e., gives the most pleasant tone combined with the longest life.

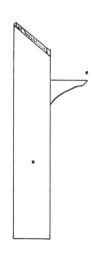

The two chief flaws of leather are its capacity to get constantly softer and more worn with use and its sensitivity to climate conditions. A third drawback is the critical plucking position required by leather; because of its strong taper it will work with one even volume only in one fixed position. The first of these flaws often changes the character of a harpsichord in the course of a few years from strong to weak, from loud to soft and from bright to dull. The change is gradual, as the leathers get worn, so that the owner will often barely notice it. The second flaw makes leather a poor choice in humid climates; the leather soaks up the humidity, becomes soggy and "bunches up" during the pluck, giving a rubbery and imprecise feel to the touch. And the third flaw calls for a precisely engineered action with practically no play between parts, again a risk in humid areas.

Many voicers accentuate the drawback of a critical plucking position by leaving the leather thick until the middle section of the plectrum and then cutting a steep taper. The taper must be gradual in order to allow the jack some leeway in plucking position. The underside of leather is less slippery than that of delrin and more likely to hang from the string on its return. The underside must be smooth and free of the slightest obstruction. A sharp blade making a smooth cut is even more necessary for leather voicing than for delrin. To prevent a final curl of the thin tip, which could prevent the leather's return, I generally cut a final and very short but steep taper at the tip. Leathers which have been used a lot can sometimes be rejuvenated by advancing all the jacks slightly toward the string and then cutting the curled-over tip off by converting it into the final taper illustrated. In all voicing, the "slow" test to catch hangers should be tried; this consists of releasing the key ever so slowly and watching if the plectrum will slip around the string. If it does this at slow playing speed, then it will perform under all conditions. To make the underside of leather more slippery, graphite from a pencil can be applied, but the graphite must not be used to make an otherwise sloppy voicing cut work properly.

H. Jack regulation. To have an instrument perform properly, whether voiced in delrin or leather, it would probably pay the owner to sit down once for a few hours and face the boring task of a complete regulation. The pleasure he will get from playing a well regulated instrument will easily compensate him for a few hours' suffering. If he decides to regulate his instrument, he must not aimlessly "spot" regulate it here and there where it needs it most. To be effective, regulation has to be done on one stop and one note at a time, and must proceed from top to bottom, catching in this painstaking process every jack in the instrument.

When regulating, it is best to start with the principal, or lower, 8′ set of jacks. I generally proceed from the top treble jack chromatically down to the bass. To do a good regulating job it is necessary only to understand the operation of one single jack. Since all jacks are alike, the rest will follow. We have already described the optimum positions and distances of the jack action but will summarize them here briefly. Before following this regulating procedure, the reader is urged to go through the rest of the chapter, since the keyboard and strings also enter into the regulating process. We will assume that the keyboard works smoothly, the slide is in its proper place, and the strings are free of rust or corrosion at the plucking points.

Each single jack must perform the following functions: (1) it must rise as soon as the key is depressed; (2) it must start the plucking process before the key is down more than one third of its total dip; (3) the plucking process itself should occupy the second third of the key travel; (4) during the pluck, the plectrum must not be strained—it must bend easily and release without a sudden snap; (5) the volume and type of tone must match that of the other jacks; (6) upon its return the plectrum must slip under the string easily, smoothly and without hesitation even when key is released slowly; (7) when key comes to rest, the jack damper must make firm contact with the string, stopping its vibrations completely; (8) during a quick repetition the jack must perform every single time; (9) jacks must pluck successively on the same key of multiple string sets.

Remedies for troubles in these nine functions. (1) If the jack does not rise instantly when the key is depressed, it will have to be made longer to reach the key. This is done by turning the end pin out, or counterclockwise, until it almost makes contact with the key. There must be a hairline gap to allow the jack to "hang" from its damper. Lost motion can also occur with the end pin the correct length, if the damper has been pulled down too far. Damper and end pin adjustment must therefore be considered together. The correct way to set both adjustments is to first position the end pin so that the plectrum is about $1/16$ in. below the string; then the damper should be set to rest firmly on the string without, however, actually lifting the jack.

(2) The moment at which the plucking process starts is again determined by the end pin. Positioning end pin as described above will result in the correct timing for the pluck.

(3) To limit the plucking process itself to the middle third of the key travel requires a flexible, yet crisp, plectrum. Plectrum must not project more than $1/32$ in. beyond the string (except in instruments possessing a half stop); for the right plectrum dimensions and shape the reader should refer back to the discussion on voicing.

(4) To achieve a pluck without excessive straining again depends on plectrum shape, dimensions and voicing already discussed.

(5) To achieve an even tone (and a resultant even action, since tone and action are related), it is necessary to compare each jack with its neighbors.

The jack adjustment screw, usually bearing on a bevel in the tongue, regulates the amount of plectrum projection and, by extension, the amount of volume. Turning the adjustment screw down (clockwise) will push back the tongue and plectrum and should result in a softer tone. Turning adjustment screw up (counterclockwise) lets the tongue come forward, resulting in increased plectrum projection and added volume. There is a limit to the amount of useful adjustment. Pushing the tongue back too far will, of course, result in the plectrum's failure to reach the string; allowing the plectrum too much projection will not increase the volume but merely make the action unplayable. It must be remembered that a delrin plectrum, unless very well tapered, will show little volume difference in different positions; and a leather plectrum needs only a small amount of adjustment to go from soft to loud. Often the volume as well as the type of tone desired is better adjusted through voicing than by way of the adjustment screw.

(6) To pass the "slow" test upon its return, the plectrum must slide past the string without hesitation upon a slow release of the key. If it doesn't, it is likely to be a "hanger," probably the most common cause of harpsichord action malfunction. Hangers can have the following causes: a. End pin may be out too far to permit plectrum's return under the string; screw in end pin. b. Damper may be down below level of plectrum; pull up damper. c. Jacks may be sticking in guides or slides; see comment under guides and slides. d. The key itself may be sticking; see comment under keyboard. e. The spring may be too strong; this is a frequent cause of hangers. Please refer back to our discussion of the jack spring and its correct tension. f. The tongue may be sticking; refer to the section on jack tongues. g. The plectrum may be projecting too far beyond the string; turn adjustment screw until projection is just enough to effect the pluck, no more. h. The plectrum may be insufficiently beveled or may have some roughness on its underside; take a very thin slice off the plectrum underside to remove the obstruction or roughness (which often can't be seen). Leather can be graphited on the underside to make it more slippery.

(7) The correct damper position has already been discussed.

(8) Good repetition can be spoiled by any of the factors causing hangers. In addition, a weak jack spring will hamper quick repetition because of its slowness in returning the tongue to rest position. Repetition can also be hampered by too much play between jack and slide; see comment under slides and guides. The bass is less likely to repeat quickly than the treble, since the strings there vibrate with greater amplitude and thus need more time to come to rest. To cope with this increased string amplitude, end pins must be slightly shorter and plectra projection slightly greater in the bass.

(9) The reason for staggered plucking of multiple jacks is to reduce the resistance of the action. When four sets of jacks pluck simultaneously, there will be four times the resistance of a single pluck. The plucking order can be regulated with the end pins. Frank Hubbard* suggests the following orders: single manual, 4′, front 8′, back 8′; double manual, 4′, lower 8′, upper 8′, 16′. He also suggests having a different plucking order if the instrument seems to insist on a different order. The important point is to stagger the plucks.

*Hubbard, Frank, *Harpsichord Regulating and Repairing*, Tuners Supply Co., Boston 1963.

II. THE KEYBOARD

To determine whether a sticking action is caused by the jack or the key, the jack must be removed entirely and the key tried by itself. If it does not return of its own accord after being depressed, or if it returns sluggishly, the key itself must be removed so that it can be eased. We have already discussed some keyboard removal under the headings of the individual makers. Some makers leave enough room between keyboard and pinblock so that individual keys can be lifted out for servicing. To try this, remove the nameboard or removeable batten above the keys. Then lift out the jack or jacks resting on the sticking key and try lifting up the key itself. A pin (the balance pin) will usually pass through the center of the key, and the key must be lifted above this pin and out. On some two-manual instruments the upper keys can also be lifted out individually, but in others, and in many singles, the whole keyboard must come out as a unit to remove individual keys.

Once the key is removed it is likely to stick at one of the three contact points with its balance and guide pins. The first is the balance hole, the un-bushed round hole at the key bottom through which the balance pin passes. By sliding the key up and down the balance pin it is often possible to feel where it binds. If the balance hole is too small, it should be drilled or reamed out slightly; enlarging the hole too much would cause a wobbling key. Next the top mortise through which the balance pin emerges must be examined. If this is bushed, the bushing should be compressed (piano tuners do it by squeezing the jaw of a "key easing pliers" inserted in the bushing) or carefully sliced a little thinner with a sharp blade. If the mortise is unbushed, a slight squeeze with a pliers should widen it enough to admit balance pin freely.

The system of guiding keys, either through front pins, rear pins, or racks may also be responsible for a sticking key. Again, bushings must be compressed and mortises widened. In piano keyboards, the guide pin is flattened out in its upper portion, and the flattened area of the pin fits into the guide bushing under the front of the key. Sometimes a pin will twist slightly sideways, so that its flattened section fits diagonally across the bushing, causing it to bind. Such a pin must be returned to its original position.

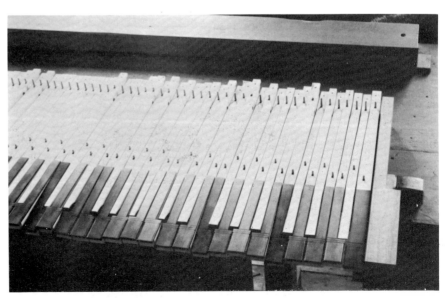

Keyboard of a Dowd harpsichord before levelling and fitting.

Keys occasionally stick because they rub against each other or because particles have fallen between them. Keys rubbing against their neighbors must be sanded or filed till they clear. An unusual cause of sticking keys is too little clearance between the sharps and naturals in front of the sharp.

To remove an entire keyboard, it is usually safest to remove the jacks as well. Theoretically the jacks "hang" from their dampers and are thus poised above the keys, so that keyboard removal should not disturb them. However, an unregulated harpsichord will have many jacks resting firmly on the key. Treble jacks sometimes have no dampers and would thus drop down, while the jacks of some makers go right into the keys themselves. Other keyboards have obstructions which may interfere with the jacks during removal. When taking out a set of jacks, place them in the order of removal on a board, and note which slide they belong to, as well as the direction in which they are facing. It is sometimes difficult to determine this once jacks have been removed.

The keyboard itself will be held either by screws from below or by screws going through the key frame itself. To get at the keyboard it is often necessary to remove the lockstrip in front and keyblocks to the side. On Neuperts and many others, the keyboard is held with only three screws, inserted diagonally under the front of the keys. These screws can generally be seen by looking at the front rail of keyboard frame. Other screws going down from the balance rail can only be exposed by removing some keys. It is a convention to mark such places on the key with a picture of a screw head, but not everyone follows this convention. When looking for keyboard screws on the harpsichord bottom, eliminate heavy screws which seem to be going into the side, braces or belly rail. In two-manual instruments with a keyboard coupler controlled by a hand stop, the coupler connection may go through the keyboard and is usually removable (see section on Neupert).

To get at the lower manual of a two-manual keyboard, the keyboard must usually come out as a unit, and the upper key frame must be removed. It will be easier to get the upper keyboard off if the coupler dogs are vertical (see pictures of Neupert coupler). In removing each item from the harpsichord, I generally put the screws back in their matching holes, so that no confusion

Double keyboard assembly of a Goble harpsichord. Fronts of naturals and sharps are still to be added. Note balance pin felts, and pins under front of keys.

can result. A job of this type must not be undertaken in a hurry, or in the presence of dogs or small children.

While the keyboard is out, the fussy player may wish to check the key dip and the key level. The dip is the amount of downward key travel, which Hubbard gives as $5/16$ in. for harpsichords. Any shorter dip than that will put a strain on the timing of multiple plucks, and may result in the uncomfortable feeling of getting the final pluck just when the key bottoms. Many piano-trained players prefer a dip of $3/8$ in., which allows still more leeway to accomplish the pluck comfortably.

The dip is usually determined by the thickness of felt and cardboard punchings under the front of the key. Adding or subtracting cardboard punchings will shorten or lengthen the dip. The dip can also be controlled with the jack rail, since a key will "bottom" when its jack hits the jack rail above it. However, jack rails should not be used for this purpose; they should be set so that the jacks barely touch the rail when the key bottoms naturally.

The key level is achieved by varying thicknesses of paper punchings under the balance rail. By holding a straight edge above the keys, punchings can be added and subtracted as needed. To build up one or two keys which are lower than the rest, punchings of ordinary paper or file card stock can be manufactured by cutting a disc $3/8$ in. in diameter with a central hole $1/8$ in. in diameter.

III. THE JACK SLIDE AND LOWER GUIDE

The first thing that must be checked about the slide is its own freedom of movement. Slides frequently jam, due to a bowing-in of the pinblock under pressure. Some makers leave very little play in the gap between pinblock and belly rail, and this small amount of play may soon disappear altogether. Needless to say, the slide *must* be free to move, not only for adjustment purposes, but for on-off or loud-soft changes. Even in an Italian harpsichord with fixed slides, a slide must be movable for tuning purposes.

When the slide is jammed so that neither hand stop, nor pedals, nor actual

Bracing of the gap in a Morley harpsichord, intended to prevent sagging of belly rail and jamming of slides.

finger manipulation will move it, all jacks must be removed. Next it should be determined if the slide has indeed jammed due to a squeeze between the other slides (if so, no play whatever between slides should be visible) or is perhaps only held rigid between the capstans. If the slide is really jammed, it must be taken out of the harpsichord. This is an operation that must be carefully investigated before an attempt is made to perform it. Some makers leave a "window" on the spine which, when unscrewed, will provide an opening through which the slides can be withdrawn. If they will not come out even when forced, the string tension must be lowered.

Other makers allow the slide to drop down, which involves the removal of the keyboards and lower guides. In Neuperts, the tension bar between belly rail and pinblock above which the slides ride has a removable bottom section, held only by pressure. With other makers the slides can be pushed up and slid under the strings, until they can be taken out at the spine by twisting them to line up from front to back. If there is no window, if the slide will not drop down, and if it cannot be taken out under the strings (the presence of a 4′ will usually rule this out), a narrow slot will have to be cut into the spine, large enough to withdraw at least one slide. (Such a cut can be made by drilling first and chiselling out the corners.) The window is later covered by a $^1/_4$ in. thick rectangular patch matching the case which should be held by screws so it will henceforth be removable.

Once the slides are out, they must be sanded, filed or sawed until they fit easily into their positions. Usually only a fraction needs to be taken off on each side. If a window is cut into the case, a block holding the capstan screw must be attached to the patch covering the window.

Next, we may check the slide's lateral position. The slide plays a role of crucial importance in a harpsichord, and a tiny movement can sometimes result in the miracle of making a totally unplayable action totally playable. The reason for the slide's critical role is its control over the overall plectrum projection. A slide which is positioned too close to the strings, thereby forcing all plectra to project an excessive amount beyond the strings, can be pulled back to allow the right amount of plectrum projection with one small adjustment. Similarly, a slide too far from the strings can cause the plectra to miss the strings altogether, and again a small adjustment can set this right.

Most slides are controlled by capstan screws which can be turned in or out with an awl or small screwdriver. If a set of jacks looks to the right, it would follow that the right capstan controls the "on" or loud position, and the left controls the "off" or soft position. Jacks looking to the left will have the "on" position controlled by the left capstan and the "off" position by the right capstan.

Some instruments have, instead of capstans, small notched wheels for slide adjustment. Others have double slotted machine screws. In almost every harpsichord, however, there will be a device to adjust the lateral position of the slide, mounted either on the case walls of the instrument or on the slide itself. Some, like Neuperts, have nuts which must be unlocked before turning capstans and re-locked afterwards or they will "wander." Instruments with pedals or knee levers often have spring-loaded slides, generally pressing towards the "on" position.

Jackslides in a Morley harpsichord. Note that slides have plenty of room in the gap to move freely without jamming.

The "window" in the spine of a Challis harpsichord to allow jackslides to be removed easily. John Challis at the instrument.

Jackslides and capstans in a Sperrhake.

Before starting to regulate a harpsichord, the serviceman must look carefully at the slide setting to determine its best position. If he is setting the slide after the instrument has been voiced, the cue of the slide position must be taken from the length of the plectra. If the plectra are to be trimmed to allow an unused plectrum portion to become the new tip, the slide must be advanced far enough to allow enough plectrum projection for trimming and still have some reserve. (When revoicing an entire set, many of the adjustment screws will be found to have been turned up all the way by a previous adjuster in an effort to get longer plectra; the slide must be advanced far enough to allow most of the adjustment screws to return to their original central positions.)

The final position of the jack slide should be such that the finished voicing will show a plectrum projection beyond the string of only $1/32$ in.; at the same time there must be room for the "off" position, allowing the retraction of all the jacks without "ghosting" (faintly sounding), and still being clear of the strings in the rear of the jacks. There must be good clearance between the backs of the jacks and the adjacent set of strings, so that the bass strings don't buzz against the backs of jack tongues.

In spinets and the De Blaise triangular harpsichords, the slide position can be changed by a front-to-back movement. We have already discussed the spinet problem of paired and facing jacks, upon which any change in the harpsichord case acts in opposite directions. Thus every other jack will advance toward the string, while its neighbor will recede, resulting in alternate loud and soft notes along the entire action. Instead of resetting each jack with the adjustment screw, the entire slide can often be pushed forward or back, allowing the evening-out of plectrum positions in one small movement. Spinet slides are often screwed down firmly, but the holes under the screws are oversized, allowing movement of the slide.

Once the position of the slide is fixed (and for purposes of voicing it should be held rigid in the *on* position), we can turn our attention to the fit between jack and slide slots. If the jacks are wooden, some play must be left for expansion during humid summer weather. The combination of wooden jacks and leather plectra often leads to trouble because leather does not tolerate easily even the small amount of variation caused by enough play for summer and winter use. If the jacks actually stick in the slide or rub against the sides of the slot, producing a squeak, the jack must be sanded until it works without obstruction. Usually it is enough to break the corners of the jack. If much filing has to be done, it will be easier to do it on the slide instead of the jack's surface.

Where there is too much play, causing a wobble, either the jack or slide has to be shimmed. I have seen jacks whose makers used postage stamps to shim them, a rather expensive way of doing it. If the jack is shimmed, two patches should be glued on the face of the jack on either side of the tongue; file card stock is usually the right thickness. Some people have used self-sticking aluminum tape, which cuts down the work if many jacks have to be shimmed. The aluminum surface provides a smooth gliding action but does not look very attractive. Other smooth tapes may work equally well. The slide, if it has any thickness, can be shimmed in preference to the jacks.

With the slide in good shape, we can turn our attention to the lower guide. This is often a source of sticking or noisy jacks. Any scratch on the jack end pin, or unevenness in the guide holes, can cause extraneous sounds. A tiny drop of oil rubbed over the surface of the end pin may eliminate the noise. The end pin holes can often be reached from above by passing a long rattail file through the slide and into the guide holes. Unlike the fit between slide and jack, the guide hole can allow the end pin a fair amount of play.

The lateral position of the guide should, of course, place the guide holes directly underneath the slide slots, and directly above the key centers. In an ideal harpsichord, the key centers, guide, and slide line up perfectly vertically and all of them are in the proper relation to the strings. With a movable jack slide, all jacks will tilt slightly in either the "on" or "off" position, since the lower guide is fixed. Ideally, the guide should be put in the center between the two positions, allowing the jacks a slight tilt in either direction.

After the jack guide has been checked, each jack should be watched as it drops down slowly after key release to see that it passes both slide and guide without hesitation.

IV. THE HAND STOP AND PEDAL SYSTEMS

Practically all harpsichords have a device to control the shifting of the jack slides, which in turn results in register changes. On the old Italian harpsichords, the slides for the 2 × 8′ were meant to be in one fixed position; their makers saw no need for register changes. Nonetheless, a piece of moulding mounted at the end of the slide allowed the changing of registers from the inside of the harpsichord, at least for tuning purposes.

Some of the Flemish instruments had push handles attached to the treble ends of the registers which went straight through the case and allowed the player to make a change by reaching around to the outside of the cheek. The modern makers copying this system may find themselves constantly replacing these handles; it is a safe bet that movers have gotten more careless through the centuries, and any item protruding from the side of a harpsichord must offer a strong temptation to modern moving men.

The most common means of changing registers are handstops which come through the nameboard and are thus accessible to the player just by lifting his hand. In the old argument between the proponents of pedals and those favoring handstops, the latter group makes a fairly strong case. Those who use handstops would point out that (1) the overwhelming majority of historical instruments had them; (2) the composers, when they desired register changes, left a pause in the music coinciding with the necessity of lifting the hand from the keyboard; (3) the presence of pedals leads the player into making frequent, unnecessary and unmusical changes; and (4) handstops are mechanically simple and make the instrument less costly.

The pedal proponents would reply that they are not concerned with history, only with the ease of playing; a pedal change can be accomplished while the hands are occupied playing the notes. In addition, quick and startling contrasts can be achieved, thus alleviating some of the harpsichord's inherent faults. It is true that in the late eighteenth century, when the harpsichord was competing with the piano, pedals were used more frequently, controlling such exotic devices as machine stops and Venetian swells. (Some 50 years later pianos were to be equipped with a pedal operating a drumstick which hit the sound-

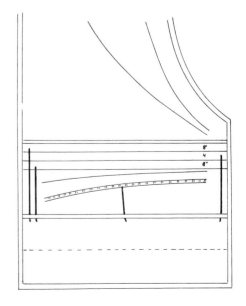

Typical arrangement of hand stops on a double harpsichord, with the two 8′ jackslides controlled from the left, the 4′ from the right, and the lute stop slide control in the center.

The simple hand stop control on a Zuckermann harpsichord.

Hand stops on a Hubbard kit harpsichord under construction.

The pedal lyre of a De Blaise harpsichord.

The central hand stop controlling the coupler on a Neupert harpsichord. The lever going through the pinblock must be detached before keyboard can be removed.

board, a device used to great effect in the piano version of Beethoven's immensely popular Battle Symphony.)

The simplest and most frequently used hand stop consists of a metal bar which is pivoted in the center, with its end connecting to the slide. The lever moves from side to side, and a push to the right, for instance, will result in a slide movement to the left. Simple slide levers are flat or square, but a more sophisticated type changes in outline at the front, so that the front section is vertical for easier manual manipulation. On simple harpsichords hand stops are on the sides, but on multi-string instruments some levers usually go through the center. These may be the levers going to the buff stop rails, so the lever must assume a somewhat tortuous shape to get through the tuning pins. A space-saving device is to stack two levers above each other, allowing the player to reverse the position of two slides with one twist.

With handstops the jack slide will not be spring-loaded, but will move freely from side to side. The pivot screw in the stop itself must therefore be fairly tight to hold the slide in position. Because of the plucking pressure, slides have a tendency to wander backwards unless held firmly in place. If the hand stop pivot screw can't be tightened, some friction or "drag" should be created between the slides themselves (i.e., a small piece of felt) so that they stay in one position. Occasionally a handstop will not have a chance to move the slide to the full extent necessary, because it is stopped by the cut-out made for it in the nameboard. Such a stop has to be either re-bent or the nameboard slot widened.

Another type of hand stop has a push-pull action (see Neupert). Push-pull stops are also sometimes used to control the half stop on instruments with pedals. In harpsichords with multiple string sets also possessing a half stop, the hand stop will not be very useful, since it will move from "on" to "off" and must be left in a non-fixable intermediate position for the half stop.

Something of a compromise between hand stops and pedals are knee levers. Many of the small German harpsichords have a knee lever controlling the 4′ stop. The lever is in the center underneath the harpsichord and is moved sideways, to the "on" position with one knee and to the "off" position with the other. Other knee levers are spring loaded, forcing the player to supply knee pressure as long as the stop is desired. Knee levers have the advantage of being easily and cheaply installed and not presenting a cumbersome moving problem like pedals.

Harpsichord pedals are more complicated than piano pedals and serve an entirely different function. While there usually are only two piano pedals, matching the two human feet and serving the function of brief changes, there can be as many as seven or eight harpsichord pedals, some needing to be held down for long periods. For that reason, harpsichord pedals must be able to move up and down, and in addition sideways, to be locked in position under a notched plate. The notches in the pedal plates will represent the "on," "intermediate" and "off" positions, in which the pedal is held under spring pressure.

The double action of the pedals requires a fairly complex mechanism; usually the pedal is made of two pieces—the front or actual pedal which pivots horizontally, and the rear which pivots vertically. In the better harpsichords the pedals themselves and the notched plates are made out of steel rubbed to a satin finish. Some makers use brass plated, horn shaped, one-piece piano pedals, which cannot easily be converted to the double action; most of the German harpsichords have pedals with a rubber washer (presumably to save the plating), which terminate in a bulky box hiding the lower pedal action. It is often necessary to open this box from below and expose the mechanism, since the essential pivot blocks are often made of soft wood and split under constant use. (I once had the unusual task of converting a Neupert pedal action to hand stops, because the instrument's owner was tired of coping with splitting pivot blocks.) A much neater way to house pedals than the large box with accompanying lyre braces is to attach the pedals to the low crossbrace of a stand, which is common practice among the better makers.

Pedals are often adjustable in three different places, which can lead to confusion. First the pedal rods running from the back of pedals to the underaction can usually be lengthened or shortened. This is done either by means of an adjustable collar at the foot of the rods or a threaded column at the top of the rods. Lengthening the rods will have the effect of pushing the underaction up and thus pushing the slide further forward, making the stop louder. Shortening the rods should have the reverse effect. The next adjustment is often contained at the treble side just below the harpsichord bottom. This will adjust the pedal underaction, consisting of horizontal rods which transmit the vertical pedal thrust laterally into the upper slide action. These rods will have nuts allowing them again to be lengthened or shortened. Last of the adjustments is our old friend, the capstan screw. The lower pedal adjustments won't do any good if the capstan is blocking their path. If, for example, more volume is desired, the capstan must be turned first. Then, and only then, if the pedal rods are too short to allow the slide to be stopped by the capstan, can the other adjustments be brought into play.

On an instrument which has pedals and half stops, the pedal should be set on the notch representing the half hitch; then the rods should be adjusted to allow minimal plectrum projection for a soft sound. Both the "off" and the loud positions should automatically fall into place from a correct setting of the half hitch, since the distances in the notch plate determine the relationships between the positions. If the "off" position allows the slide to go too far back, the off capstan can be advanced to stop the slide earlier. In the "off" position, the plectra should just miss; in multi-string set harpsichords, the 4′ should be left on the soft side since it has a tendency to be shrill and overpower the other

Push-pull, or draw stops on a Neupert.

Jackslide controls on a Dolmetsch (activated by pedals).

233

stops. The key to pedal adjustments, as to everything else in a harpsichord, is a thorough understanding of how each single part works. One lever alone should be worked at a time and its effects carefully observed.

V. THE STRINGS AND SOUNDBOARD

Harpsichord strings are much thinner than piano strings, and are usually made of spring wire; steel in the tenor and treble sections, and brass or phosphor bronze in the bass. In most cases it is best to get replacement strings from the maker, especially the non-standard covered or overspun low brass strings. Most piano supply houses carry wire in harpsichord sizes, although some of them sell only to the trade.

The following is a stringing list given by Frank Hubbard as typical for North European harpsichords. This list would also apply to most modern harpsichords with average scales. Also given is Hubbard's suggested list for short-scaled, lightly built Italian harpsichords. Below this is given a simplified stringing list as used in the Zuckermann kit harpsichord, consisting of only 6 instead of 9 sizes. The switching of sizes close to each other will generally not result in a critical change of tone.

The most frequently broken strings are the thinnest sizes of brass wire. Brass wire is very soft and any kinking or marring is likely to result in a break. When replacing a string, it is neatest to copy the style used on that particular instrument. There are two common styles of making hitchpin loops, and two styles of treating the tuning pin winding.

Wireloop Style A. The most commonly used and neatest way to make the loop is also the most difficult to make for an amateur. One needs either three hands, one assistant, or a loop making device. The actual loop is perhaps ⅛ in. in diameter, and the length of the twisted winding about 1 in. The loops can be made by putting an eye hook on the chuck of a hand drill held by one person, while a second bends over about three inches of the wire end, putting the crook of the bend into the hook. The wire holder then spreads both sections of the wire (the main stem and the bent over end) so that they diverge from the hook in 45 degree angles. In this style of loop-making, one section of wire is *not* wound around the other, but both are evenly intertwined. The assistant then turns the drill while the holder keeps the wire taut. When one inch of winding has been accumulated, wire end is clipped with a little reserve, and the remains are wound tightly on the end. This type of loop will slip or unravel unless the wire ends are held taut and at an angle.

Wireloop Style B. This easier though perhaps less attractive loop can be handled by one person. The loop is made by bending over a one or two inch end of the wire all the way around without allowing it to make a sharp kink, and then holding the bent over section (perhaps ⅛ in. diameter) with pliers. (Some people find it easier to make the loop around a headless nail driven into the bench.) Next the loose end of the wire is wound on the main stem at right angles for about four or five coils. The winding need not be neat or close. The loose end is then clipped off, leaving an end ⅛ in. long sticking out at right angles to the wire. This little end must go *under* the wire when the loop is placed on the hitchpin. Under tension this loop will tighten close around the hitchpin, and the little end will prevent its unravelling. If string tension

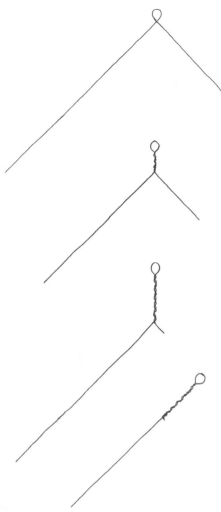

Hitchpin loop Style A

Hitchpin loop Style A

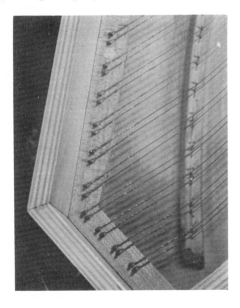

alone will not close the loop, screwdriver pressure should be applied against it until the loop winding is neat and close together.

Once the loop is made, we can turn our attention to the tuning pin end. Here, again, there are two styles, one requiring the tuning pin out of the

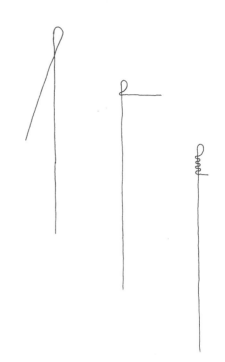

Hitchpin loop Style B

TYPICAL STRINGING OF NORTHERN EUROPEAN HARPSICHORD

EIGHT FOOT CHOIR

Note	No. of String Courses	Wire Size in Thousandths	Material
f‴—g′	23	.009	Steel Music Wire
f#′—c	7	.010	Steel Music Wire
b—a	3	.011	Steel Music Wire
g#—f#	3	.012	Steel Music Wire
f—G#	10	.014	Steel Music Wire
G—D#	5	.014	Spring Brass Wire
D—C	3	.016	Spring Brass Wire
BB—AA#	2	.018	Spring Brass Wire
AA—GG#	2	.020	Spring Brass Wire
GG—FF	3	.022	Spring Brass Wire

FOUR FOOT CHOIR

Note	No. of String Courses	Wire Size in Thousandths	Material
f‴—c′	30	.008	Steel Music Wire
b′—c	12	.009	Steel Music Wire
b—G	5	.010	Steel Music Wire
F#—E	3	.012	Steel Music Wire
D#—C	4	.014	Steel Music Wire
BB—GG#	4	.014	Spring Brass Wire
GG—FF	3	.016	Spring Brass Wire

TYPICAL STRINGING OF ITALIAN HARPSICHORD

Note	No. of String Courses	Wire Size in Thousandths	Material
d‴—f′	10	.008	Steel Music Wire
e″—a#	19	.009	Steel Music Wire
a—g	3	.010	Steel Music Wire
f#—f	2	.011	Steel Music Wire
e—d#	2	.012	Steel Music Wire
d—G#	7	.013	Steel Music Wire
G—F#	2	.014	Steel Music Wire
F—D#	3	.014	Spring Brass Wire
D—C	3	.016	Spring Brass Wire

Hitchpin loop Style B

SIMPLIFIED STRINGING ON A ZUCKERMANN KIT HARPSICHORD WITH SHORT BASS STRINGS

Note	No. of String Courses	Wire Size in Thousandths	Material
f^3—a^1	21	.009	Steel Music Wire
$g\#^1$—g#	13	.011	Steel Music Wire
g—c	8	.013	Steel Music Wire
B—G	5	.016	Brass Spring Wire
F#—C#	6	.020	Brass Spring Wire
C—AA	4	.025	Brass Spring Wire

235

instrument altogether, the other just a turning up of the pin. If there are many windings of wire on the tuning pins, it is likely to be style "A." If the pins have only four or five windings, using style "B" will result in a better match.

Tuning pin winding Style A. Unwind and take out the tuning pin needing string replacement. Place the wire loop on the hitchpin and unravel enough wire to bring it to about a foot (somewhat less in the bass) past the tuning pin position. Hold the tuning pin horizontal with the squared end to the right, insert wire end in the tuning pin hole and start turning the pin in a clockwise movement, coiling on the wire until all of the excess is on the pin. Rolling the pin between the fingers and maintaining tension on the string, the loops (about 15 coils) should wind on the pin close together and in neat order. The pin is then tilted vertically, inserted in its wrestplank hole, and hammered down to the height of its neighbors. The last two coils on the pin may have to be pushed down to achieve enough downbearing from the nut. Make sure wire is against its proper bridge and nut pin. Giving the string a tug by hand will stretch it out and allow it to hold like its neighbors.

Tuning pin winding Style B. Wind up the pin needing the replacement string six full turns. Then bring wire about 3 inches past the tuning pin and clip, holding on to the wire all the time. (A spring-loaded clothes pin placed over the hitchpin will prevent the loop from slipping off the hitchpin.) Next thread the end of wire into tuning pin hole, letting it stick out about $1/16$ in. since it will slip back a bit. This will create a 3-inch slack which is to be wound on the tuning pin. The tuning wrench is held with the right hand, turning down the pin (clockwise), while the left hand feeds the wire carefully, allowing it to coil neatly, each coil lying directly below the preceding coil. The last coil may have to be slipped down to establish some downbearing with respect to the nut. Check the position of the string to make sure it is against its nut and bridge pin.

Aside from breaking, the strings can cause trouble if they are rusty or corroded, especially at the point of contact with the plectrum; roughness on the string can cause a hanger. If the rust or corrosion feels rough to the touch, it should be cleaned off with steel wool or a hard rubber eraser. To remove dust on the soundboard from under the strings, use a large, soft bristled, new paint brush, wiping right through the strings. Dust can be collected in the corners and vacuumed out. Reversing the vacuum to blower will get the dust out even more thoroughly, though it may settle on the remaining furniture of the room.

When a harpsichord goes out of tune in what seems to its owner an un-usual fashion, the first thing he will often blame are the tuning pins, having learned that this is the cause in pianos which don't hold pitch. It must be remembered that, in a harpsichord, tuning pins are not loose if they cannot be turned with the *fingers of one hand.* Before the harpsichord owner jumps to unwarranted conclusions about loose pins and chemical tighteners, he should realize that loose pins on harpsichords are extremely rare and are more likely to occur because of faulty fits from pin to plastic bushing then on wooden blocks.

The most common causes of tuning instability (not including inherent structural characteristics) are given here approximately in the order of their importance:

Tuning pin winding Style A, with a short coil in the middle of the pin and the final windings pushed down to provide bearing on the nut.

Tuning pin winding Style B, with a single winding of about four coils.

1. A poor tuning job; the harpsichord will be out of tune before the tuner puts down his wrench.
2. A radical change in weather from very dry to very humid.
3. New strings which need stretching out to their limits.
4. A brand new and "unweathered" case.
5. "Frictional retardation," i.e., overly strong string angles on a double-pinned bridge.
6. Slipping hitchpin loops.
7. Loose hitchpin rail, or loose or missing frame members (if strings go consistently and radically down).

The two commonly blamed causes for poor tuning stability—loose tuning pins and the movers—can practically be ruled out. We have seen that harpsichords can be moved across the Atlantic without much loss in tuning accuracy, but once the instrument has arrived, one day of radical weather change can put an end to all that. In order to enable the harpsichord owner to know if his instrument is exhibiting unusual tuning instability, he must, of course, have a norm or a frame of reference. What, indeed, is tuning instability, and how often must a harpsichord be tuned in the ordinary course of events?

When I was in the Army, the lieutenant teaching us warfare would answer any question about tactics from the soldiers with the stock reply, "It depends on the situation and the terrain." Something very similar could be applied to tuning stability. It varies from one hearer to another, from one tuner to another, from one harpsichord to another, from one climate to another. It must be remembered that multi-string set harpsichords, which must agree in unisons, will require much more frequent tuning than a single set of strings which will rise and descend more or less in a fixed relation. More frequent tuning will also be necessary in ensemble playing with a fixed pitch; many times an instrument will be quite acceptable, but a quarter tone high or low. Keeping all of this in mind, tuning anywhere from once a week to once a month is average; any more than that may be considered unstable, any less extremely stable.

Coming now to the soundboard we must again divest ourselves of everything we have learned about pianos. Harpsichord soundboards may be very wavy, warped up or down, without causing any serious problems except when the up-warp is great enough to touch the strings and the down-wrap is enough to bring the bridge below the level of the strings. Similarly, cracks have no ill effect unless they cause a buzz or pull the soundboard completely apart. Soundboards which have sunk far enough to give the strings no bridge bearing at all can be fixed quickly with a "happiness" bar, a dowel with a coil spring on top. The half-inch dowel is squeezed between the harpsichord bottom (an opening may have to be made) and the bridge underside. The coil spring will presumably allow the board to "breathe."

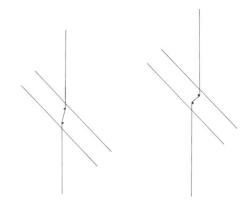

Safe and dangerous angles for strings on double-pinned bridges. The acute angle of the string at the right can cause tuning instability since the friction at the bridge can prevent the entire string length from taking an equal tension.

Diagram of a typical wavy soundboard. Unless the waves are actually touched by the sounding strings, such distortions seem to have no affect on the tone of the instrument.

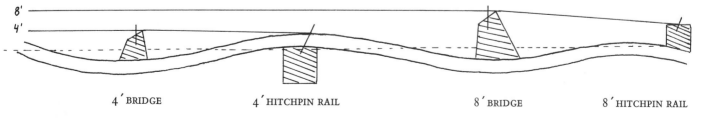

4′ BRIDGE   4′ HITCHPIN RAIL   8′ BRIDGE   8′ HITCHPIN RAIL

A soundboard which is warped up is harder to repair. One extra rib may have to be installed from underneath under the area of greatest warpage. The extra rib should be as thin as possible. The easiest way to get the rib to stay on a flattened soundboard is to put glue on the rib and then nail it in from the top with small half-inch nails, whose holes have been pre-drilled to establish the rib's position. The nailheads, which will show on the soundboard's surface, can be touched up with a color matching that of the board. This repair, although perhaps not as neat as it should be, does flatten the board and does not interfere with the tone. It is a lot easier than replacing the soundboard itself.

Soundboard cracks should be left alone unless the repairer feels competent to shim them. Tapered shims are available from the piano supply houses, but their taper is usually too steep for thin harpsichord soundboards. Vellum or cloth was often glued under soundboard joints or cracks. Hubbard suggests epoxy resin for filling some cracks, but the wood is likely to shrink away from the filler which itself does not expand or contract with the wood, causing a new crack along its border. To locate a buzz, one person should play the buzzing note while a second person probes the soundboard, putting finger pressure on all its areas. If the buzz is caused by the soundboard, it should change or disappear (sometimes for good) during such probing.

VI. THE REST OF THE HARPSICHORD

After having considered the action, soundboard and strings, we are left with the cabinet and some general considerations which we will discuss under the headings of (a) the jack rail, (b) the legs, (c) the cabinet, (d) moving, crating and storage and (e) emergency repairs.

A. The jack rail. This wooden slat, which is fixed above the jacks, is the only part of the cabinet which bears directly on the touch of the action. The rail, which should have felt or rubber padding on its underside, must be set so that the jacks just touch it when the keys are down as far as they will go. Jack rails can cause an unsatisfactory action if they are too high, too low, too loose, or too flexible. A jack rail which is too high will let the jacks bounce up after the key has bottomed, delaying their return. A low jack rail will decrease the amount of key dip and make the action uncomfortable to play. A simple test of a low jack rail is to leave the rail in its regular position but unfastened and then strike the keys; if the jacks themselves push up the rail it is too low, inhibiting their travel upwards. A loose rail will cause a rattle, clattering as the jacks bounce against it. Whatever system is used to fasten the jack rail to the case sides always allows its easy removal and is usually also adjustable in height. A rail too flexible will permit a rubbery touch in the center of the keyboard, where the jacks will not experience a firm resistance as they push against the rail above them.

B. The legs. Many harpsichords are shaky or swing from front to back because of a poor connection between their legs and the cabinet. The sturdiest base for a harpsichord is a stand, but many makers prefer the much more easily made legs. A stand, which should be collapsible for transportation, generally consists of a front section, a rear section, and two connecting rails. To make the stand collapsible it is necessary to provide the rail ends with hidden nuts which match bolts from the front and rear sections. The important thing about the legs is the method attaching them to the underside of the case. Some makers use thin ($^1/_4$ in.) bolts going into little nuts, resulting in give between the leg tops and the instrument bottom. The bolts should be steel and at least $^1/_2$ in. thick, going into threaded steel plates, against which the entire leg top surface must bear firmly. This type of connection also allows the leg to be screwed on and off without the use of tools. The German system, copied from the piano, of using male and female plates matched by press fits usually has just enough play to result in a shaky harpsichord in spite of the thick and heavy legs. Wooden threads and matching threaded wooden plates will usually wear out with a fair amount of use.

C. The cabinet. A thorough discussion of cabinet repairs and finishes would not be within the scope of this book and is, in any case, easily available. In general, harpsichords are not finished in the highly polished tradition of pianos and television cabinets, but usually show a rubbed oil finish. If the owner can be certain that his instrument has this kind of finish, he can apply further coats of oil (boiled linseed). We have found that scratches and spots can be touched up with an eyebrow pencil which comes conveniently in the various shades of natural wood and has enough of a greasy base to adhere well. (Frank Hubbard has found that Miss Clairol hair dye—light or sable brown—gives the right shade for matching Italian boxwood keys.)

Most harpsichord owners are nervous about making such changes to their cases as the addition of mouldings, hinges or soundboard decorations, thinking that these may interfere with the tone. By now it should be apparent to the reader that although the thickness of the case and the weight of the frame members are important to the tone, minor alterations to the outside cabinet are going to make no difference whatsoever.

D. Moving, crating and storage. To move harpsichords it is best to own a heavy padded canvas cover with straps and buckles, which is fitted to the particular instrument. (John Challis, in addition to making every detail on his harpsichords, also sits down at the sewing machine to make the cover.) In lieu of a cover, the harpsichord can be wrapped and tied into a quilted mover's pad. During transport, the instrument should either rest on its spine, lashed to

Shipping crate for a harpsichord showing rigid brace along bentside, and lifting tapes left in position for removal.

the side of the truck, or lie flat on its bottom, provided no pedal underaction protrudes below the level of the leg mounting blocks.

For long distance shipping, a simple rectangular crate can be made, consisting of 1-in. pine sides and $1/4$-in. plywood top and bottom, reinforced with a few struts. The crate must have one diagonal brace (see illustration) to fit the particular instrument. When constructing the crate, a one inch space should be left all around the instrument for stuffing tight with shredded or crumpled newspaper. The instrument can be covered with wax or oil paper. Two canvas straps should be used to lower it into position (coffin fashion); these straps are left in and will later be used to lift it out again. There should be more paper between the top of the harpsichord and the lid of the crate. The crate lid should be screwed on, so that it can be opened with ease. The legs, pedal lyre, and accessories can be packed in the small triangle formed in the crate by the diagonal brace.

When storing harpsichords for long periods of time, especially during the summer, it may be a good idea to tune the whole instrument down one full tone to forestall the possibility of the strings going up a tone or more above pitch (something quite common in harpsichords) and thus leading to string breakage.

E. Emergency Repairs. By this I mean getting an instrument ready for a performance with a minimum of tools and time. I sincerely hope the reader will not experience a situation in which an entire orchestra and its famous conductor, plus the engineering staff of a recording studio, twiddle their thumbs, whiling away the precious minutes (each costing hundreds of dollars), while a lone harpsichord tuner struggles with that instrument. I would also hope the reader is spared tuning a concert harpsichord on the stage of Carnegie Hall for a recital of Bach's *Well Tempered Clavier* (thus demanding special care in tuning) while an impatient mob of harpsichord enthusiasts is milling in front of the hall's closed doors and the head usher is nervously demanding more speed.

Complete calm and a light hearted attitude are necessary to cope with such situations. If some jacks fail to work and the instrument is slightly out of tune, the player will at least have a chance to blame his performance on the harpsichord. I have never yet heard a harpsichord recital in which the performer did not miss a good number of notes, so one may be doing him a favor to provide an easy alibi.

To prevent a last minute panic, it is better to tune and check the instrument carefully before it has gone to the concert hall. One should not rely on the excuse that it will only need tuning and adjustment all over again after the move. The condition the harpsichord leaves in is almost certainly the condition in which it will arrive.

If at the last minute a broken string is discovered, and if the tuner has a replacement, the string should be tugged and pulled vigorously to stretch it out in order to avoid its almost certain descent. If a balky jack is encountered which absolutely defies regulation under stress, the tuner may try exchanging it with an extreme treble or bass jack of a note not much used. The jacks of a harpsichord are usually numbered consecutively from No. 1 in the bass, and are often fitted to their particular slot, so exchanging jacks may not work and should be used only in emergencies. (Judging by the total disarray of the order of many jacks I have seen, switching is a common practice.) If a plectrum has snapped and the tuner has no replacement, he may try his own toenail clipping; since this is much softer than delrin and heavily curved, it should be left on the short side.

THE TUNING SYSTEMS

The average harpsichord owner struggling with his tuning wrench may feel somewhat better to learn that Leonard Bernstein failed completely in his first attempt to tune his harpsichord. The possession of what is commonly known as "perfect pitch" will not aid in the setting of an equal tempered bearing; on the contrary, it may well interfere, allowing the possessor of this gift to hear perfect intervals instead of the adjusted relationships between notes which constitute modern, equal tempered tuning.

The Greek philosopher Pythagoras examined the relationships between the vibration of stretched strings. The philosopher, who believed that the essence of things could be expressed numerically, found that the relationships between consonant intervals could be expressed in ratios of whole numbers. If A, for instance, gives off 440 vibrations per second, then the A an octave lower will produce 220 v.p.s. or a ratio of 1:2. If the E above the lower A gives off 330 v.p.s. it will yield a pure or beatless fifth; the relationship between 220 and 330 can be expressed by the ratio 2:3. When the frequencies of two strings are not in such simple mathematical relationships, the vibrations clash and set up pulsating waves or "beats" at the points where the vibrations do not coincide.

Pythagoras found that an octave derived from a cycle of 12 pure or perfect fifths (3:2) will not yield a perfect octave (2:1) as well. It will result in a larger or *wider* octave, and the difference between the actual result and the perfect octave is known as the "Pythagorean comma." Since octaves sound in unison, and anything less than a perfect octave is immediately recognized by the ear, the Pythagorean comma has to be absorbed by other intervals. Most tuning systems or temperaments are attempts to absorb the Pythagorean comma gradually, or hide it where it will show least.

We must remember that tuning becomes a problem only on an instrument in which each note has a fixed chromatic pitch. On most instruments the player has some control over pitch and can make necessary adjustments himself. When keyboard instruments came into use, players were forced to recognise the problem of how to tune them. Different eras have supplied different answers, generally in response to the music being written at the time. When composers were not concerned with harmony or vertical relationships, they did not need to worry about how chords would sound together.

We can thus distinguish between tuning systems like the Pythagorean, meantone, well-tempered tuning, and equal temperament. Because the reader may well want to try some of these earlier systems, it will be instructive to go into them in some detail. We must realise that the modern equal tempered tuning is the most colorless of all systems, since it achieves an exactly equal division between all semitones. It thus makes very little difference whether a piece is played in the key of C, A, or G sharp, aside from the actual pitch; a composition will sound the same, because the relationships between the notes in a given key are always the same as those between notes of another key.

To tune a Pythagorean scale of perfect fifths, it is first necessary to find out what the sound of a perfect fifth is like. A fifth is an interval comprising $3^{1/2}$ full tones, like the intervals A-E, G-D and F#-C#. Aside from the octave, the sound of a perfect fifth is perhaps the most well known. It is what all string players use when they tune their instruments; the perfect fifths have a flat, absolutely beatless sound which is easily recognized. We may try this tuning order as given below, keeping in mind that all the fifths must be perfect or beatless fifths. The bearing or guide octave is going to be contained within the span f-b′ (F below middle C to the B above middle C). Whenever a fifth lies outside this range, we must tune an octave up or down to bring it within that space.

A "Pythagorean" Tuning

1. Tune beatless fifths forward (up) from middle C to G# as follows: C up a fifth to G; G down an octave to G; G up a fifth to D; D up a fifth to A; A down an octave to A; A up a fifth to E; E up a fifth to B; B down an octave to B; B up a fifth to F#; F# down an octave to F#; F# up a fifth to C#; C# up a fifth to G#; G# down an octave to G#.

2. Tune beatless fifths backwards (down) from middle C to E flat as follows: C down a fifth to F; F up an octave to F; F down a fifth to B flat; B flat up an octave to B flat; B flat down a fifth to E flat.

3. Tune the rest of the instrument in octaves from the bearing.

We will now have arrived at a tuning in which the comma has been absorbed in one fifth, G sharp–E flat, which is completely wild. Four of the thirds should be approximately perfect, and the remaining thirds wider than perfect by an equal margin.

Moving now to the most important of the early tuning systems, meantone tuning, we discover that, while the Pythagorean scale had perfect fifths and wide thirds, just intonation had perfect fifths and some perfect thirds, meantone has perfect major thirds and narrowed fifths. Thus we encounter the narrow fifth, the mainstay of equal tempered tuning, for the first time. The fifth was "as narrow as the ear can bear" (much narrower, indeed, than in equal tempered tuning); that is, the tuner left it before it started the out of phase beats which sound unpleasant or "sour." Unlike equal tempered tuning, in which the major thirds have a very strong beat, meantone has beatless thirds. Now the presence or absence of beats in major thirds is far from an abstract question over which scholars may quibble. Unlike the slowly beating narrow fifth (perhaps 2 or 2 beats per second) equal tempered major thirds around middle C have as many beats as the ear can comfortably take in, resulting in a buzzy, pulsating sound. Beatless thirds, on the other hand, sound absolutely flat and heavenly pure. When a C major triad is sounded in an equal tempered scale, the chords pulsate with the nervous energy of our modern age; the same triad in meantone has a calm, otherworldly ring.

Why, the reader may ask, isn't meantone tuning used on all harpsichords if most of the harpsichord music was written while this system was in common use? Well, in the first place, the system is little known nowadays, and although it is certainly no more difficult (probably less so) than equal tempered tuning,

The wrong and the right way to grapple with a tuning hammer. Sense of touch is important; one wants to feel the pin as one listens to the tone. Unlike piano pins, which may need a firm grip, harpsichord tuning pins should respond with finger pressure. After tuning, listen to the tone with hands off the hammer, or, better still, with hammer off the pin. Good tuners pull the pin very slightly above pitch (very slightly), and then gently ease the pin down to pitch. The hammer should float in the hand—any pressure up or down on the handle of the hammer will strain the pin from its normal position and lead to a harpsichord that is out of tune before the tuning is finished.

few modern tuners know how to set a meantone bearing. Secondly, the system is only good for keys up to three sharps or two flats without retuning the enharmonic black keys, making it cumbersome for a good deal of the later literature, and impossible for most nineteenth-century music. It was this weakness, of course, which introduced the equal tempered scale into which any key can fit equally well, though each key will be "out of tune" by the same amount.

Meantone derives its name from the division of a third into two equal whole steps. The resultant temperament achieves a distinct coloring for each of the eight principal meantone keys, to which composers attached emotional significances. According to Yates,* composers of the later meantone period used the dramatic and pathetic effects of the temperament to great effect, and he cites as an example the "Fall of Goliath" in Kuhnau's "David and Goliath." Meantone's most important use, according to Yates, was to "build in by modulation changes of registration more variable and subtle than those that can be produced by pedal changes on a modern instrument." Let us, then, follow Yates' suggested tuning order for meantone, adding enough detail to his sketchy diagram to enable the average tuner to follow it easily.

When checking the accuracy of narrowed fifths with beatless thirds at the checkpoints given, the tuner must keep in mind that a third possessing beats could be either wide or narrow, that is outside or inside of smooth (or beatless). As soon as any interval gets away from smooth and is widened or narrowed, it will start beating; the only way the tuner can tell whether he is on the inside of smooth or on the outside is to continue widening or narrowing the interval. If a third C-E, for example, is wide (or outside of smooth) and if the C is in tune, than the E must be sharp. Lowering the E will make the interval beat more slowly until the beats disappear and the third is perfect. Lowering the E still further will narrow the interval and the beats will start increasing at the same rate at which they slowed down.

Tuning Meantone Temperament

1. Tune narrow fifths forward from middle C. This is done by tuning a perfect fifth first, and then *lowering* the *upper* note of the fifth until a slow beat can be heard. (If you have trouble hearing beats, tune a perfect octave and then tune down the upper note *very* slowly; listening carefully you will hear slow pulsations, getting faster as you proceed with tuning it down, until the octave sounds "sour.") The beat of the fifth must be fairly slow, but clearly audible. Octaves are beatless.

Tune from C up a fifth to G; G down an octave to G; G up a fifth to D; D up a fifth to A; A down an octave to A; A up a fifth to E.

2. Now check the major third C-E both of whose notes have already been tuned. It should be beatless; otherwise the narrowed fifths have not been set correctly.

3. Continue tuning narrow fifths forward as follows: E up a fifth to B; B down an octave to B; (check beatless third G-B); B up a fifth to F# (check beatless third D-F#); F# down an octave to F#; F# up a fifth to C# (check beatless third A-c#); C# up a fifth to G#; G# down an octave to G#.

*Peter Yates, *Amateur at the Keyboard*, New York 1964.

4. Tune narrow fifths backwards from middle C. This time the *lower* note of the fifth is *raised* slightly to narrow it: C down a fifth to F (check beatless third F-A); F up an octave to F; F down a fifth to B flat (check beatless third B flat-D); B flat up and octave to B flat; B flat down a fifth to E flat.

5. Enharmonic intervals are tuned sharp or flat as the key requires. Thus if A flat is desired, it should make a beatless third with C. If G sharp is wanted it is tuned to a beatless third with E.

6. Tune the rest of the instrument in octaves from the bearing.

When the later Baroque composers started to write music in all the different keys, including those not covered by meantone tuning, it became important to make compromises with the meantone temperament. Thus composers tried to achieve a *well-tempered* tuning which would preserve the distinction between the individual keys but allow all of them to be played harmoniously. These attempts led to the famous well-tempered tuning of J. S. Bach.

Turning now to our modern equal temperament, we find that this tuning system is designed for chords and vertical relationships, which will sound equally harmonious (or dissonant) anywhere on the keyboard. There are many methods of setting an equal temperament, but the result should not be capable of any variation. Modern tuning starts with A-440, although in recent years the concert pitch, which was arrived at by international agreement, has been driven up mercilessly by the big orchestras. The string players think they sound better (certainly shriller) slightly sharp, so that the New York Philharmonic now sets A at 442 v.p.s., while the Metropolitan Opera and the Berlin Philharmonic use A-444.

Equal temperament is based on narrow fifths, wide fourths, and very wide major thirds. The major thirds beat faster as they ascend, and this characteristic is used by professional tuners to check the accuracy of their narrowed fifths and widened fourths. In the octave F-F around middle C there is a progression of 8 major thirds; the F-A has about 6 beats per second, while each successive major third increases its speed just recognizably faster until the last third C-E is almost a blur.

Before proceeding, we must briefly turn our attention to the handling of the tuning hammer. Because harpsichord strings are thin, the slightest movement of the tuning pins will result in a pitch change. On many harpsichords the tuning pins stick out far enough so that any sideways pressure against the pin results in a pitch change. Therefore the wrench should be set perfectly vertically on the pin. A "T" hammer is probably better from that point of view but I prefer an "L" shaped wrench because the tuner can get more leverage to move pins which are sometimes extremely tight.

Piano tuners "set" the pin—they leave it just a hair above the true pitch, so that when the pin winds downward due to string pressure, it will go "into" rather than out of tune. In harpsichords the pin itself is rarely the cause of a string going out of tune. More important than "setting" the pin is the ability to leave the pin in the exact position required and check the pitch *after* the tuning wrench has been removed from the pin. The act of lifting off the wrench can sometimes result in a pitch change, especially if the tuner "leans" on the pin.

Harpsichords which are completely out of tune (half tone sharp or flat) should be quickly and roughly tuned to pitch before attempting a fine tuning; if the tuner fine-tunes such an instrument, his bass will go out while he tunes the treble and vice versa. Harpsichords which are sharp should be rough-tuned somewhat *below* pitch ($^1/_8$ tone) since they will have a tendency to creep back up; similarly flat harpsichords should first be quickly pulled slightly *above* pitch. One suggestion for getting around the necessity for three hands when holding and sounding a tuning fork, striking a key, and handling the hammer is to strike the fork and use the vibrating fork itself to depress the key.

The tuning procedure for equal temperament described here is the simplest one for the amateur to follow. It does not require any comparisons with thirds, nor any tuning of fourths. Nor does it entail any thought on the part of the tuner when and how to widen or narrow his intervals. It is a simple cycle of narrowed fifths going only forward, so that the top note of the fifth is lowered in each case to make the fifth narrow. Equal-tempered fifths are not as narrow as meantone fifths; they are just a little bit under a perfect or beat-less interval. The tuner should set a beatless fifth and then tune the upper note down a fraction of a turn, stopping long before the interval sounds wild. The average ear may not, at first, hear the difference between a beatless fifth and an equal-tempered fifth; the equal tempered fifth has a slow, lazy wave to it, which must be listened to carefully.

Equal Tempered Tuning

1. Tune *slightly* narrowed fifths forward from A as follows: A-440 down an octave to A-220; A up a fifth to E; E up a fifth to B; B down an octave to B; B up a fifth to F#; F# down an octave to F#; F# up a fifth to C#; C# up a fifth to G#; G# down an octave to G#; G# up a fifth to D#; D# up a fifth to A#; A# down an octave to A#; A# up a fifth to F; F down an octave to F; F up a fifth to C; C up a fifth to G; G down an octave to G; G up a fifth to D; D up a fifth to A.

2. The last fifth, D-A, is the checkpoint. If it is slightly narrow without beating wildly, the temperament will be correct. As another check, the tuner may try ascending thirds, starting with f-a, and compare their increasing speeds.

3. Tune the rest of the instrument in octaves, the bass first.

When tuning a multi-string set harpsichord, start with the principal 8′ set and tune it completely. Then put on the second 8′ and tune it to the first set, starting from the top and going down chromatically. Try the unisons in octaves to see that there are no beats. Next, take off the second 8′ and put on the 4′ set. The original 8′ set stays on all the time as the guide from which the other sets are tuned. After the 4′ has been tuned to the first 8′, try all three sets together by octaves. If there is a 16′, shut off all but the original 8′ and tune the 16′ to it. Then try the entire harpsichord coupled together. Playing octaves with both hands on a four string-set harpsichord will produce 16 notes, which must all sound in unison. Any tuner who can turn out a faultless tuning of this kind is ready for Carnegie Hall.

Thus we leave the reader, with his well tempered and well regulated harpsichord. May it be, to him, a thing of beauty and a joy forever.

Glossary

Adjustment screw   the jack screw regulating the amount of plectrum projection.

Arcade   the keyfront on many antique keyboards and modern copies, which consists of a series of round arches formed by a rotating cutter.

Back eight foot   the row of jacks farthest from the player, activated by the lower manual, which pluck the string a distance from the nut and thus produce a fluty tone.

Back rail   the rear cross member of the key frame, covered with cloth or felt (back rail felt).

Balance pin   the pin passing through the center of a key, acting as its pivot.

Balance rail   the central cross member of the key frame, carrying the balance pins.

Bearing   the downward or sideward thrust of strings on bridge or nut. Also the guide octave in which a temperament is set.

Beat   the waxing and waning caused when two notes are sounded which are not in exact mathematical relationships. When an A-440 v.p.s. and an A-444 v.p.s. are sounded together they will produce 4 beats per second.

Belly rail   the harpsichord frame member running under the front edge of the soundboard. The bellyrail and pinblock edge form the gap which contains the action.

Bentside   the curved or right hand side of the harpsichord case. On some instruments the "bentside" is not curved.

Box slide   the type of jack slide or register which is deep enough to hold the jacks upright without requiring a lower guide.

Bridge   the curved strip glued to the soundboard over which the strings pass. The bridge transmits the string's vibrations to the soundboard.

Bridge pin   the pin driven into the bridge to position the strings and define the end of the string's vibrating segment.

Bristle   the jack spring whose function it is to return the tongue after it glides around the string upon the jack's return after plucking. Originally made of hog's bristle, this spring is now usually made of nylon or music wire, but is often still called a bristle.

Buff stop   a series of leather or felt pads mounted on a rail, which create a pizzicato or harp effect when brought into contact with a set of strings. This stop is called *harp* stop in England and *Lautenzug* in Germany, which is sometimes erroneously translated as "lute" stop. In Germany the buff on a 16′ is called a *theorbo* stop.

Cap moulding   the moulding on the upper edge of Italian harpsichords

Capstan   a heavy screw with four holes in its head used for regulating the position of action parts such as jack slides.

Cembalo   the German term for harpsichord.

Cheek   the short side piece in a harpsichord case, to the right of the keyboard.

Clavecin   the French term for harpsichord.

Clavichord   a rectangular keyboard instrument possessing metal blades (tangents) which strike the string, but unlike piano hammers have no escapement action.

Coupler   a device connecting the upper keyboard to the lower, so that strings normally played from the upper keyboard can be added to registers played on the lower keyboard.

Cutoff bar   the largest soundboard rib, usually placed diagonally to the spine, and roughly parallel to bridge and bentside.

Coupler dog   an upright prong either mounted on the lower keys or hanging from the upper keys which connects the two keyboards.

Covered strings   bass strings which have a soft wire winding wrapped around a hard wire core to increase their weight. Such strings are needed when the bass is shortened from its natural or ideal length.

246

Damper   the felt pad on the jack which damps the string.

Delrin   a modern plastic often used in harpsichord plectra.

Dip   see "key dip."

Disposition   the arrangements of stops on a harpsichord.

Docke   the German term for jack.

Dog   see "coupler dog."

Dogleg jack   a jack which can be operated from both the upper and lower keyboard.

Double harpsichord   an instrument with two manuals.

Double virginal   an instrument possessing two virginals, one in 8´ and one in 4´ pitch.

Down bearing   the amount of downwards pressure exerted by the strings.

Eight foot   a set of strings in a harpsichord tuned to normal pitch (at unison with the piano). The term derives from organ building where the pipe for note CC is eight feet long.

End pin   the vertical lower screw on the jack which regulates its height.

Equal tempered tuning   the modern setting of the temperament dividing the octave into 12 equal semi-tones.

Foreshortening   the shortening of the bass strings so that they deviate from the mathematical ideal of doubling the length of each octave.

Four foot   a set of strings tuned an octave higher than 8 foot or normal pitch.

Frame   the inner structural members in a harpsichord case.

Front rail   the front cross member of the key frame.

Front pin   the key pin driven into the front rail which serves to guide the key in many modern keyboards.

Gap   the space between belly rail and pinblock which contains the action.

Ghosting   the faint sound produced when the plectra of a set of jacks brushes the strings when in the "off" position.

Half hitch   see "half stop."

Half stop   a mechanism allowing a set of jacks to pluck at half strength (near their plectras' tip) to produce a soft or *piano* tone.

Hand stop   a hand operated mechanism for changing registration.

Harp stop   see "buff stop."

Harpsichord   a plucked instrument possessing strings running parallel to the spine, as distinguished from virginals and spinets.

Hitchpin   the pin holding the string at its terminus beyond the bridge.

Hitchpin rail   the strip of wood or metal containing the hitchpins.

Inner case   the harpsichord proper in Italian instruments with a separate outer case. In some modern harpsichords, a complete inner frame.

Jack   the plucking device in a harpsichord, spinet or virginal.

Jack guide   see "lower guide."

Jack rail   the bar with a felted or cushioned underside, which is positioned above the jacks to limit their upward motion.

Jack slide   the narrow rail with punched slots which serves as the upper guide for the jacks, and whose motion allows the jack to be brought in and out of play.

Jack spring   see "bristle."

Just scale   the scale in which the string length is doubled for each successive octave.

Keyboard   the unit comprising the key levers mounted on the key frame.

Key blocks   the wooden blocks at either end of the keyboard.

Key button   a block of wood on some modern keyboards, with a rectangular, felted slot through which the balance pin passes at the top of the key.

Key dip   the amount a key travels downwards at its front.

Key frame   the structure supporting the key levers.

Key front   the vertical front of natural keys.

Key lever   the actual key, especially the part hidden under the action.

Key top   the covering applied to a natural key.

Knee in Italian harpsichords, a triangular brace holding the case sides.

Knee lever a device operated by the player's knee, to change registration.

Lid stick the stick which props up the lid.

Liner the strip running along the case to which the soundboard is glued.

Lock strip the board in front of the keyboard which often holds a lock.

Lower guide the fixed lower rail through which the jack bottoms or end pins pass.

Lute stop a row of jacks plucking very close to the nut and producing a nasal tone; not to be confused with the buff stop.

Machine stop a device operated by pedal or knee lever which allows a shift in several registers at once for a sudden *piano* effect.

Manual a keyboard.

Meantone tuning a tuning system used in most of the early music, in which thirds were beatless and fifths were considerably narrowed.

Music wire the thin steel wire used for stringing in harpsichords.

Name batten a narrow strip of wood above the keys screwed to the pinblock, which often bears the maker's name.

Name board the board above the keys running the width of the instrument.

Naturals any of the octave's seven keys with wide tops, reaching to the front. The "white keys" as distinguished from the "black" keys called "sharps" or "accidentals."

Nut the front bridge, usually glued to the pinblock near the line of jacks.

Overspun strings see "covered strings."

Peau de buffle buffalo hide; a stop using this soft leather which strokes rather than plucks.

Pedal a foot operated device to change the stops.

Pedal harpsichord a harpsichord possessing an organ pedal board which can be operated by the player's feet.

Pinblock the hardwood, laminated, or metal block holding the tuning pins.

Pitch c the pitch of c^2, an octave above middle C, used as the standard for comparing length of scale in harpsichords.

Plectrum the piece of quill, leather or plastic projecting from the jack, which actually does the plucking.

Plucking point the point at which a string is plucked, relative to the overall length of the string.

Punchings the small felt or paper washers which regulate key dip and key level.

Push coupler see "shove coupler."

Quill the material (i.e., crow and raven) used for plucking on the old harpsichords. Also, any plectrum.

Quint a set of strings tuned a fifth (or an octave and a fifth) above 8′ pitch.

Rack the board in back of the keyboard with vertical cuts in which the keys were guided on antique instruments.

Ravalement the French term for the change of Flemish harpsichords to a wider compass and more useful disposition.

Register see "jack slide."

Rib the bars glued to the underside of the soundboard at an angle to the cutoff bar.

Rose the ornamental rosette set into the soundboard.

Scale the string lengths of an instrument, generally expressed by citing the length of c^2.

Sharp Any one of the octave's five accidental keys which do not reach to the front.

Short octave on antique instruments, the lowest octave in which some keys have been omitted, and others are tuned to lower notes to extend the range.

Shove coupler a keyboard coupler which is disengaged by pulling the upper keyboard toward the player and engaged by shoving the keyboard backwards.

Sixteen foot stop a set of strings tuned an octave below 8′ pitch; also the row of jacks which plays such a set.

Soundboard   the thin vibrating board underneath the strings, which carries the bridge.

Spine   the straight (left) side of a harpsichord.

Spinet   the triangular or polygonal harpsichord with strings running at an angle to the front.

Square   an oblong-shaped instrument, generally an early piano.

Stop   a row of jacks (like the 8′ or 4′), or a device (like the buff stop) which is capable of altering the tone.

String band   the width and outline of the space which the strings occupy.

Tail   the small rear case piece which forms the end of the harpsichord.

Tangent   a metal blade which strikes the string in a clavichord.

Tongue   the pivoting member of the jack carrying the plectrum.

Tuning hammer   the wrench used to turn the tuning pins; sometimes used to tap in the pins.

Tuning pin   the steel pin with a threaded bottom and square head which holds the string at one end.

Unisons   two notes, or sets of strings, of the same pitch.

Venetian swell   a stop operating a lid with Venetian slats which could be opened when playing for loud-soft effects.

Virginal   an oblong harpsichord with strings running parallel to the front.

Voicing   the operation of shaping the plectra to achieve the optimum sound from a harpsichord.

Wrest plank   see "pinblock."

Appendix—
By a
Harpsichord
Kit Builder

HARPSICHORD KIT—A superb, authentic, full toned instrument, in kit form for easy home workshop assembly, $150. Same instrument as owned by Metropolitan Opera, Philadelphia Orchestra and RCA Victor Records. Also Clavichord kit, $100. For free brochure please write to: Zuckermann Harpsichords, Dept. O. 115 Christopher St., N.Y.C. 10014.

The relationship between Wally Zuckermann of Zuckermann Harpsichords, Inc. and the author of this book is perhaps too close to make possible that olympian detachment as well as the warmth and severity with which he has dealt with the other makers in this book. What Wolfgang Joachim Zuckermann has written about Zuckermann Harpsichords has been printed in its entirety, but since Mr. Zuckermann, who is responsible for more harpsichords in America than all other makers combined, is self-effacing to a degree, and since the publisher wants this book to be as complete and informative as possible, it may serve the interest of the reader, and the cause of even-handed justice, if one of his customers appends this note. It will serve, by extension, to represent in this book the largest class of harpsichord makers in America—the ten or twelve thousand amateurs (and some professionals) who have constructed a harpsichord from a kit.

My first visit to Zuckermann Harpsichords took me up a back stairs in a loft building in Greenwich Village into a small office with a harpsichord on one side and a clavichord on the other, and parts of instruments displayed on the walls. Through doorways to the left and right could be seen a number of people working on a number of instruments, including two very pretty girls walking back and forth stringing. To one side were several old harpsichords in various stages of repair.

Zuckermann himself is an intense wiry man, with gray sideburns and a manner of speaking—at once shy and harrassed—that made me think he would rather have been anywhere else but in the midst of all that bustle. Shortly after that he did abandon production of finished harpsichords and concentrated on kits only. By casual questions over a considerable period of time I learned that he came to this country in 1938, and that he is the son of an academician father who presided at family musical evenings. He plays the cello, and of course the harpsichord. Besides the Christopher Street office he has another shop farther west in the outskirts of the Village near the docks, and he lives nearby in a charming old house on a tiny cobbled lane. The largest room in his house, between the kitchen and the bedroom, contains a lathe, a drillpress and a large workbench.

As can be imagined, he spends a considerable portion of his time talking to customers on the telephone and answering their letters. He takes all of the troubles and failures of his customers personally, as though they were his own fault; he is constantly rewriting instructions to make them clearer or to warn against still another possibility of disaster. Only a small percentage of his builders have trouble, but he suffers with those who do. "How is it possible," he will ask sadly, "for a soundboard to sink under the bridge at the *treble*? *That* never happened before." And he will try to think of something that will help.

Since his customers all seem to have their troubles in the middle of the night (and their enthusiasm often seems to keep them working long after they should have knocked off for a good night's sleep and clearer heads), he has had to list his home phone under an assumed name. Tony Vivaldi was a recent one, and the present, and equally improbable, *nom de telephone* is so far known only to those who do *not* make harpsichords in the middle of the night.

He recently purchased a thirteenth-century house in Devonshire, England, where he dreams of retiring for a part of each year to work out improvements in his instruments, and then write the instructions clear enough so that no one can make a mistake.

Like thousands of others, I had seen the little ad that promised a "superb, authentic, full toned instrument, in kit form for easy home workshop assembly, $150." If the word "superb" seemed to promise much, the price was modest, at least. Being an amateur musician of sorts, and knowing other amateur musicians, especially those

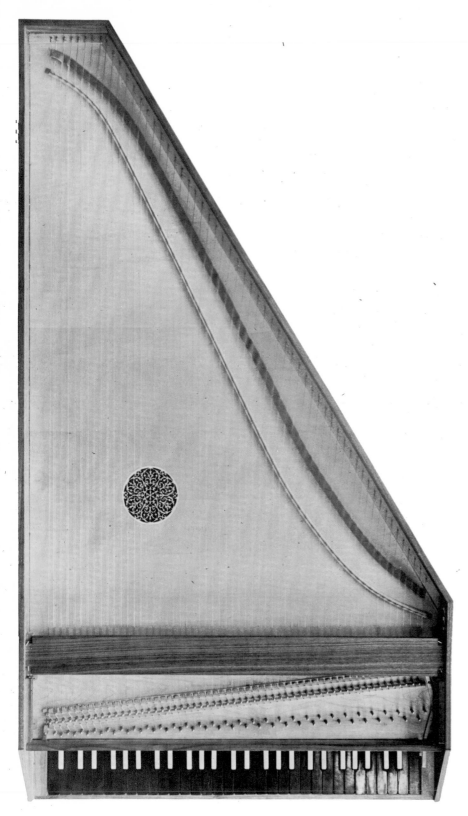

Not exactly classic proportions, but there are many apartments that could not allow the extra foot in length that longer bass strings would require.

interested in baroque music (I once published a teaching method for the recorder), I had long wanted a harpsichord of my own. I once fell in love with a Dolmetsch spinet whose owner would not let me play it because its tuning and mechanism were so fragile that he only used it for ensemble work in performance—all practice and preparation was done with an old upright piano.

Since such fragility, however beautiful, seemed impractical, I bought a decrepit grand piano from the dank basement of a second-hand dealer, and patiently restored it to playable condition.

I have now described in myself the essential qualifications of a Zuckermann kit builder—a liking for music, especially baroque, some ability with my hands and tools, and the patience to putter with things to make them work.

Meanwhile, a friend of mine bought a Zuckermann kit and was extremely pleased—with himself because he had achieved a playable instrument, and with the kit because the materials were of excellent quality, the instructions were clear, and the cabinet work (which costs an additional $150) was beautifully mitered and fitted. However, he soon received a massive put-down when a gushing cocktail party hostess introduced him as a "harpsichord maker" to the new owner of a Rutkowski and Robinette double: "We were discussing musical instruments," said the R & R owner when my friend confessed that he had built a Zuckermann kit.

Soon after this I saw a Zuckermann harpsichord at the home of a composer friend, one of the few constructed by Zuckermann himself in his own shop, but entirely from kit parts. It was indeed a playable instrument, although out of tune, since the owner did not have even the patience to use his Conn electronic strobo-scopic tuning machine. After admiring the harpsichord, we retired to another room and made music around an old upright—which was less out of tune than the harpsichord because the piano tuner had been there recently.

When I moved from the suburbs to a tiny New York apartment, the grand piano had to go. As consolation my wife gave me a Zuckermann kit as a birthday present. Three times Railway Express tried to deliver the bulky package when we were not at home, and in desperation we drove through the back streets of New York's West Side to pick up our kit; we drove home with it tied to the top of the car.

That evening we unwrapped our packages and turned the apartment into a harp-sichord factory, in which condition it remained for the next three weeks. The dining table became the jack factory, and then the keyboard factory since we wanted a "reverse" keyboard with black naturals and ivory accidentals. Everything fitted, everything worked. If something went wrong it was always because I had gone ahead too eagerly without reading the instructions carefully enough. We spent a total of about 80 hours on the project, using only a hammer, screw driver, pliers, small hand mortise saw (for cutting veneer), and an electric drill.

A crisis developed in the matter of the rose. I was ready to string the instrument, and anxious to plow ahead. But my wife wouldn't hear of it. What is a harpsichord without a rose? All work was stopped and the rose hunt began. Finally on a street near the docks in Brooklyn we found a maker of ouds, the Arabian lutes, ancestors of our own lutes and guitars, which are still to be found all over the Arab world. We bought several oud roses for a few dollars, and mortised the prettiest one into the soundboard.

The joy of knowing that you have put together all the parts without leaving any-thing out, or sanding and finishing a new and rather handsome piece of furniture— all these are shared by the "home craftsman," the kitbuilders who put together ship models, beach buggies, furniture, and grandfather clocks. But, as the R & R man said, we were discussing musical instruments.

I have been playing my harpsichord steadily now for three years. It works. One of the reasons it works is that I have learned how to tune it, to voice it, to fix it. If I could not do this, I do not think I would still have a harpsichord. I don't like things to be out of whack. In the end I learned to tune and voice and make small repairs to the action of my piano, since piano tuners are becoming increasingly sloppy—not to mention their prices.

As between a piano and harpsichord, the harpsichord is much easier to keep in top playing condition. Tuning and voicing a piano is a chore, and is impossible without the proper tools, tuning felts, wedges, etc. Even a touch-up job in between complete tunings is a production. Since a piano in active use could use a tuning once a month, and *must* be tuned several times a year as the seasons change, most

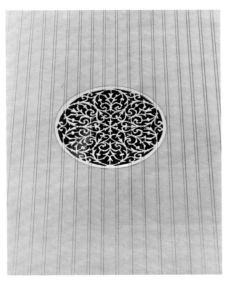

The rose from an Armenian oud makes a handsome rose for a harpsichord.

pianos are out of tune most of the time; you get used to it. Because of the nature of the harpsichord tone, and also because of the kind of open, horizontally textured music one plays on it, an out-of-tune harpsichord is more objectionable than a piano out of tune to the same degree. The triple stringing of the piano, and the average tuner's version of equal temperament, tend to blur the beats of out-of-tune strings into a progressively rougher whine. On the harpsichord, the single strings out of tune become much more annoying in the general tone texture. I find that I want the harpsichord more accurately in tune than I did the piano.

And to tune the harpsichord completely requires only the tuning wrench and about 15 minutes. However, I find that rather than tune the instrument when it has gone out of tune, I now *keep it in tune*, which is quite a different thing. Much as a violin or guitar player will check his tuning before playing, I will touch up as necessary—a matter of a minute or so. On my harpsichord the baritone register tends to be very stable, and to stay in tune with itself. The lowest bass and highest treble may need smoothing up by matching octaves out of the baritone register every two or three weeks. So far as I can judge, my Zuckermann needs tuning no more often than any other harpsichord, and in reality no more often than a piano if it were kept to the same degree of accuracy.

The onlie begetter of Zuckermann Harpsichords, Wolfgang Joachim Zuckermann, otherwise known as Wally. He has made life interesting for 6000 builders.

The jack is the heart of the harpsichord mechanism, and the Zuckerman jack was obviously designed to be widely adjustable to allow for the maximum correction of amateur errors in spacing and construction. But one gets better tone by voicing the plectra with a knife instead of forcing the tongue to the limit of its adjustment. His new jacks make changing the delrin plectra very easy, and the square hole for leathering is satisfactory. His instructions used to call for .009 wire to be used as tongue springs; this was too light and he now calls for .011 wire, which is adequate. My instrument is a 2 × 8′, using one course of quill and one of leather.

I have long thought that the jack slide was the poorest part of the instrument, and I would prefer channel brass or a solid wood slide. He has changed his old plywood slide for a new one using several pieces of flat brass (adjustable in four different places to allow for errors of spacing the strings). This is better than the old slide, and when properly installed gives no trouble. He is now working on a new system for holding the jack rail; the four little brass hooks worked, but did not make a very handsome job.

Mechanically the Zuckermann harpsichord works, and works remarkably well. What does it sound like? Is it possible to say anything about the tone of an instrument in general that has been put together by thousands of different "makers"? To answer this question I think we have to speak of what is possible to achieve in tone quality, rather than the average. I have played on or listened to some eight or ten Zuckermanns, some constructed in his shop, some made by amateurs. The difference among these various instruments was enormous, but at least 90 percent of that difference was in voicing. While anyone reasonably handy with tools can make a Zuckermann *capable* of very satisfying performance, it is probable that only a small percentage of the instruments that have been made come any where near their potential in musical sound, since expert voicing may take a long time to learn. Nothing a good harpsichord maker gives his customers is quite so valuable as that final step, when, knowing what the instrument should sound like, he sits down and makes it speak with the maximum sonority and brilliance possible to that particular instrument. (And nothing is so quickly lost from a good instrument if the owner himself does not know how to voice it and turns the job over to a piano tuner.)

I have voiced my own instrument, using both leather and quill, from a soft organ tone (cutting the leather plectra to damp out upper partials, leaving only the first two harmonics as in piano tone), to the metallic and somewhat nasal twang of quill plucking close to the nut. All of these voicings resulted in excellent and well-balanced musical tone. I have not heard an instrument of comparable size (52-in. maximum string length) that sounds as well as mine, although I have no doubt there are many. As for volume, I have more than I can use in a (now somewhat larger)

New York apartment, and I did not cut holes in the bottom. I feel that I have a better musical instrument than any factory-made instrument I could buy, and that it is surpassed only by those instruments made by a few dedicated makers.

What then does the Zuckermann instrument lack, and how could it be made to sound better? The greatest improvement would be to add a foot to its length, to improve the lower bass octave. My soundboard is the new one of three-ply basswood, $^1/_8$ in. thick. The outer plies run crossways from spine to bentside; I think the tone of the instrument, especially in the bass would be improved if the grain of this soundboard ran lengthwise of the instrument. I think that spruce, with its alternating grain of hard and soft layers would probably make a better soundboard than basswood. I think the soundboard ribs are too heavy, and should not extend as they now do to the very edge of the board. I think the top of the inner case might be narrowed all around, including the belly rail, to give more effective soundboard area.

Further changes than this would probably destroy the chief virtue of the design. The inner-outer case construction is admirably suited for amateur construction with a minimum of tools. The inner case is several times stronger than it really needs to be —and still some builders who make sloppy joints have trouble when they try to string it. I believe a curved bentside (with a soundboard having its plies lengthwise of the instrument) would make possible a more uniform resonance throughout the scale (resonance as my instrument stands favors the top of the treble and the baritone register; this is compensated for by voicing, but results in more difference in the timbre of various parts of the scale than there should be). In short, if the whole case of the Zuckermann harpsichord were allowed to participate in the resonance, in line with classical construction, and the bentside were curved to allow equal proportionate resonance to all parts of the scale, I think it would be a better instrument.

But would such an instrument be so foolproof in the hands of the amateur constructor?

A builder of a Zuckermann harpsichord tunes the second 8′ choir in unison with the first.

I keep my instrument in meantone, and do not mind occasionally changing the A flat to G sharp; there are only four of them. And yes, I play all of Bach in meantone —as he did whenever he played on anything but his own personal harpsichords and clavichords at home. More nonsense than sense has been written about the discords of meantone—the composers avoided them, and the total effect is of greatly *increased* consonance and sonority.

I use quill instead of delrin because it makes a difference. As Hugh Gough says, God made crows for harpsichords—what else? But it must be good, tough, black quill, with all the pith trimmed away. If for nothing else one should try quill to find out what kind of sound a plectrum should make—and then voice the delrin accordingly. If delrin is thinned carefully with a very sharp knife to about .010 thickness (half its original thickness) it can be made to give a very good imitation of quill as long as you are not trying for maximum volume. The curve of the quill in cross section (I think this is the reason) allows a louder, clearer pluck than I have been able to get from delrin.

My Zuckermann harpsichord is not a toy and not a gadget, but a musical instrument in constant use. It could be better, and if he brings out an improved model with curved bentside and greater length and better soundboard I will buy and build it. Meanwhile it serves, and serves very well.

D.J.W.

Printed in the U.S.A. by Clarke & Way, Inc., New York
Format by the Bert Clarke Design Group

COM